Patterns of
ENGLISH Pronunciation

J. Donald Bowen

Cover design by Lois Jefferson Kordaszewski

NEWBURY HOUSE PUBLISHERS, INC.

Language Science
Language Teaching
Language Learning

ROWLEY, MASSACHUSETTS 01969

Copyright © 1975 by Newbury House Publishers, Inc. All rights reserved. No part of this book may be reproduced or transmitted in any form or by any means, electronic or mechanical, including photocopying, recording, or by any information storage and retrieval system, without permission in writing from the Publisher.

ISBN: 0-88377-044-X

Library of Congress Card Number: 75-24702

First printing: August, 1975
Second printing: April, 1978
       7 6 5 4 3
Printed in the U.S.A.

Patterns of ENGLISH Pronunciation

J. Donald Bowen
University of California, Los Angeles

NEWBURY HOUSE PUBLISHERS, Inc. / ROWLEY, MASSACHUSETTS

To KAY
with gratitude and with love

ACKNOWLEDGMENTS

Many contributors have assisted in the preparation of this manual, some knowingly, but most innocently. It is extremely difficult to keep track of the sources of ideas that have accumulated over a period of almost twenty years, so a complete and proper acknowledgment is virtually impossible.

Three books are exceptions. One is *Patterns of Spanish Pronunciation* by J. Donald Bowen and Robert P. Stockwell, published in 1960. The present text derives from a similar conceptualization, with the difference that the audience in the United States for English as a Second Language, rather than Spanish, does not permit the assumption of a single background language. A second, more recent, text is *Pronunciation Contrasts in English* by Don L. F. and Alleen Pace Nilsen, which was most helpful in devising minimal pair sentences for the contrast drills in Chapters 2 and 3. The third is *Modern English: A Textbook for Foreign Students* by William Rutherford, whose ingenious and innovative pronunciation exercises are in large part a model for the synthesis attempted in Chapter 9.

I owe much to my colleagues in a general way—for their stimulus and the opportunities they gave me to discover that some ideas really weren't so good after all, thus sparing me some of the criticism that reviewers would justly deliver. I am especially grateful for a critical reading and tryout of most of the chapters by Professors Marianne Celce-Murcia, Thomas P. Gorman, and Harold S. Madsen and to Miss Elizabeth Jeremenko. Their suggestions have been most helpful. I also gratefully express my appreciation to two groups of Russian students who worked through generous samples of the material while at the University of California, Los Angeles during the summers of 1972 and 1973. I sincerely appreciated their enthusiastic reception of the exercises, which has encouraged me to hope they will be useful for other students.

Finally I gratefully thank my wife Kay for a formidable job of typing and manuscript preparation, which she undertook in spite of many other demands on her time and talents. As she typed she also provided patient and careful criticism that really amounted to technical editing.

The errors and deficiencies are of course my own.

J. Donald Bowen

English Language Institute
American University in Cairo
July, 1975

PREFACE

When one wishes to write a pronunciation manual for a language to be studied in a classroom, and especially when that language is English, certain unavoidable problems have to be met. One is the choice of dialect to be taught, since English is a language that is widely spoken over vast areas of the earth and occurs even in the United States in various dialect forms; another is the way sounds are to be represented on the printed page; a third is the degree of abstraction and technical detail to be included in the explanations. There are pedagogical implications for each of the choices, and it is well to discuss some of these before proceeding to a description of the text which follows.

The dialect selected can be designated as general American normalized in the direction of all practical simplicity. Recognizably regional variants (New England, Southern, etc.) are avoided, and if there is a balanced choice between the presence or absence of a contrast, the absence is assumed, a decision made in the interest of simplicity. Thus while certain words are distinguished by some speakers of American English, they are homophonous for others. The interpretation of "two words pronounced the same way" is accepted on the assumption that learners of English do not need contrasts that substantial numbers of native speakers do without. Thus no distinction is shown between *wear/where, horse/hoarse,* or *merry/marry/Mary,* despite the fact that many Americans do recognize and observe differences. On the other hand, certain distinctions are observed in the text which some Americans do quite well without: *pin/pen, cot/caught, collar/caller,* and *law/lore,* for example. Which are to be represented and which submerged is a matter of judgment, but the assumption that governs the decision is majority usage (or what is assumed to be the usage of the majority of speakers in the major dialect areas).

The problem of how sounds are to be represented by visual symbols on the printed page arises, since the author, not being present to personally interpret what he sets down, has to rely on visual configurations to represent sounds. The traditional writing system would probably be satisfactory for some languages, but not English, where spelling frequently obscures pronunciation. English spelling is fine, if you already speak English, but it leaves much to be desired as a guide to pronunciation for second-language learners. So it is considered advisable to utilize a transcription to show pronunciation in a clear and unambiguous way. The transcription used in this text tries to be clear and unambiguous (employing a separate representation for each significantly different sound) but also attempts to stay as close to spelling tradition as possible, at least as far as the consonants are concerned. The analysis of vowel sounds varies somewhat from traditional spelling, since there are not only numerous patterns to choose from, but it is felt advantageous to use a representation that displays the phonetic relationships between vowels and diphthongs as explicitly as possible.

How to indicate the "suprasegmental" features of stress and intensity, pitch and pitch change, intensity or overall prominence, syllable length, and transitional features is a more complex problem, since these features are only rarely (and then quite indirectly) shown in the traditional written forms of English. An attempt has been made to employ devices that are visually suggestive, such as relative length of a line for syllable length, relative height with respect to reference lines to show pitch, arrows to show the direction of pitch change, and accent marks commonly used in professional literature.

A variety of representational devices is used to (1) highlight the particular problem being discussed and (2) help promote flexibility in student use of such devices, rather than freezing associations with a single system.

The third problem is the amount of technical detail to discuss and to represent in the respelling. The generalization followed in this text is "no more than the student can accept as guidance" (to the extent this stricture can be interpreted and observed for the unseen audience that may use this text). As an example, the aspiration that accompanies the *p* of the word *pill* may be shown as this feature of the *p* is discussed, perhaps as [pʻɪl], but this marking of aspiration should not be generally included in transcribing English. After all, the student must get used to regular spelling, where it is not marked (as this pronunciation feature is automatic for speakers of English, and there is therefore no need to mark it). But perhaps a better reason is that a proliferation of such representations would make the transcription much more difficult to interpret, and many students, especially those who question the wisdom of learning a "temporary" spelling system, would consider such a transcription too much of a burden for the help they could expect to derive from it. User morale is important, and it is this consideration that leads to the expensive decision to include a double representation of each drill in the text: regular spelling and a transcription respelling. Hopefully, exposure to this twofold representation will promote a clear understanding of the pronunciation problems and contrasts and at the same time will encourage familiarization with spelling forms and the traditional conventions of representing English sounds.

I feel that a visual representation of sounds for the purpose of guiding students' pronunciation should be suggestive. In observance of this criterion in a few instances the rule of a single symbol for a single sound is not followed: the digraph /ng/ is used for the velar nasal in *sing,* the digraph /sh/ is used for the initial sibilant of *ship,* and a few others. These do introduce a few problems, but can be justified because they take advantage of symbol associations the students are already familiar with, or anticipate associations that will eventually be needed in reading English. In theory, symbols are completely arbitrary, and this may hold in analytical research. But in practical teaching, the suggestive power or potential of a symbol is of enormous importance and is very much a relevant criterion in making decisions of pedagogical application. In the final analysis a pragmatic judgment must prevail: if a device serves its purpose well, keep it—if not, discard it. The salient features of the system utilized in this book (though not all the details) have been widely applied in texts for teaching English and found to be generally helpful.

But what if a particular representation doesn't match the pronunciation of a particular teacher? For example, what if *either* is represented /íydhər/, but the teacher's normal pronunciation, and the only one he feels comfortable with, is /áydhər/? There are several options: (1) write a correction in the text and ask your students to do likewise, (2) introduce your pronunciation as a variant and inform students of the alternatives, (3) cross out the item, skip it, and let students learn the item in context (especially if they're studying in the United States or somewhere else where an out-of-class standard will emerge), (4) go along with the recommendation of the text and try to conform. The teacher can confidently accept any of these solutions without being especially concerned about the consequences. My own choice would probably be number 2 for *either,* though other problems might justify explaining or correcting or ignoring.

Some examples of variation do not concern dialect area or level of formality but occur in free variation in the language. Thus the word *regard* may occur as /rəgárd/ or as /riygárd/, with no consequence of meaning, dialect, register, or style level. It represents a variation under weak stress of /ə ~ iy/ that is allowed in the kind of English presented in this text. Similarly one may hear (or say) /prədúws/ or /prowdúws/ for *produce,* with a permitted variation between weak-stressed /ə ~ ow/, or even medial stressed /ôw/. The policy of the text is to use both permitted variants in such words, in hopes of building tolerance for these variations in the student that can match the speech and expectations of native speakers.

The present volume is not a textbook in the usual sense of the term, but a supplementary manual designed to help a motivated student work toward the perfection of his pronunciation of English. It is therefore intended to be used along with a text, preferably in short, regular sessions that use only five or ten minutes of the class hour. This pattern of attention to pronunciation problems accords with the generally accepted belief that while pronunciation is an important concern for the beginning-level student, there is a limit to the proportion of classroom teaching time that can profitably be devoted exclusively to pronunciation: the student has other, usually more motivating responsibilities (grammar, lexicon, culture, etc.), and other more rewarding activities (reading, conversing, listening) than just practicing sounds, even when these appear in sentence contexts.

Also there is the problem of providing incentives for a good pronunciation beyond minimum intelligibility, and an excessive concentration on pronunciation to the neglect of other aspects of the full learning task may damage the motivation of some students. It seems advisable to introduce pronunciation drills in moderate quantities and look for progress to stimulate continued interest in further improvement.

It would be convenient for learning purposes if English could be dissected and we could find some logical way to put the pieces back together one at a time. Then no sound or sound feature would appear in the text before it had been formally presented (identified, described, discussed, illustrated, and practiced). Unfortunately this seems not to be possible, and sounds other than the one we wish to focus our attention on appear in every exercise.

Another solution, since the individual sounds and features of English come in patterned sequences and communicate through their totality, would be to try to concentrate simultaneously on all the sounds and features of an utterance. This may be in large part what happens when learning occurs under so-called "natural" circumstances, where a particular feature comes to the conversants' attention only when it is absolutely crucial (Did you say *surface* or *service*?) But in a classroom where language is analyzed and various features are formally presented, concentrating on everything at once seems impossible. Indeed concentrating on even two things at the same time is rather like keeping both ends of a teeter-totter down.

Trying to decide how to present and practice all the pronunciation skills a student needs leads to problems of priority for which there are no ideal solutions, so we compromise. We introduce pronunciation features one at a time, to focus the student's attention on them. It is hoped that with understanding and guided practice, the student will achieve an improved mastery over each feature. At the same time an attempt is made to minimize the occurrence of too many difficult and unfamiliar sounds and features which can be a distraction. It is often not possible to avoid some of these, but when possible an environment of easier or familiar features is used.

How do we know that one sound is easier than another? Actually we don't; it is especially hard to generalize for an expected audience of many background (native) languages. But experience with many students suggests that some sounds are generally no great problem for most learners (for example /m/) and others are difficult for many (as is /th/).

An attempt is made to sequence the sounds and features on the basis of importance and difficulty, though this criteria—applied on the basis of experience and intuition—are occasionally modified in the interest of convenience in teaching, such as discussing similar features together.

This manual can be used in several ways. For beginning- or elementary-level students the sequence of the text can be followed, assuring a reasonably complete coverage of the general problems of English pronunciation. For an intermediate or advanced class, or for remedial work, the teacher can identify problem sounds or contrasts and find an appropriate presentation and drill by consulting the index. Then present the information and practice exercises on the particular point which the class finds difficult. For any section on which the class is performing satisfactorily I would advise simply skipping the material that seems not to be needed. There is no purpose served in going over material just because it's there. It is often observed that motivation may suffer if students feel they are not progressing, and it may be encouraging to a group of students for the teacher to suggest stopping in the middle of a presentation, since they have satisfactorily mastered the points included. For most pronunciation problems an adequate amount of exercise material is included so the instructor may feel free to pick and choose.

In talking about pronunciation it is customary to distinguish segmental and suprasegmental elements. The segmental units are the string of vowel and consonant sounds that are uttered in sequence, forming the words and sentences of the spoken language. The suprasegmental units are the features of prominence and transition that are added to the string of vowels and consonants to facilitate the interpretation of spoken utterances. These mainly include features of pitch and stress. The names segmental and suprasegmental are not particularly important and need not be taught to students, but the distinction helps explain the needs of the learner and the organization of the present text as it attempts to meet these needs.

Suprasegmental features seem more difficult to master for second-language students and this suggests they should be presented early. Yet it is clearly impossible to add suprasegmental modifications in any meaningful way unless there is a segmental string of sounds they can be applied to, which suggests that segmental units must be introduced first. The compromise adopted in this text is to intersperse suprasegmentals and segmentals. The text is organized in three parts or cycles. Part One is an introduction of selected features of pitch and stress and an inventory of the vowels and consonants, with contextual illustrations of contrasts that have proved generally to be problems. The inventory includes Chapters 1, 2, and 3. Part Two presents some of the patterns commonly associated with combinations of features of intonation, vowels, and consonants, including the effects of vowels and consonants. The patterns are described in Chapters 4, 5, and 6. Part Three recycles the same sequence on the construct level, with Chapter 7 devoted to suprasegmental and Chapter 8 to segmental constructions. By this time it becomes quite obvious that these elements are so mutually interdependent that separate treatment is neither strictly possible nor productively desirable. Chapter 9 therefore offers assorted exercises in which a synthesis of features and patterns is attempted in more complex environments and constructions.

In the three cycles the text moves from very simple concepts to rather complex problems which are given a more technical treatment. It is therefore possible, and I think desirable, to use the exercises over a period of time (about two years) as the pronunciation component of courses for beginning, intermediate, and advanced students, selecting from the cycle most appropriate to the students' needs and interests at each level.

Perhaps a few suggestions for ways to use the text would be helpful. It will be quickly noticed that a rather informal style of English is described and practiced in the exercises. This may be controversial, since there is a time-honored tradition in our schools that specifies formal English as appropriate to education generally and most particularly to the language classroom. Some teachers may feel that a careless or even sloppy kind of English is being taught. This is true if careless and sloppy are merely paraphrases (albeit emotional paraphrases) of "informal." We have noticed for a long time that foreign students come to the United States after years, sometimes eight or ten years, of studying English and find that they cannot understand even the relatively formal English of course lectures. Ordinary conversation (unless directed specifically to them—and doctored accordingly) and television programs are out of the question—totally incomprehensible.

In my opinion the reason for their trouble with spoken English is not lack of language-learning aptitude or low-quality education in schools abroad, but simply a lack of familiarity with the informal registers of spoken English—with English as people really do use it. We have deluded ourselves about how our language sounds and have adopted unrealistic standards for classroom teaching that produce a kind of competence that doesn't match usage among native speakers in the real world. This text deliberately tries to teach the features and patterns that have long been neglected.

The exercises can be used in a classroom context by any teacher who has a good command of informal English and who is not averse to using informal style in the classroom. Or the exercises can be used in lessons prepared for the language laboratory. For both of these usages it is crucial to point out that a structured sequence of presentation is followed throughout the text, a sequence which must be adapted to the needs of the classroom. If /sh/ and /ch/ are being presented in a minimal sentence pair exercise, /sh/ always comes first. *But,* when given as a classroom exercise the order must be randomized, so the student will be required to *learn* the difference and not simply learn which is assumed to come first in a contrasted sequence. To fail to supply this randomization can vitiate much of the value of doing the exercises.

Students working in groups can employ the same cue identifications for each other that the teacher and the laboratory recording supply. Of course productions must be reliably accurate, or it will be unfair to expect the listener to make discriminations. A student working alone can read the descriptions of how the sounds or features are produced, sequenced, interrelated, etc. and can practice producing the exercise sentences. He will of course be limited by his own skill of self-critiquing and cannot benefit from the independent feedback of an outside judge.

A serious effort has been made to provide or at least suggest contextualizations to support different contrasts associated with pronunciation differences. The minimal pair principle has been followed, applied not just to sounds, but rather to words and, whenever possible, to sentences and situations. Except when dealing with sounds or features having a very low frequency of occurrence, it has usually been possible to devise reasonably acceptable context, where expectations are not overpoweringly in favor of one option of a choice. Extensive use has been made of paraphrase and association to build the concept of contrastive identification into a more inclusive situation. The presentation of contextualized exercises can be done in various ways. My own suggestions are the subject of an article which appeared under the title "Contextualizing Pronunciation Practice in the ESOL Classroom" in the *TESOL Quarterly* 6:1 (March 1972) 83-94, reprinted in the *English Teaching Forum* 11:1 (January-February 1973) 1-7. Essentially, contextualization means finding ways of making material meaningful in the widest possible range of associations.

It is my sincere hope that this manual will prove helpful, especially to students who wish to develop improved listening comprehension, or who hope, for whatever reasons, to improve their facility in English communication by increasing their own accuracy and fluency in pronunciation.

CONTENTS

Acknowledgments	v
Preface	vii
1. Elements of Intonation	1
2. The English Vowel System	12
3. The English Consonants	29
4. English Stress and Intonation Patterns	75
5. English Vowel Patterns	95
6. English Consonant Patterns	131
7. Constructs of English Intonation	175
8. Constructs of English Vowels and Consonants	199
9. Functional Synthesis	228
Index	261

Patterns of
ENGLISH Pronunciation

Chapter 1
ELEMENTS OF INTONATION

It is noted in many languages, and particularly in English, that some parts of an utterance are more prominent than others. This prominence is achieved by means of contrasts in stress (loudness) and pitch (height on a musical scale). Prominence is usually associated with a syllable and in the present text will be marked by placing an accent mark (´) over the vowel of the most prominent syllable of a word (e.g., *abúndance*). In discussing prominence in this manual the term stress will be used, even though more than loudness is involved, following a precedent that has been widely observed in teaching texts.

We will find it useful for purposes of description to distinguish stress as applied to words, and as applied to phrases. Within words there are three levels of stress: strong, medial, and weak. Stress distinctions in phrases will be discussed in a later chapter.

One of the characteristics which marks English as distinctive is the fact that weak stress is very weak indeed, with very little prominence given to weak-stressed syllables. The exercises given below show a strong syllable followed or preceded by a weak syllable. Notice that the weak syllable is very briefly pronounced in comparison to the strong syllable. This is shown in the heading for the exercise by placing a line (—) in the position of the strong syllable and a dot (˙)

in the position of the weak syllable. These represent both loudness and the actual length of time devoted to the pronunciation of each syllable. The weak-stressed syllables are very briefly pronounced and the strong-stressed syllables are held for a longer time.

In citation form it is normal for the strong-stressed syllables to be pronounced on a higher pitch than the weak-stressed. This is shown in the notation of the column heading in the exercises that follow by a difference in the height of the dots and lines. When the weak-stressed syllable follows (as in the column to the left), the line to indicate strong stress and high pitch is located near the top reference line; the dot which indicates weak stress and low pitch is located near the bottom reference line. When the weak-stressed syllable precedes (as in the column to the right), the dot is located mid way between the two reference lines, and the line representing the strong-stressed syllable starts near the top line and then angles down to show the drop from high to low pitch.

The following exercises are composed of lists of two-syllable words, the first made up of a strong syllable followed by a weak syllable, the second of a weak followed by a strong syllable. Try to imitate the pronunciation of your teacher in a way that reflects the difference in prominence, keeping in mind that the weak-stressed syllables are very brief and lightly pronounced.

1.1 Two stress levels—strong and weak: two-syllable patterns
Presentation of patterns; read down:

ɛ́niy	əbáwt	any	about
mɛ́niy	əbə́v	many	above
bániy	əláyv	Bonnie	alive
dɛ́biy	əgɛ́n	Debbie	again
kǽndiy	əgów	candy	ago
ɛ́mə	əpán	Emma	upon
ówpən	məstéyk	open	mistake
pɛ́nsəl	məshíyn	pencil	machine
téybəl	səpówz	table	suppose
mínət	pəlíys	minute	police
ǽləs	biykɔ́z	Alice	because

It is interesting and relevant to note that only certain vowel sounds can appear in English weak-stressed syllables. Only two of these are shown above: /iy/ and /ə/. This limitation will be discussed further later on.

Certain contrasts of similar forms occur in English in which stress distinguishes the function of related words. An example of these is given below.

1.1a Noun-verb patterns
   Comparison of pattern; read across:

NOUN	VERB		
âbjəkt	əbjɛ́kt	object	object
dɛ́zərt	dəzɚ́rt	desert	desert
prɛ́zənt	prəzɛ́nt	present	present
rɛ́bəl	rəbɛ́l	rebel	rebel
rɛ́kərd	rəkɔ́rd	record	record
sâbjəkt	səbjɛ́kt	subject	subject

Note that the conventional English spelling gives no hint of which pronunciation is appropriate. English speakers get this information from the way the word is used, whether as a noun or as a verb. This emphasizes the need for understanding how the system works and shows the hazard of depending on traditional spelling to guide pronunciation.

1.2 Two stress levels—strong and weak: three-syllable patterns
   Presentation of pattern; read down:

kǽbənət	əlɛ́vən	cabinet	eleven
prɛ́zədənt	əréysər	president	eraser
kǽpətəl	dətɚ́rmən	capital	determine
kwâlətiy	prəsíydɪŋ	quality	proceeding
âpəzət	rəléyshən	opposite	relation
ɛ́nəmiy	əkâstəm	enemy	accustom
hâspətəl	shəkâgow	hospital	Chicago
dâmənow	kəsâbə	domino	casaba
kǽləndər	təméytow	calendar	tomato
ɛ́ləfənt	pətéytow	elephant	potato

4 Patterns of English Pronunciation

In some of the above words the vowel sounds /ɪ/ and /ow/ appear in weak-stressed syllables (*proceed<u>ing</u>, domin<u>o</u>, tomat<u>o</u>*, etc.). The complete vowel system for weak-stressed syllables will be presented in Chapter 4.

1.3 Two stress levels—strong and weak: four-syllable patterns
   Presentation of pattern; read down:

˙˙˙	˙ ˙˙		
pɛ́nətrəbəl	ɪmpásəbəl	penetrable	impossible
ǽdmərəbəl	rəmárkəbəl	admirable	remarkable
krɛ́dətəbəl	rəláyəbəl	creditable	reliable
hǽbətəbəl	əfə́rmətəv	habitable	affirmative
márkətəbəl	fətágrəfiy	marketable	photography
láyənəsəz	əbílətiy	lionesses	ability
kǽpətələst	sənílətiy	capitalist	senility
pə́rsənəliy	təlɛ́grəfiy	personally	telegraphy
nǽshənəliy	kətǽstrəfiy	nationally	catastrophe
lǽtərəliy	kəpǽsətiy	laterally	capacity

1.4 Two stress levels—strong and medial or weak: two-syllable patterns
   Presentation and comparison of pattern; read down, then across:

˙ ˙	˙ –		
fíybəl	fíymèyl	feeble	female
thímbəl	thə́mnèyl	thimble	thumbnail
pɛ́nsəl	pɛ́nsɛ̀l	pencil	pen cell
éykər	éykɔ̀rn	acre	acorn
sə́pər	sə́spɛ̀kt	supper	suspect
kə́vər	kánvə̀rt	cover	convert
práfər	prówfàyl	proffer	profile
prúwvən	prówgræ̀m	proven	program
kámɪk	kántæ̀kt	comic	contact
sə́niy	sə́ndày l	sunny	sundial
wíndiy	wíndmìl	windy	windmill
kániy	kándə̀kt	Connie	conduct
ríytə	ríytèyl	Rita	retail
réylɪŋ	réylròwd	railing	railroad

1.4a Two stress levels—weak or medial and strong: two-syllable patterns
   Presentation and comparison of pattern; read down, then across:

•⏋	-⏋		
əpɛ́nd	ə̀pɛ́nd	append	upend
əpír	ə̀pstɛ́rz	appear	upstairs
əpɔ́l	ə̀phówld	appall	uphold
əbɛ́t	à̀wtbíd	abet	outbid
əbrɛ́st	ə̀pbréyd	abreast	upbraid
əjə́st	ə̀njə́st	adjust	unjust
əshɔ́r	ə̀nshɔ́r	assure	unsure
əprúwvd	ə̀nprúwvd	approved	unproved
əbówd	ə̀nbówd	abode	unbowed
əkrɔ́s	ə̀nkrɔ́s	across	uncross
əntíl	ə̀ndə́n	until	undone
ɪnə́rt	ə̀nnə́rv	inert	unnerve
riypéyd	prìypéyd	repaid	prepaid
məstéyk	mìstráyl	mistake	mistrial

One of the tests of a weak-stressed vowel is its potential substitution by the neutral vowel symbolized above by /ə/. Thus in the next-to-last pair of words above *repaid* can be pronounced /riypéyd/ or /rəpéyd/, but *prepaid* can only be pronounced /prìypéyd/.

1.4b Noun-verb patterns
   Comparison of pattern; read across:

-⏋	•⏋		
Noun	Verb		
kándə̀kt	kəndə́kt	conduct	conduct
kánflìkt	kənflíkt	conflict	conflict
kánvə̀rt	kənvə́rt	convert	convert
ínsə̀rt	ɪnsə́rt	insert	insert
ínsə̀lt	ɪnsə́lt	insult	insult
prájèkt	prəjɛ́kt	project	project
sə́spèkt	səspɛ́kt	suspect	suspect
prówdùws	prədúws	produce	produce
pə́rmìt	pərmít	permit	permit

Again note that the spelling offers no assistance in the appropriate interpretation of these forms; the student must gain a feeling for the association of form and function.

The contrasts presented above are contextualized in the following exercise. Read each sentence and select the interpretation (of noun or verb stress) that is appropriate. As a test cover the stress symbols in the column to the right while doing the exercise.

1.4c Noun-verb patterns contextualized
Selection of pattern; read each sentence:

1. Their (conduct) is proper. / ´ ` /
   They (conduct) themselves properly. / ˇ ´ /
2. There's a (conflict) of ideas. / ´ ` /
   Their ideas (conflict). / ˇ ´ /
3. Put the (insert) on page ten. / ´ ` /
   (Insert) the paragraph on page ten. / ˇ ´ /
4. That's an (insult). / ´ ` /
   Don't (insult) me. / ˇ ´ /
5. The soldiers will certainly (rebel). / ˇ ´ /
6. Where shall we unload this (produce)? / ´ ` /
7. How many weeks do they (project)? / ˇ ´ /
8. There's a (conflict) of interest. / ´ ` /
9. The (suspect) fled from the scene. / ´ ` /
10. Do you have your parking (permit)? / ´ ` /
11. The schedule will (conflict) with my plans. / ˇ ´ /
12. The soldier said he wouldn't (desert). / ˇ ´ /

The following series of exercises shows all three levels of stress in single words.

1.5 Three stress levels—strong, medial, and weak: three-syllable patterns

Presentation of pattern; read down:

`• _`	`_ •` ⌐		
ǽpətàyt	ìntərvíyn	appetite	intervene
fówtəgræ̀f	ìntrədúws	photograph	introduce
télofòwn	sèventíyn	telephone	seventeen
háydəbèd	æ̀ftərnúwn	hide-a-bed	afternoon
dípləmæ̀t	èntərtéyn	diplomat	entertain
séntrəlàyz	pèrsənél	centralize	personnel
téləkæ̀st	rèkəménd	telecast	recommend
múltətùwd	gèrəntíy	multitude	guarantee
rídəkyùwl	kòrəspánd	ridicule	correspond
ǽvənùw	fìftiytúw	avenue	fifty-two

1.5a Noun-verb patterns

Comparison of pattern; read across:

`• _`	`_ •` ⌐		
Noun	**Verb**		
ə́ndərwèr	ə̀ndərwént	underwear	underwent
ə́ndərdɔ̀g	ə̀ndərstǽnd	underdog	understand
ə́ndərwə̀rld	ə̀ndərráyt	underworld	underwrite
ə́ndərpæ̀s	ə̀ndərmáyn	underpass	undermine
ə́ndərbrə̀sh	ə̀ndərbíd	underbrush	underbid
ə́ndertòwnz	ə̀ndərtéyk	undertones	undertake
ówvərsìr	òwvərhír	overseer	overhear
ówvərɔ̀lz	òwvərhɔ́l	overalls	overhaul
ówvərbɔ̀rd	òwvərbíld	overboard	overbuild
ówvərshùwz	òwvərshúwt	overshoes	overshoot
ówvərkòwt	òwvərkə́m	overcoat	overcome
ówvərdræ̀ft	òwvərdrɔ́	overdraft	overdraw

1.5b Adjective-verb patterns
Comparison of pattern; read across:

˙ ˙	˙ ‒		
dámənənt	dámənèyt	dominant	dominate
váyələnt	váyəlèyt	violent	violate
sírkyələr	sírkyəlèyt	circular	circulate
régyələr	régyəlèyt	regular	regulate
məltəpəl	məltəplày	multiple	multiply
byúwtəfəl	byúwtəfày	beautiful	beautify
térəbəl	térəfày	terrible	terrify
édəbəl	édəfày	edible	edify
íykwəliy	íykwəlàyz	equally	equalize
káləniy	kálənàyz	colony	colonize

1.5c Noun/adjective-verb patterns
Comparison of pattern; read across:

˙ ˙	˙ ‒		
Noun/Adjective	Verb		
éstəmət	éstəmèyt	estimate	estimate
síndəkət	síndəkèyt	syndicate	syndicate
grǽjəwət	grǽjəwèyt	graduate	graduate
áysələt	áysəlèyt	isolate	isolate
désələt	désəlèyt	desolate	desolate
ǽdvəkət	ǽdvəkèyt	advocate	advocate
mádərət	mádərèyt	moderate	moderate
ǽnəmət	ǽnəmèyt	animate	animate
kánsəmət	kánsəmèyt	consummate	consummate
ǽgrəgət	ǽgrəgèyt	aggregate	aggregate
déləgət	déləgèyt	delegate	delegate
dúwpləkət	dúwpləkèyt	duplicate	duplicate
ímpləmənt	ímpləmènt	implement	implement
kámpləmənt	kámpləmènt	complement	complement

This is a highly productive pattern with a great many examples, none of which are marked for contrast in the regular spelling. Also, there are numerous four-syllable examples, such as *appropriate*, *associate, coordinate, expatriate, affiliate,* etc. that admit both interpretations. But not all *-ate* words will follow the full pattern; many which take only /ət/ are adjectives or nouns only (*temperate, inviolate, delicate, intricate, immaculate, consulate, ultimate, obstinate, passionate, fortunate, disparate, literate, accurate, adequate*), while many others take only /-èyt/ and are verbs (*dominate, educate, violate, repatriate, conjugate, vindicate, irrigate, originate, regulate, obligate*).

The contrasts presented above are contextualized in the following exercise. Read each sentence with the stress pattern (for a noun or adjective or for a verb) that is appropriate. As a test, cover the stress symbols in the column to the right while doing the exercise.

1.5d Noun/adjective-verb patterns contextualized
Selection of pattern; read each sentence:
1. The (estimate) is wrong. / ´ ˇ ˇ /
   We (estimate) two days. / ´ ˇ ˋ /
2. They want (separate) rooms. / ´ ˇ ˇ /
   (Separate) the students. / ´ ˇ ˋ /
3. It's an (animate) noun. / ´ ˇ ˇ /
   (Animate) the cartoon. / ´ ˇ ˋ /
4. He's a (moderate). / ´ ˇ ˇ /
   (Moderate) your argument. / ´ ˇ ˋ /
5. He's my (advocate). / ´ ˇ ˇ /
   I (advocate) another solution. / ´ ˇ ˋ /
6. He's a (consummate) fool. / ´ ˇ ˇ /
   They will (consummate) their marriage. / ´ ˇ ˋ /
7. The (implement) is dull. / ´ ˇ ˇ /
   (Implement) the treaty. / ´ ˇ ˋ /
8. It's a (delicate) operation. / ´ ˇ ˇ /
9. Why did the students (demonstrate)? / ´ ˇ ˋ /
10. We have to (irrigate) tonight. / ´ ˇ ˋ /
11. That's an (accurate) answer. / ´ ˇ ˇ /
12. You're very (fortunate). / ´ ˇ ˇ /
13. Make a (duplicate) copy. / ´ ˇ ˇ /
14. He'll (graduate) this June. / ´ ˇ ˋ /
15. The noun is the (complement). / ´ ˇ ˇ /

1.6 Three stress levels—strong, medial, and weak: four-syllable patterns

Presentation of pattern; read down:

• – • •	– • • •		
ǽpətàyzɪŋ	sɚ̀rkyəléyshən	appetizing	circulation
éjəkèytəd	dìpləmǽtɪk	educated	diplomatic
kálənàyzɚr	mòwtəvéyshən	colonizer	motivation
kǽtəgɔ̀riy	ìrəgárdləs	category	irregardless
sékəndɛ̀riy	əpərtúwnliy	secondary	opportunely
dísəntɛ̀riy	æ̀dəlésənt	dysentery	adolescent
nésəsɛ̀riy	dɛ̀məkrǽtɪk	necessary	democratic
háyərɑ̀rkiy	kòwəlíshən	hierarchy	coalition

As implied by the comparisons made earlier, some of the stress patterns are related to each other, often in interesting and regular ways. One of the strongest of these correlations is shown below.

1.6a Verb-noun and noun-adjective patterns

Comparison of pattern; read across:

• • –	– • • •		
Verb-Noun	**Noun-Adjective**		
kɑ̀nstətúwt	kɑ̀nstətúwshən	constitute	constitution
ìnstətúwt	ìnstətúwshən	institute	institution
rɛ̀gyəlèyt	rɛ̀gyəléyshən	regulate	regulation
èjəkèyt	èjəkéyshən	educate	education
áysəlèyt	àysəléyshən	isolate	isolation
dípləmæ̀t	dìpləmǽtɪk	diplomat	diplomatic
ɔ́təmæ̀t	ɔ̀təmǽtɪk	automat	automatic
mɑ́nəlìth	mɑ̀nəlíthɪk	monolith	monolithic
tɛ́ləskòwp	tɛ̀ləskɑ́pɪk	telescope	telescopic
máykrəskòwp	màykrəskɑ́pɪk	microscope	microscopic

The stress patterns discussed and illustrated to this point are very typical of English. They do not at all exhaust the possibilities of English words, which can become quite long and complex, as illustrated by a word like *internationalization* /ı̀nternæ̀shənəlezéy-shən/. But such words are made up of stems and affixes.

nation	néyshən
national	nǽshənəl
international	ı̀nternǽshənəl
internationalize	ı̀nternǽshənəlàyz
internationalization	ı̀nternæ̀shənəlezéyshən

The ways in which complicated words are built up is an interesting study, one which must include an effort to determine the English patterns of stress placement and vowel alternations, and later on in the text we will more fully illustrate some of these patterns.

Stress is crucially important in English and can never be ignored or even slighted if an acceptable mastery of spoken English is a learning goal. For the purposes of introducing the concept of stress and illustrating the basic important patterns, the exercises presented should be sufficient at this time. So we turn now to an introduction of segmental units: the vowel and consonant sounds.

Chapter 2
THE ENGLISH VOWEL SYSTEM

The vowel system in English is rather complex, but an acceptable pronunciation of English vowels can be accomplished by any serious student who makes an effort to understand the basic features of the system and to conscientiously apply what he learns.

Unlike consonants, which can usually be described quite definitely in terms of where they are produced, vowels can be characterized mainly by their relation to each other. Every human mouth is a cavity of roughly the same size and shape, and the space it contains is the location of various tongue positions that are crucial to producing the resonances that are characteristic of vowel contrasts. The open mouth, from the side, looks something like this, with dotted lines approximating the space available between the top of the tongue and the roof of the mouth:

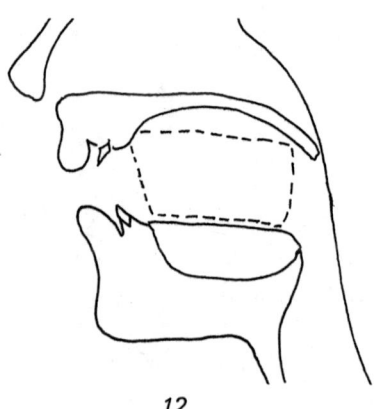

The tongue moves up and down (aided by a similar movement of the jaws) and forward and back, to change the size and shape of the mouth cavity, which acts as a resonance chamber to produce the vowel sounds. The space to represent tongue positions can be normalized in the shape of a square and divided into nine compartments, as follows:

This figure constitutes the basic frame of reference for the description of vowels as presented in this text. You will note that it has two dimensions, one up and down and one front to back. The nine squares can be labeled for purposes of identification as follows:

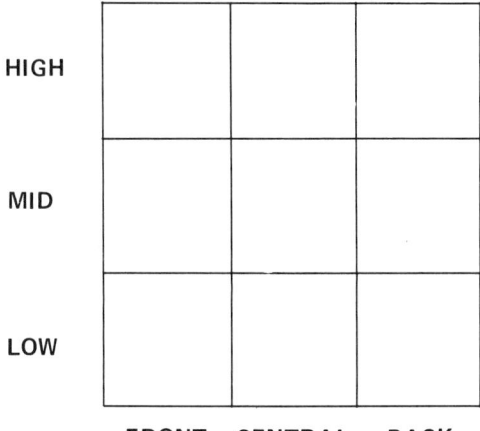

We can describe a vowel as having a high front position, a low front position, mid central, low back, etc. For our purposes the grid needs one modification: the elimination of the line in the central column that separates high and mid, to produce:

The elongated space represents a sound that is characteristic of English and will require special description to understand and specific practice to master; further information and special exercises will appear later in another chapter.

English distinguishes simple vowels and diphthongs (sometimes called simple and complex, sometimes short and long). We will present the simple vowels first, illustrated in short, one-syllable words. The boxes below contain the symbols that represent the seven simple vowels of American English:

I		U
ɛ	ə	
æ	ɑ	ɔ

ɪ	sɪt	sit
ɛ	sɛt	set
æ	sæt	sat
ə	sət	Sutt
ɑ	sɑt	sot
ɔ	sɔt	sought
ʊ	sʊt	soot

2.1 The English simple vowel set
Presentation and comparison of patterns; read across, then down:

1. sɪt	bɪk	kɪd	tɪk	pɪt	ɪt	pɪl	dɪn
2. sɛt	bɛk	kɛd	tɛk	pɛt	ɛt	pɛl	dɛn
3. sæt	bæk	kæd	tæk	pæt	æt	pæl	dæn
4. sət	bək	kəd	tək	pət	ət	---	dən
5. sɑt	bɑk	kɑd	tɑk	pɑt	ɑt	pɑl	dɑn
6. sɔt	bɔk	kɔd	tɔk	---	ɔt	pɔl	dɔn
7. sʊt	bʊk	kʊd	tʊk	pʊt	--	pʊl	---
sit	Bic	kid	tick	pit	it	pill	din
set	Beck	Ked	Tech	pet	et	pell	den
sat	back	cad	tack	pat	at	pal	Dan
Sutt	buck	cud	tuck	putt	Utt	---	dun
sot	bock	cod	tock	pot	Ott	Poll	Don
sought	balk	cawed	talk	---	ought	pall	dawn
soot	book	could	took	put	---	pull	---

The vowels in all the examples cited above are in closed syllables (in syllables that end in a consonant). This is typical of English simple vowels—although there are some exceptions. Confusions are more likely between some pairs of vowels than others; generally speaking, the nearer the vowels are in sound, the more likely they are to be confused.

The exercise sentences that follow are presented in minimal pairs. These consist of two sentences (or they could be two words or two phrases) which are alike except for one sound. Both sentences make sense, so we can say there is a minimal-pair situation. Which situation (or sentence or phrase or word) is interpreted depends on the accuracy of producing or hearing the appropriate member of the pair. Considering both possibilities in the same drill gives the student an opportunity to practice the contrasting pair in a context. It is no doubt true that both members of a minimal pair rarely occur in the same real-life conversation (or story or article or speech), but it is also true that when one of the pair occurs, it can sometimes be mistaken for the other.

The drill sentences contain two minimal-pair words (which make the sentences also minimal) separated by a slash. Following the sentences, in parentheses, are two words (or sometimes phrases) that paraphrase the meanings of the minimal-pair words. These serve to identify and differentiate each member of the pair, since the paraphrase items, unlike the original pair, do not sound alike and will therefore not be easily confused. It is suggested that a student working by himself should already understand the meaning of each of the two sentences by associating each in turn with the appropriate paraphrase. So he thinks: "After the play the audience left—they departed" compared to: "After the play the audience laughed—they giggled." In this way the appropriate meaning for this context is assigned to "left" and "laughed."

If two students are studying together, one can choose one member of the sentence pair and say it. The other then gives what he thinks is the correct paraphrase. If the two students consistently agree, they have communicated in a satisfactory way. If not, either the pronunciation or the comprehension is deficient. In a classroom the teacher will be able to use the paraphrases, either to identify or to cue members of the pair. Sometimes the concepts presented by minimal pairs can be represented pictorially or by actual items, such as the contrast between "men" and "man," or can be mimed, such as "pet" (by stroking) and "pat" (by tapping lightly with the extended fingers). These modes of identifying meanings are excellent ways to differentiate the sentence-pair and should be used whenever practical. The important principle is to show convincingly that differences in pronunciation—even small differences—are used to signal different meanings.

Following is a series of exercises designed to help students distinguish between vowels that may sound similar. A student should practice only those pairs which he finds difficult to tell apart.

2.1a English /ɪ/ and /ɛ/

dɪn/dɛn   1. I heard a roar over the din/den. (noise/cage)

pɪnd/pɛnd   2. He pinned/penned a note on her desk. (attached/wrote)

lɪft/lɛft   3. Take the lift/left to get to the office. (elevator/turn)

chɪr/chɛr   4. Let's have a big cheer/chair for Dick. (shout/seat)

bítər/bétər   5. To spank some children makes them bitter/better. (angers them/improves them)

2.1b English /ɛ/ and /æ/

mɛn/mæn   1. Will the men/man come? (group/person) or (many/one)

pɛn/pæn   2. This pen/pan leaks. (Don't write/cook with it.)

pɛt/pæt   3. Don't pet/pat the dog. (stroke/tap) (or gestures)

lɛnd/lænd   4. I hope you will lend/land me a fish. (loan/bring in)

lɛft/læft   5. After the play the audience left/laughed. (departed/giggled)

2.1c English /æ/ and /ɑ/

kæd/kɑd   1. The old cad/cod looked terrible. (man/fish)

ræk/rɑk   2. Darwin fell on the rack/rock. (frame/stone)

æks/ɑks   3. The farmer lost his axe/ox. (tool/animal)

blækt/blɑkt   4. The soldiers blacked/blocked out the camp. (made dark/traced)

rǽkət/rɑ́kət   5. The racket/rocket was deafening. (noise/space vehicle)

2.1d English /æ/ and /ə/

dæm/dəm	1. My damn/dumb teacher said no. (accursed/unintelligent)
ræg/rəg	2. Throw that old rag/rug out. (worn cloth/carpet)
kæf/kəf	3. He stumbled and tore his calf/cuff. (lower leg/pant leg)
bækt/bəkt	4. The horse backed/bucked unexpectedly. (reversed/reared)
ǽngkəl/ə́ngkəl	5. My ankle/uncle is broke. (foot joint cracked/relative insolvent)

2.1e English /ə/ and /ɑ/

pəp/pɑp	1. My pup/pop is very good natured. (dog/father)
wən/wɑn	2. The one/wan boy looks sick. (first/pale)
shət/shɑt	3. He shut/shot up the consul. (silenced/wounded)
rəbd/rɑbd	4. Somebody rubbed/robbed the paint on the table. (applied/stole)
kə́lər/kɑ́lər	5. Her color/collar is just not right. (pigment/neck of garment)

2.1f English /ɑ/ and /ɔ/

dɑn/dɔn	1. When will Don/dawn come? (Donald/daybreak)
hɑk/hɔk	2. William thinks he'll have to hock/hawk his watch. (pawn/sell)
stɑks/stɔks	3. He paid too much for the stocks/stalks. (corporation shares/corn stems)
bɑ́diy/bɔ́diy	4. This looks like a body/bawdy shop. (auto repair, indecent)
nɑ́tiy/nɔ́tiy	5. That's really a knotty/naughty problem. (complex, evil)

2.1g English /ə/ and /ʊ/

bək/bʊk	1. I lost a buck/book yesterday. (dollar/bound volume)
pət/pʊt	2. He'll have to putt/put the ball in the cup. (stroke/place)
tək/tʊk	3. The girls tuck/took up the hem. (fold/shortened)
lək/lʊk	4. He gave me this awful luck/look. (misfortune/glance)
həks/hʊks	5. These are Huck's/hooks. (belong to Huck/curved fasteners)

Stressed simple vowels have a relatively steady quality. They can be characterized by a set of dots, referring more specifically to tongue position, placed on the frame of reference, as follows:

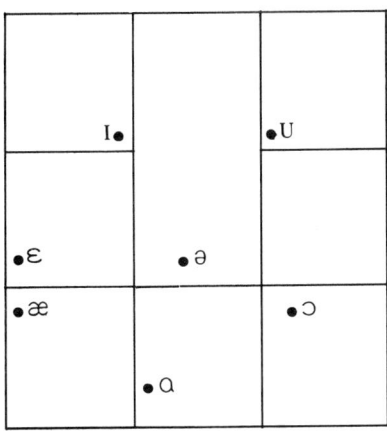

American English diphthongs (or complex vowels or long vowels) consist of a vowel plus an offglide, for which the tongue moves up in the mouth. The offglide is represented as a semivowel (/y/ for a glide toward a higher front position and /w/ for a glide toward a higher back position). The seven diphthongs common in American English are represented by dots and arrows (the dot for the vowel and the arrow for the semivowel glide) on our frame of reference as follows:

20 Patterns of English Pronunciation

iy	biy	bee, be, Bea
ey	bey	bay, bey
ay	bay	buy, by, bye
oy	boy	boy
aw	baw	bough, bow
ow	bow	bow, beau
uw	buw	boo

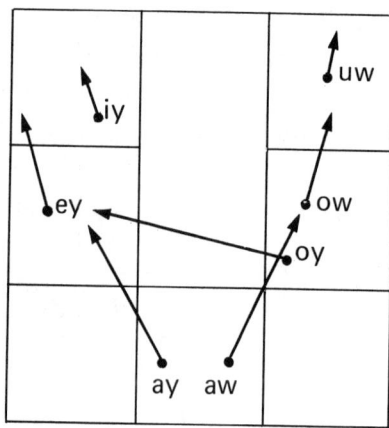

2.2 The English diphthong set

Presentation and comparison of patterns; read across, then down.

1. biy	siy	fiyl	tiyl	diyn	liyn	biyt
2. bey	sey	feyl	teyl	deyn	leyn	beyt
3. bay	say	fayl	tayl	dayn	layn	bayt
4. boy	soy	foyl	toyl	----	loyn	----
5. baw	saw	fawl	tawl	dawn	----	bawt
6. bow	sow	fowl	towl	down	lown	bowt
7. buw	suw	fuwl	tuwl	duwn	luwn	buwt
bee	sea	feel	teal	dean	lean	beat
bay	say	fail	tail	deign	lane	bait
buy	sigh	file	tile	dine	line	bite
boy	soy	foil	toil	----	loin	----
bough	sow	fowl	towel	down	----	bout
bow	sew	foal	toll	Doane	loan	boat
boo	sue	fool	tool	dune	loon	boot

The diphthongs cited above occur in open and in closed syllables (in syllables where the diphthong is the last sound and in syllables where a consonant follows). The pronunciation of diphthongs in English is usually somewhat relaxed, with no great hurry to finish the glide. Note also that to pronounce the glide the tongue moves *in the direction of* /y/ or /w/, but usually doesn't go all the way to the top of the mouth where /y/ and /w/ are made when they begin a word.

This is especially noticeable in the lower diphthongs /ay, oy, aw/ where the glides do not reach the area of the roof of the mouth. Note also that the lower glides are longer and more noticeable, since there is more space for the tongue to rise, whereas the high vowels in the diphthongs /iy/ and /uw/ are already quite near the roof of the mouth and there is just a little space available for a further rise.

It is very common and very easy to confuse simple vowels and diphthongs. The drills which follow contrast the diphthongs with the most closely similar simple vowels. Be sure you can hear and produce the difference.

You will notice that the letter symbol used for the simple vowel alone is not quite the same as the one used in the related diphthong: /ɪ/ in the simple vowel but /i/ in the diphthong /iy/. In other words the /i/ only appears in this text when accompanied by the /y/. There is no real reason for this, though the vowel sound alone and in the diphthong are probably slightly different, with the /y/-glide influencing the vowel it follows. The intention of the respelling is always to clearly represent different sounds, and experience tells us that the /ɪ/ and /iy/ sounds are easily confused by students. To try to be helpful, the respelling marks the difference both by using different vowel-letter symbols and by a separate representation for the glide. Thus the simple vowel symbols are /ɪ-ɛ-ɑ-ɔ-ʊ/ and the diphthong symbols are /i,e,a,o/ plus /y/ or /a,o,u/ plus /w/.

2.2a English /ɪ/ and /iy/

bɪt/biyt	1. Who bit/beat Mr. Jones? (wounded with teeth/hit with a stick)
hɪt/hiyt	2. The smithy has to hit/heat the horseshoe. (with a hammer/with a fire)
wɪn/wiyn	3. I hope you win/wean the puppy. (gain/stop from suckling)
rɪm/riym	4. He dropped the whole rim/ream. (wheel/paper)
mɪl/miyl	5. They talked about the mill/meal. (flour grinder/dinner)

Note that the contrasts cited are in closed syllables, since simple vowels typically occur before a consonant.

2.2b English /ɪ/ and /ey/

gɪv/geyv	1. They always give/gave generously. (all the time/previously)
sɪv/seyv	2. You should sieve/save this flour. (strain/keep)
stɪl/steyl	3. The water is very still/stale. (quiet/not fresh)
chɪn/cheyn	4. The blow broke his chin/chain. (jaw/shackles)
tíntəd/téyntəd	5. He sees the world through tinted/tainted glasses. (colored/tarnished)

2.2c English /ɛ/ and /ey/

sɛl/seyl	1. Why don't you sell/sail this boat? (for money/for pleasure)
lɛs/leys	2. I like dresses with less/lace ruffles. (fewer/needlework)
wɛd/weyd	3. I wed/weighed my spouse a year ago. (married/measured heaviness)
tɛst/teyst	4. Test/taste this to see if it has enough salt. (examine/touch with tongue)
pɛnd/peynd	5. I shudder to think of his penned/pained expressions. (written/distressed)

2.2d English /æ/ and /ay/

dæm/daym	1. I wouldn't give a damn/dime for his opinion. (disparagement/ten cents)
kæt/kayt	2. He grabbed the cat/kite by the tail. (feline animal/flying toy)
tæp/tayp	3. I'll tap/type out a message. (on the telegraph key/on the typewriter)

2.2d (continued)

læk/layk   4. The president will never lack/like authority. (feel the absence/be pleased by)

snæpt/snaypt   5. She really snapped/sniped at him. (spoke discourteously/criticized disparagingly)

2.2e English /ɑ/ and /ay/

kɑt/kayt   1. She pulled down the cot/kite. (bed/flying toy)

dɑk/dayk   2. The boat smashed into the dock/dike. (pier/sea wall)

bɑnd/baynd   3. This is the bond/bind that hurts. (connection/difficulty)

blɑnd/blaynd   4. His daughter is blonde/blind. (fair haired/sightless)

trɑd/trayd   5. They trod/tried that path many times. (walked/attempted)

2.2f English /ɑ/ and /aw/

rɑt/rawt   1. The dry rot/route is dangerous at night. (decay/road)

plɑd/plawd   2. They plod/ploughed over the field. (trudge/made furrows)

pɑnd/pawnd   3. His dog ended up in the pond/pound. (water/animal shelter)

dɑnd/dawnd   4. He donned/downed the nightcap. (put on the head covering/drank the brew)

dɑ́təd/dáwtəd   5. He dotted/doubted his i's/eyes. (put a point over/disbelieved)

2.2g English /ɔ/ and /oy/

ɔl/oyl	1. Do you need the awl/oil? (tool/lubricant)
kɔl/koyl	2. The snake was ready to call/coil. (appear on the scene/form rings)
fɔl/foyl	3. The tree broke his fall/foil. (descent/rapier)
bɔld/boyld	4. He looks like a bald/boiled eagle. (white headed/cooked in water)
lɔnz/loynz	5. His lawns/loins have dried up. (no more grass/no more children)

2.2h English /ɔ/ and /ow/

fɔn/fown	1. Bambi answered the fawn/phone. (young deer/communication device)
bɔl/bowl	2. They are all dressed to go to the ball/bowl. (formal dance/outdoor concert)
hɔl/howl	3. The crowd soon filled the hall/hole. (auditorium/excavation)
ɔd/owd	4. Within a week he awed/owed everybody in town. (fearfully impressed/was indebted to)
pɔz/powz	5. Her pause/pose was hard to explain. (hesitation/temporary position)

2.2i English /ə/ and /ow/

kət/kowt	1. She got an ugly cut/coat at the sale. (wound/garment)
kəm/kowm	2. Come/comb through the house carefully. (proceed/search)
həl/howl	3. This ship has a dangerous hull/hole. (body/opening)
gəl/gowl	4. The gull/goal was too high to reach. (bird/target)
bəst/bowst	5. That was quite a bust/boast last night. (party/brag)

2.2j English /ʊ/ and /ow/

kʊk/kowk	1. Where's the cook/coke I asked you about? (kitchen artist/soft drink)
bʊl/bowl	2. There was a black bull/bowl in the corner. (male bovine/concave container)
pʊld/powld	3. They pulled/poled the boat upstream. (tugged forward/pushed with a long stick)
hʊks/howks	4. Have you read the recent book about the Hookes/hoax? (well-known family/deception)
stʊd/stowd	5. He stood/stowed the tall statue in the closet. (placed upright/put away)

2.2k English /ʊ/ and /uw/

lʊk/luwk	1. I saw it in Look/Luke. (picture magazine/the third gospel)
fʊl/fuwl	2. No one but a full/fool kid would do that. (amply fed/silly)
pʊld/puwld	3. They pulled/pooled their resources. (drew out/combined)
kʊd/kuwd	4. Do you think the dove could/cooed? (would be able/murmured)
stʊd/stuwd	5. She stood/stewed and fussed. (remained in place/worried)

Usually students don't confuse the diphthongs with each other. Some, however, especially those whose native language does not have structurally distinct diphthongs, do confuse English diphthongs with each other. The following exercises are included to illustrate the relevant contrasts. Notice that since diphthongs are being compared, contrasts in open syllables (not ending in a consonant other than the glides /y/ and /w/) are possible.

2.3 English /iy/ and /ey/

siy/sey	1. Did you see/say what I told you to? (perceive visually/utter)
tiym/teym	2. We can easily team/tame these two horses. (pair/domesticate)
hiyt/heyt	3. The battle produced tremendous heat/hate. (hotness/ill will)
wiyd/weyd	4. We had to weed/wade in the rice paddy. (remove unwanted plants/walk through water)
wiyl/weyl	5. That's the biggest wheel/whale I ever saw! (rotating device/huge fish)

2.3a English /ey/ and /ay/

sey/say	1. Why did he say/sigh so much? (speak/lament)
teyp/tayp	2. We'll tape/type a letter to her. (record in sound/write on a machine)
leys/lays	3. She has lace/lice on her collar. (needlework/small insects)
feyts/fayts	4. The fates/fights have left him discouraged. (destiny/conflicts)
kleymd/klaymd	5. Balboa claimed/climbed the mountain. (declared ownership/ascended)

2.3b English /ay/ and /aw/

nay/naw	1. The prophet said the time is nigh/now. (near at hand/the present time)
bay/baw	2. Your servant seems to buy/bow too much. (purchase/bend at the waist)
ayl/awl	3. They finally spotted the green isle/owl. (island/wise bird)
dayn/dawn	4. They want to go dine/down. (eat/descend)
faynd/fawnd	5. They want to find/found a monastery. (locate/establish)

2.3c English /aw/ and /oy/

baw/boy — 1. The bough/boy fell out of the tree. (limb/child)

saw/soy — 2. Over there is the sow/soy field. (female hog/Asian bean)

awl/oyl — 3. That owl/oil is pretty slippery. (wise bird/viscous liquid)

fawld/foyld — 4. He really fouled/foiled the pitcher. (hit crooked/thwarted)

pawnts/poynts — 5. A pair of hawks pounce/points at the rabbit. (spring toward/indicate toward)

2.3d English /aw/ and /ow/

waw/wow — 1. He uttered a loud "wow/whoa." (ejaculation of delight/message to horse to stop)

bawt/bowt — 2. It was the first bout/boat he'd been in. (boxing match/floating vehicle)

dawst/dowst — 3. She doused/dosed him with saltwater. (threw over/administered as medicine)

fawnd/fownd — 4. He at last found/phoned his sister. (located/called by telephone)

bawnd/bownd — 5. She bound/boned the turkey. (tied securely/removed skeletal pieces)

2.3e English /oy/ and /ow/

koyn/kown — 1. She had one coin/cone for lunch. (piece of money/serving of ice cream)

soyl/sowl — 2. Ploughing is good for the soil/soul. (land/spirit)

oyld/owld — 3. The engine was oiled/old. (lubricated/aged)

hoyst/howst — 4. A good hoist/host keeps things moving. (lifting device/party giver)

2.3e (continued)

poyzd/powzd	5. Marianne was poised/posed for the picture. (in readiness/placed in position)

2.3f English /ow/ and /uw/

sow/suw	1. They're going to sew/sue for peace. (work with needle/petition)
blow/bluw	2. The winds blow/blew every day. (still do/used to)
sowp/suwp	3. She makes her own soap/soup. (cleansing agent/dinner appetizer)
kowld/kuwld	4. The weather's cold/cooled today. (has no heat/has become less warm)
rôwstɪŋ/rûwstɪŋ	5. The chicken is roasting/roosting. (cooking/resting)

Chapter 3
THE ENGLISH CONSONANTS

Whereas the vowels and diphthongs have an open and sonorous production (and appear in virtually every syllable) the consonants, the sounds that "go with" the vowels in most syllables, are produced by restricting, or even stopping, the air flow in various ways. The consonants that fully interrupt the air stream are called "stops" or "stop consonants." A special kind of stop is referred to as an "affricate." Another set of consonants is characterized by noisy breath friction and called "fricatives." Another set has the air flow diverted through the nose and is called "nasal." A further set—"liquids"—is produced with almost no friction. And finally there are two "semiconsonants" which function similarly to the semivowels that occur with vowels to form diphthongs as described in the last chapter. All of these types will be illustrated below.

But first we should understand two other dimensions by which consonants are defined. The first of the two refers to the location in the mouth where the consonant is produced, the "place of articulation." This ranges from the lips, through the teeth, alveolus, palate, and velum to the pharynx and the glottis. The place of articulation is the location in the mouth where the fixed articulators (just listed) are approached, or in the case of the stops, "touched," by the moving articulators attached directly or indirectly to the jaw (the lower lip and the tongue) or to the velum (the uvula), shown in the following diagram:

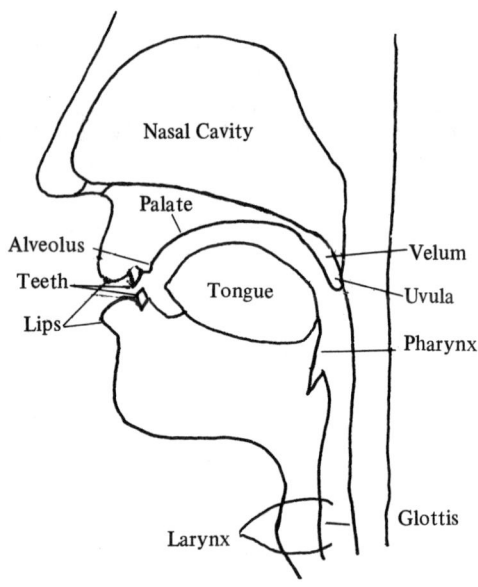

The other dimension that is relevant to the production of consonant sounds is the voicing of the articulation. For some consonants the vocal chords or bands are in motion (vibrating), as they are for all English vowels; for other consonants the vocal chords are at rest and usually relaxed and open (not vibrating), as they are when we whisper any sound. Our frame of reference for consonants is somewhat similar to the one used for vowels, though we are usually interested in points along the speech tract, rather than in areas that produce resonance chambers. We have a front-to-back dimension that shows place of articulation. The up-and-down dimension of the figure is used to show type of articulation and is not concerned with tongue height, as in the figure for vowels. The third dimension is shown within each box, where two separate symbols may appear; the ones in the top of a square are voiceless, the ones in the bottom, voiced.

The figure that shows the organization of English consonant sounds in terms of their place, type, and voicing of articulation is on the facing page.

Type of Articulation	Place of Articulation							
	Lips	Lips-Teeth	Teeth	Alveolus	Palate	Velum	Pharynx	Glottis
Stop	p b			t d		k g		*
Affricate					ch j			
Fricative		f v	th dh	s z	sh zh		h	
Nasal	m			n		ng		
Liquid				l	r			
Semiconsonant				y		w		

The glottis column is included because there is one variant of the English /t/ sound that has a glottal articulation, but this will be discussed at length later. Remember in looking at this chart and getting familiar with the symbols that six sounds are represented by digraphs (two letters together): /ch, sh, zh, th, dh, ng/. These are all single sounds (the /ch/ will be described as a possible exception to this statement) in spite of being represented by two letters. The symbols have been chosen because they are readable and helpfully suggestive—if this were a book for professional linguists we would probably use the symbols /č, š, ž, θ, ð, ŋ/. This would mean learning symbols that are new for most students and that will not have so useful a carryover to reading in the traditional alphabet. There are some disadvantages, but it has seemed better to violate the linguistic canon "one sound one symbol" in the interest of suggestive representation of sounds for students, who are either familiar with the English alphabet or will have to become familiar with it.

A consonant may appear at the beginning or at the end of a syllable (i.e., before or after the vowel nucleus). In words of more than one syllable a single consonant may end one syllable and/or begin the next. That is to say, in a word like *baby,* there is no clear way to tell whether the second /b/ is the end of the first syllable (as in /beyb-/) or the beginning of the second (as in /-biy/). Fortunately it usually doesn't make much difference for purposes of learning to pronounce /béybiy/, so the question can be safely left to the phoneticians. Another feature of the arrangement of consonants is of concern to the student: consonants in either initial or final position in a syllable can occur singly or in clusters or groups. As many as three consonants may appear in an initial cluster and as many as four may occur finally. That means that if the right words are put together, as many as seven consonants can occur in a sequence. This is indeed a major problem for students of English whose native language allows only one or at most two consonants in sequence.

This chapter will present the consonant sounds alone, usually in one-syllable words. Chapter 6 will deal with the problems of consonant clusters.

We begin with three consonants: /m, n, s/. These are chosen because they are very simple to produce, and since similar sounds occur in most of the world's languages, they usually do not cause many difficulties to students. This presentation will introduce consonant sounds in simple words, at the beginning and at the end of syllables, and in a few cases, single consonants between syllables. The words cited all have meanings in English, but what they mean is not very important. (Most of the capitalized words are proper names, which really have no "lexical" meaning.) Our concern is for the syllable structure, which will carry over into other, longer words. The word /nəm/ (spelled *numb*) may be relatively unimportant because it doesn't occur frequently, but it may be found in other very common words, such as /nə́mbər/ (spelled *number*). To help identify words, they are given both in transcription and in traditional spelling.

3.1 English /m/, /n/, and /s/

Presentation of pattern; read down:

/m - m/		/n - n/		/s - s/	
1a. mɪm	mim	2a. næn	Nan	3a. sɪs	sis
b. mɛm	mem	b. nən	none	b. sæs	sass
c. mæm	ma'am	c. nayn	nine	c. sɔs	sauce
d. mɑm	mom	d. nawn	noun	d. siys	cease
e. məm	mum	e. nown	known	e. saws	souse
f. meym	maim	f. nuwn	noon		
g. maym	mime				

Distribution of pattern; read across in pairs:

	/m-/	/-m/		
1a.	mæn	næm	man	Nam
b.	mən	nəm	Mon	numb
c.	meyn	neym	main	name
d.	mown	nowm	moan	Nome
e.	mɪs	sɪm	miss	Simm
f.	mæs	sæm	mass	Sam
g.	məs	səm	muss	some
h.	meys	seym	mace	same

	/n-/	/-n/		
2a.	næm	mæn	Nam	man
b.	nəm	mən	numb	Mon
c.	neym	meyn	name	main
d.	nowm	mown	Nome	moan
e.	nəs	sən	Nuss	son
f.	niys	siyn	niece	seen
g.	nays	sayn	nice	sign
h.	nuws	suwn	noose	soon

	/s-/	/-s/		
3a.	sɪm	mɪs	Simm	miss
b.	sæm	mæs	Sam	mass
c.	səm	məs	some	muss
d.	seym	meys	same	mace
e.	sən	nəs	son	Nuss
f.	siyn	niys	seen	niece
g.	sayn	nays	sign	nice
h.	suwn	nuws	soon	noose

There will be few difficulties with these three sounds, although some students may tend to overnasalize vowels adjacent to nasal consonants. Even this is not a serious flaw, since many English speakers show the same influence. Nasal quality of vowels is particularly noticeable when a nasal consonant occurs both before and after a vowel, as in /mæn-nən-neym-mown/, etc. Note that in English a final nasal consonant is clearly pronounced and doesn't become just a nasalization of the preceding vowel. Note also that /m/ and /n/ are voiced, and that /s/ is voiceless.

The next set of sounds should also be relatively easy for most students—the voiced stops. These sounds completely interrupt the flow of the column of air from the lungs, the /b/ by the two lips coming together, the /d/ by the front part of the tongue touching against the alveolus, and the /g/ by the back part of the tongue against the velum. In initial position voicing begins just before the air stream is released by opening the lips, etc. In final position (when silence follows) voicing terminates very quickly as the air stream is closed. Except in very strongly emphasized speech the final stop usually is just a closure, though when speaking loudly or in anger a devoiced release may be heard.

3.2 English /b/, /d/, and /g/

Presentation of pattern; read down:

	/b - b/			/d - d/			/g - g/	
1a.	bɪb	bib	2a.	dɪd	did	3a.	gɪg	gig
b.	bæb	Bab	b.	dɛd	dead	b.	gæg	gag
c.	bəb	bub	c.	dæd	dad	c.	gɑg	Gog
d.	bɑb	Bob	d.	dəd	dud			
e.	beyb	babe	e.	dɑd	Dodd			
f.	buwb	boob	f.	diyd	deed			
			g.	deyd	Dade			
			h.	duwd	dude			

Distribution of pattern; read across:

	/b-/	/-b/			
1a.	bɑm	mɑb		bomb	mob
b.	bɪn	nɪb		bin	nib
c.	bæn	næb		ban	nab
d.	bən	nəb		bun	nub
e.	bɑn	nɑb		Bonn	knob
f.	bəs	səb		bus	sub
g.	bæd	dæb		bad	dab
h.	bæg	gæb		bag	gab

	/d-/	/-d/			
2a.	dɪm	mɪd		dim	mid
b.	dæm	mæd		dam	mad
c.	dəm	məd		dumb	mud
d.	dɛn	nɛd		den	Ned
e.	dɑn	nɑd		Don	nod
f.	days	sayd		dice	side
g.	duws	suwd		deuce	sued
h.	dəb	bəd		dub	bud

3.2 (continued)

	/g-/	/-g/		
3a.	gæm	mæg	gamb	mag
b.	gəm	məg	gum	mug
c.	gɔl	lɔg	gall	log
d.	gæs	sæg	gas	sag
e.	gɪb	bɪg	gib	big
f.	gæb	bæg	gab	bag
g.	gəb	bəg	gub	bug
h.	gæt	tæg	gat	tag

In some languages the voiced stops change noticeably when they occur between syllables. Not so for English /b/ and /g/. The /d/ sound does change, but this depends on stress patterns and other considerations which will be discussed in more detail later, when this feature of /d/ and /t/ will be dealt with. For now, just imitate the model.

3.2a English /b/, /d/, and /g/ between syllables
Pattern details; read down:

	/-b-/			/-d-/	
1a.	ǽbiy	Abby	2a.	ɛ́diy	Eddie
b.	tə́biy	tubby	b.	mə́diy	muddy
c.	hə́biy	hubby	c.	bə́diy	buddy
d.	nɑ́biy	knobby	d.	bɑ́diy	body
e.	bɑ́biy	Bobbie	e.	gʊ́diy	goodie
f.	lɪ́biy	Libby	f.	kɪ́diy	kiddie
g.	méybiy	maybe	g.	léydiy	lady
h.	əbə́v	above	h.	ədúw	ado
i.	əbáwt	about	i.	ədɔ́r	adore

	/-g-/	
3a.	ǽgiy	Aggie
b.	mə́giy	muggy
c.	bə́giy	buggy
d.	bɑ́giy	boggy
e.	bówgiy	bogey
f.	pɪ́giy	piggy
g.	lɛ́giy	leggy
h.	əgów	ago
i.	əgɛ́n	again

Note the occurrence of the stress in the second syllable on the last two items in each column. In all the examples cited the stop consonants interrupt and break the air column.

The next group of sounds are also stop consonants, the voiceless set. The /p, t, k/ are the voiceless counterparts to the /b, d, g/ just presented. In initial position the onset of voicing (for the following vowel, which is normally always voiced) comes well after the release, which sets the column of the air in motion. In fact, air pressure is built up while the passage is closed, so that when the opening comes, the air escapes forcefully with a noticeable puff. This puff of air is called aspiration and is an important characteristic of English voiceless stops when they occur at the beginning of a stressed syllable (i.e., always when a word of one syllable is cited). In final position (before silence) the /p, t, k/ are usually unreleased, unless the word is pronounced very forcefully or emphatically (in this respect they are like /b, d, g/). Listen for and try to produce aspirated versions of the voiceless stops—this is the feature that identifies them for English speakers. If initial /p, t, k/ are pronounced without aspiration, they are very likely to be interpreted as /b, d, g/. The student should have no trouble hearing the right version—that's not difficult. What is difficult, and important, is to remember to produce aspirated variations when they are appropriate.

3.3 English /p/, /t/, and /k/

Presentation of pattern; read down:

	/p - p/			/t - t/			/k - k/	
1a.	pɪp	pip	2a.	tɪt	tit	3a.	kɪk	kick
b.	pæp	pap	b.	tæt	tat	b.	kɑk	cock
c.	pəp	pup	c.	tət	tut	c.	kɔk	calk
d.	pɑp	pop	d.	tɑt	tot	d.	kuk	cook
e.	piyp	peep	e.	tɔt	taut	e.	keyk	cake
f.	payp	pipe	f.	tiyt	teat	f.	kayk	kike
g.	powp	pope	g.	tayt	tight	g.	kowk	coke
h.	puwp	poop	h.	tuwt	toot	h.	kuwk	kook

Distribution of pattern; read across:

	/p-/	/-p/			
1a.	pæm	mæp		Pam	map
b.	pæn	næp		pan	nap
c.	peyn	neyp		pain	nape

3.3 (continued)

	d. pæs	sæp	pass	sap
	e. piys	siyp	peace	seep
	f. puwd	duwp	poohed	dupe
	g. peyt	teyp	pate	tape
	h. powk	kowp	poke	cope

	/t-/	/-t/		
2a.	tɪn	nɪt	tin	knit
b.	tæn	næt	tan	gnat
c.	tiym	miyt	team	meat
d.	taym	mayt	time	might
e.	tɔs	sɔt	toss	sought
f.	təb	bət	tub	but
g.	təg	gət	tug	gut
h.	towd	dowt	toad	dote

	/k-/	/-k/		
3a.	kɪn	nɪk	kin	nick
b.	kæn	næk	can	knack
c.	kɪs	sɪk	kiss	sick
d.	kəm	mək	come	muck
e.	kiyp	piyk	keep	peak
f.	keym	meyk	came	make
g.	keys	seyk	case	sake
h.	kəd	dək	cud	duck

Remember that the first of each pair has an aspirated /p, t, k/ because it's at the beginning of a syllable. In citation form the syllable final /p, t, k/ are typically unreleased, but even when they *are* released, the release is normally unaspirated. We can see this difference when the voiceless stop comes between syllables (i.e., between vowels in a two-syllable word). The consonant usually goes with the vowel that carries strong stress, whether this is the first or second syllable. Thus when the first syllable carries strong stress, the medial /p, t, k/ is not aspirated; when the second syllable carries strong stress, the medial /p, t, k/ *is* aspirated.

In the following drill be sure to listen for and to produce unaspirated stops in the words in the first column, aspirated stops in the second.

3.3a Medial /p/ and /k/
Distribution of pattern; read across:

/´p-/	/-pˊ/		
1a. ápər	əpír	upper	appear
b. sápər	səpówz	supper	suppose
c. ǽpəl	əpláy	apple	apply
d. hǽpiy	əpíyl	happy	appeal
e. ówpən	əpénd	open	append
f. ówpəs	əpówz	opus	oppose
g. ówpəl	əpɔ́l	opal	appall
h. píypər	əpíyz	peeper	appease

/´k-/	/-kˊ/		
2a. éykər	əkɔ́st	acre	accost
b. béykən	əkín	bacon	akin
c. sákər	səkám	succor	succumb
d. bíykən	biykám	beacon	become
e. ówkər	əkə́r	ocher	occur
f. ówkiy	òwkéy	Okie	O.K.
g. dákiy	diykráy	ducky	decry
h. dékèyd	diykéyd	decade	decayed

Medial /t/ is comparable in part to medial /p/ and /k/; it is aspirated when the stressed syllable follows. But when the stressed syllable precedes medial /t/ the complexity of this most complicated of English consonants becomes obvious. The next six exercises will try to illustrate some of the versions of /t/.

Medial /t/ after a stressed syllable and *not* followed by /n/ or /l/ becomes a rather different sound, described as a "flap." In pronouncing a flap /t/ in a word like *pretty* the tongue begins low in the mouth and then rises rapidly and flicks past the alveolar ridge behind the upper teeth. The resulting "brush past" is the flap /t/. It is difficult to practice because it is a sound that cannot be slowed down—without a considerable change in acoustic effect. This sound is interpreted as an *r* in many languages, but English speakers will hear it as a /t/, particularly in medial position between vowels after stress (the conditions of its occurrence in English). Listen carefully and try to imitate as closely as you can. The /t/ of the first column will be flapped, of the second column will be aspirated.

3.3b Medial /t/ between vowels
Distribution of pattern; read down and then across:

/ˈt-/	/-tˊ/		
1. átər	ətɛ́nd	utter	attend
2. ɔ́tow	ətówn	auto	atone
3. ǽtɪk	ətǽk	attic	attack
4. krítɪk	krɪtíyk	critic	critique
5. átər	ətáp	otter	atop
6. áytəm	ətɛ́st	item	attest
7. prítiy	pətíyt	pretty	petite
8. dɛ́tər	dətə́r	debtor	deter
9. sítiy	sɛtíy	city	settee

This pattern is often seen in related words where the stress is shifted when an ending is added to a word. This is illustrated in the following drill where the /t/ in the first column is a flap and the "same" /t/ in the second column is aspirated.

3.3c Medial /t/ between vowels in morphologically related words
Distribution of pattern; read across:

/ˈt-/	/-tˊ/		
1. ǽtəm	ətámɪk	atom	atomic
2. ɔ́təm	ətə́mnəl	autumn	autumnal
3. mǽtər	mətíriyəl	matter	material
4. ítəliy	ɪtǽlyən	Italy	Italian
5. sǽtərəst	sətírɪk	satirist	satiric
6. sǽtərn	sətə́rniyən	Saturn	Saturnian
7. rɛ́tərɪk	rətɔ́rəkəl	rhetoric	rhetorical
8. ártəkəl	àrtíkyuwlèyt	article	articulate
9. váytəl	vàytǽlətiy	vital	vitality

It is noted that the flap /t/ occurs after a strong-stressed syllable *only* when it follows a vowel or a vowel plus /r/ (with one exception to be taken up presently). Note the following exercise that presents examples in the same stress pattern, but with an /s/ before the /t/. In this pattern, the medial /t/ in the words in the first column are unaspirated (but not flapped) and in the second column, as expected, the /t/ is aspirated.

3.3d Medial /t/ after /s/
Distribution of pattern; read across:

/´st-/	/-st´-/		
1. də́stər	dəstə́rb	duster	disturb
2. bə́stər	biystə́r	Buster	bestir
3. mɪ́stɪk	mɪstɪ́yk	mystic	mystique
4. mɪ́stər	məstɛ́r	mister	mystere
5. sɪ́stər	səstéyn	sister	sustain
6. áwstər	ɔstɪ́r	ouster	austere
7. ɛ́stər	əstéyt	ester	estate
8. ǽstər	əstə́r	aster	astir

It should be observed that the pattern is more general than having /t/ just after /s/. It can occur following /f/ as the pair /ǽftər ~ ə̀ftówsə/ *(after ~ aftosa)* shows, with the first /t/ unaspirated and the second aspirated. But the occurrence of /t/ after /s/ is much more common.

Actually the pattern of /st/ is matched by /sp/ and /sk/, which follow the general pattern of stress distribution and its effect on aspiration. Examples (first column unaspirated, second aspirated) are:

/´sC-/	/-sC´-/		
rɛ́spət	dəspáyt	respite	despite
rɪ́skiy	rɪskéy	risky	risqué

The flap sound that characterizes the /t/ when it occurs medially after stress (*3.3b* and *c* above) is also the realization for /d/ under the same stress and position conditions. This is mainly true when a very informal style of speaking is observed. This means that words like *catty* and *caddy* can have the same pronunciation. The following exercise illustrates the potential confusion between medial /t/ and /d/.

3.3e Medial /t/ and /d/
Comparison of pattern; read across:

	/ˊt-/	/ˊd-/	flapped /t/*		
1.	kǽtiy	kǽdiy	kǽtiy	catty	caddy
2.	kĭ́tiy	kĭ́diy	kĭ́tiy	kitty	kiddy
3.	ḗtiy	ḗdiy	ḗtiy	Ettie	Eddie
4.	mĭ́tiy	mĭ́diy	mĭ́tiy	Mitty	middy
5.	fǽtiy	fǽdiy	fǽtiy	fatty	faddy
6.	dáwtiy	dáwdiy	dáwtiy	doughty	dowdy
7.	hártiy	hárdiy	hártiy	hearty	hardy
8.	mǽtər	mǽdər	mǽtər	matter	madder
9.	lǽtər	lǽdər	lǽtər	latter	ladder
10.	lĭ́ytər	lĭ́ydər	lĭ́ytər	liter	leader
11.	sĭ́ytər	sĭ́ydər	sĭ́ytər	seater	seeder
12.	ə́tər	ə́dər	ə́tər	utter	udder
13.	átər	ádər	átər	otter	odder
14.	bə́tər	bə́dər	bə́tər	butter	budder
15.	bĭ́tər	bĭ́dər	bĭ́tər	bitter	bidder
16.	ǽtəm	ǽdəm	ǽtəm	atom	Adam
17.	fyúwtəl	fyúwdəl	fyúwtəl	futile	feudal

Though in normal pronunciation these are not differentiated, they may be if necessary for precise understanding. But this will be done only at the expense of a somewhat exaggerated articulation. Understandably, the speaker and hearer depend considerably on context for accurate interpretation. Sentences like the following are particularly subject to confusion:

1. You should really invite Ettie/Eddie. (Esther/Edward)
2. That's a futile/feudal custom. (ineffectual/medieval)
3. We enjoyed a hearty/hardy friendship. (cordial/enduring)
4. Whose kitty/kiddie is that? (cat/child)
5. His books were often rated/raided for good ideas. (ranked highly/used as a source)

---

*substitutable for either /ˊt-/ or /ˊd-/

Students should be familiar with the possibility of dual interpretation with the loss of this contrast.

The pronunciation of /t/ that is most difficult to relate to the voiceless alveolar stop is the variant that precedes the so-called syllabic /n/ in words like *button, cotton, mountain, fountain*. This version of /t/ before syllabic /n/ is typical of American English and is present in a wide variety of speech styles, found in all but the very most formal pronunciation. To describe this variant of /t/ takes some explanation. Both the /t/ and the /n/ are normally alveolar, so they are in a sense coarticulated. The tongue rises to make contact with the alveolus for the /t/; at the same time the glottis (vocal chords or bands) is closed. The release of the /t/ sound is made by opening the glottis, maintaining the tongue in complete contact with the alveolus, which closes the oral passage through the mouth. But since /n/ is a nasal sound the oral passage is not needed, and the air passes out through the nose. The glottal /t/ occurs only before syllabic /n/ and only in weak-stressed syllables following a stressed syllable. Note that the words in the first column have a glottal /t/ and a syllabic /n/ (transcribed without a vowel and with a dot below the letter). Similar words that differ in stress placement are listed in the second column, showing the usual aspirated /t/ before a stressed syllable.

3.3f Medial /t/ before /n̩/
   Distribution of pattern; read across:

/ˊ t-/	/-tˊ/		
1. séytn̩	ətéyn	Satan	attain
2. sǽtn̩	sætíyn	satin	sateen
3. máwntn̩	mèyntéyn	mountain	maintain
4. fáwntn̩	səstéyn	fountain	sustain
5. sə́rtn̩	æ̀sərtéyn	certain	ascertain
6. brítn̩	diytéyn	Britain	detain
7. kə́rtn̩	pərtéyn	curtain	pertain
8. bə́tn̩	bətán	button	baton
9. kátn̩	kæntíyn	cotton	canteen

Medial /t/ and /d/ do not fall together before syllabic /n/ which is after a stressed syllable, but they are pronounced in a way that may encourage confusion. The /d/ is released directly into the /n̩/ without a perceptible intervening vowel. The tongue rises to the alveolar ridge, and at the moment of contact the velum moves away from the back of the pharynx, thus opening the nasal passage to the air flow.

3.3g Medial /t, d/ before /n̩/
Comparison of pattern; read across:

	/ˊt-/	/ˊd-/		
1.	íytn̩	íydn̩	Eton	Eden
2.	sǽtn̩	sǽdn̩	satin	sadden
3.	rítn̩	rídn̩	written	ridden
4.	sə́tn̩	sə́dn̩	Sutton	sudden
5.	bítn̩	bídn̩	bitten	bidden
6.	mítn̩	mídn̩	mitten	midden
7.	mǽtn̩	mǽdn̩	matin	madden
8.	léytn̩	léydn̩	Layton	laden
9.	bə́rtn̩	bə́rdn̩	Burton	burden

Since a contrast is observed between medial /t/ and medial /d/ occurring after strong stress and before a syllabic nasal /n̩/, it is relatively easy to design contextualized exercises that illustrate the difference, such as exercise *3.13* further on in the present chapter.

One additional special kind of /t/ is the variant that precedes syllabic /l̩/ (transcribed like syllabic /n̩/ without a vowel and with a dot below the letter). In the sequence /tl̩/, following a stressed syllable, the tongue rises to contact the alveolus to produce the /t/. Immediately on contact, one side of the tongue drops to produce the /l̩/. The quality of the /t/ is suggestive of the flap variant (*3.3b*), but before /l̩/ it has a characteristic pronunciation not matched in any other position. Listen for the contrast that occurs as the stress is shifted.

3.3h Medial /t/ before /l̩/
    Distribution of pattern; read across:

/ˊt-/	/-tˊ/		
1. sêtl̩	sɔ̀tɛ́l	settle	Sawtelle
2. ræ̂tl̩	rìytɛ́l	rattle	retell
3. pêtl̩	pɑ̀tɛ́l	petal	Patel
4. mâtl̩	mòwtɛ́l	mottle	motel
5. bæ̂tl̩	bətǽlyən	battle	batallion
6. tôwtl̩	tòwtǽlətiy	total	totality
7. mɔ̂rtl̩	mɔ̀rtǽlətiy	mortal	mortality
8. féytl̩	fətǽlətiy	fatal	fatality
9. fə̂rtl̩	fərtɪ́lətiy	fertile	fertility
10. fyûwtl̩	fyùwtɪ́lətiy	futile	futility

It is perhaps useful to note that as in the case of the flapped /t/, /t/ and /d/ fall together before /l̩/ (following a stressed syllable). This can be seen in the spelling of homophonous words like *metal/medal, petal/pedal, wattle/waddle, futile/feudal,* etc. and by comparing the pronunciation of *metal/medal* (where /t/ and /d/ fall together) with *metallic/medallion* (where they do not).

The next group of sounds to be discussed is the fricative group. These are sounds made by restricting the air stream rather than interrupting it; hence where stops are perceived by reason of the initiation (or cessation) of the column of air, fricatives are perceived as the air column is squeezed on its outward passage. Therefore, while stops are instantaneous (the air is moving or not moving and the transition is inherently brief), fricatives can be prolonged or extended for as long as a lung full of air lasts. Two of the fricatives, one voiceless and one voiced, are made by a constriction of the lower lip against the upper teeth, often called "labiodentals" or "lip-teeth" consonants. Examples of these are:

3.4 English /f/ and /v/
    Presentation of pattern; read down:

/f - f/	/v - v/		
/fiyf/	/vælv/	fief	valve
/fayf/	/vərv/	fife	verve

3.4 (continued)
Distribution of pattern; read across:

	/f-/	/-f/		
1a.	fow	owf	foe	oaf
b.	fowl	lowf	foal	loaf
c.	fɪt	tɪf	fit	tiff
d.	fæg	gœf	fag	gaff
e.	fiyl	liyf	feel	leaf
f.	fayl	layf	file	life
g.	feys	seyf	face	safe
h.	fayn	nayf	fine	knife

Distribution of pattern; read across:

	/v-/	/-v/		
2a.	viy	iyv	"V"	Eve
b.	viyl	liyv	veal	leave
c.	vayl	layv	vile	live
d.	veys	seyv	vase	save
e.	veyg	geyv	vague	gave
f.	veyn	neyv	vein	knave
g.	vɪyp	pɪyv	veep	peeve
h.	vowts	stowv	votes	stove

The next pair of consonants are a problem for students of many background languages, since they seem not to be commonly found among the world's languages. These are the voiceless and voiced dental fricatives, both spelled with the digraph *th.* To produce them the tongue is brought lightly to the bottom of the upper teeth and air expelled between tongue and teeth. Sometimes these sounds are described as interdental, with the tongue said to be inserted between upper and lower teeth. This would produce a very exaggerated pronunciation, and it is more natural and more accurate to make these sounds with the tongue out of sight, behind the upper teeth. These two sounds do not have a wide distribution in English, though the /dh/ is extremely common in actual occurrence, since it appears in the definite article, all four demonstratives, several pronoun forms, and certain common adverbs. Furthermore the /th/ is certainly not uncommon, occurring in such frequently used words as *thick, thin, three, thumb, thing, thank,* and in many proper names, such as *Ruth, Beth, Arthur, Thelma, Thatcher,* etc.

3.5 English /th/ and /dh/

Presentation and distribution of pattern; read down and across:

	/th-/	/-th/		
1a.	thəd	dəth	thud	doth
b.	thɪk	kɪth	thick	kith
c.	thɔrn	nɔrth	thorn	north
d.	thərd	dərth	third	dearth
e.	thərm	mərth	therm	mirth
f.	thruw	ruwth	through	Ruth
g.	throw	owth	throw	oath
h.	thriy	riyth	three	wreath
i.	thrɑb	brɔth	throb	broth

	/dh-/	/-dh/*		
2a.	dhiyz	siydh	these	seethe
b.	dhow	klowdh	though	clothe
c.	dhay	taydh	thy	tithe
d.	dhiy	tiydh	thee	teethe
e.	dhɪs	shiydh	this	sheathe
f.	dhey	leydh	they	lathe
g.	dhowz	lowdh	those	loathe
h.	dhaw	swɑdh	thou	swathe

A quick look at the list of words beginning with /dh/ shows that some of the most frequently appearing words in the English language are included: *the, this, that, these, those, they, them, their, then,* etc. So in spite of the relatively short list of /dh/ -words in English, the sound is very important, usually appearing one or often more times in any typical sentence.

It may be worth a brief note to mention that both /th/ and /dh/ are regularly spelled *th* (cf., *ether* and *either*), though in some common English names *th* used initially spells /t/: *Thomas, Thompson, Thames, Thai,* etc.

---

*A glance at the list of words for the comparison of /dh-/ and /-dh/ shows that the examples given are not mirror images as in the case of other presentation drills. English seems to lack words for better matches.

48 Patterns of English Pronunciation

The next group of sounds are the "hissing" or s-like fricatives often called "sibilants." We have already introduced the /s/, so there are just three more: /z, sh, zh/. The /z/ is the voiced counterpart of /s/, made with the tip of the tongue approaching the lower teeth and the front part of the tongue behind the tip arched up close to the alveolus. The /sh/ and /zh/ are made with the tip of the tongue curled up and back near the palate, and with the lips rounded. It is important to listen carefully and imitate closely, because slight modifications of tongue position noticeably affect resonance quality.

3.6 English /z/, /sh/, and /zh/

Presentation of pattern; read down:

/z - z/	/sh - sh/		
ziyz	shɪsh	Z's	shish
zuwz	shəsh	zoos	shush
zowz		Zo's	

Distribution of pattern; read across:

/z-/	/-z/		
1a. zuw	uwz	zoo	ooze
b. zow	owz	Zo	O's
c. ziyl	liyz	zeal	lees
d. zeyn	neyz	Zane	neighs
e. zown	nowz	zone	nose
f. zuwm	muwz	zoom	moos
g. zuws	suwz	Zeus	sues
h. zawndz	dawnz	zounds	downs

/sh-/	/-sh/		
2a. shæk	kæsh	shack	cash
b. shæl	læsh	shall	lash
c. shɑp	pɑsh	shop	posh
d. shiyl	liysh	she'll	leash
e. shuwd	duwsh	shooed	douche
f. shɛlf	flɛsh	shelf	flesh
g. shərk	kərsh	shirk	Kirsch
h. shrəb	brəsh	shrub	brush

In English the sound /zh/ has a very limited distribution, occurring almost exclusively in medial and in some dialects final position, though many speakers substitute /j/ when final. (This substitution of final /-j/, however, is felt by many English speakers to be at least mildly substandard).

Distribution of pattern; read down:

/-zh-/	/-zh/ (~ /-j/)		
1. mézhər	beyzh	measure	beige
2. plézhər	ruwzh	pleasure	rouge
3. trézhər	gərázh	treasure	garage
4. líyzhər	məsázh	leisure	massage
5. síyzhər	bərázh	siezure	barrage
6. ǽzhər	kǽməflázh	azure	camouflage
7. klówzhər	kɔrtézh	closure	cortège
8. vízhən	prɛstíyzh	vision	prestige
9. líyzhən	mənázh	lesion	menage
10. swéyzhən	mərázh	suasion	mirage
11. várzhən	kɔrsázh	version	corsage
12. fyúwzhən	sǽbətázh	fusion	sabotage
13. yúwzhuwəl	éspiyənázh	usual	espionage

One pair of English sounds partakes of the characteristics of both stops and fricatives. These are the two affricates, voiceless /ch/ and voiced /j/. They are produced by raising the tongue to the palate (behind the alveolar ridge), which causes the tongue tip to curl back somewhat. The air column is interrupted as in a stop articulation, but instead of the tongue being drawn sharply away for a following vowel, the release of the air column is restricted as for a fricative pronunciation. And the lips are rounded, just as for /sh/ and /zh/. In a way, these are complex sounds with two components—a stop followed closely by a fricative release: /ch/ is a kind of /t/ plus /sh/, and /j/ is a /d/ plus /zh/. Listen and imitate carefully, clearly distinguishing voiceless /ch/ from voiced /j/.

3.7 English /ch/ and /j/
Presentation of pattern; read down:

/ch - ch/	/j - j/		
chərch	jəj	church	judge
	jɔrj		George

3.7 (continued)

Distribution of pattern; read across:

/ch-/	/-ch/		
1a. chaw	awch	chow	ouch
b. chɪn	nɪch	chin	niche
c. chəm	məch	chum	much
d. chɛk	kɛch	check	ketch
e. chɪp	pɪch	chip	pitch
f. chiyp	piych	cheap	peach
g. chiyt	tiych	cheat	teach
h. chowk	kowch	choke	coach

/j-/	/-j/		
2a. jey	eyj	jay	age
b. jeyp	peyj	jape	page
c. jeyk	keyj	Jake	cage
d. jæm	mæj	jam	Madge
e. jæb	bæj	jab	badge
f. jɛl	lɛj	jell	ledge
g. jɪr	rɪj	jeer	ridge
h. jərm	mərj	germ	merge

The next two consonants are not related to each other in any way: the light fricative /h/ and the nasal /ng/. They have in common the fact that each has a restricted or deficient distribution—/h/ appears only at the beginning of a syllable, /ng/ only after the vowel. The /h/ is produced by allowing the air column to proceed almost unimpeded (past a mild constriction in the pharynx). The /h/ is voiceless, but quickly voices and to some extent takes the quality of the vowel that follows. This can be illustrated by listening alternately to the whispered pronunciation of *he* and *who*. One also notes the breathy quality of /h/ in *he's* and *whose* that is absent in *ease* and *ooze*. The velar nasal /ng/ occurs only after the syllable vowel nucleus. It is produced by raising the back of the tongue until it makes contact with the velum (as for the /g/). This interrupts the air flow through the mouth, but the velum moves away from the back of the pharynx and allows the air to move through the nose. As in the case of other nasal consonants, /ng/ is normally voiced.

3.8 English /h/ and /ng/

Presentation of pattern; read down:

/h - ng/
hæng	hang
həng	hung
hɑng	Hong

Distribution of pattern; read down:

	/h-/	/-ng/		
1a.	hiy	sɪng	he	sing
b.	hey	sæng	hey	sang
c.	hay	səng	high	sung
d.	hoy	sɑng	hoy	song
e.	haw	rɪng	how	ring
f.	how	ræng	hoe	rang
g.	huw	rəng	who	rung
h.	hɪk	rɑng	hick	wrong
i.	hɛk	bɪng	heck	bing
j.	hæk	bæng	hack	bang
k.	hək	bəng	huck	bung
l.	hɑk	bɑng	hock	bong
m.	hɔk	dɪng	hawk	ding
n.	hʊk	dæng	hook	dang
o.		dəng		dung
p.		dɑng		dong

The /ng/ sound is very common in the verb suffix -*ing*, which can attach to almost any verb stem in the language.

For various reasons (the light pronunciation of /h/, the optional dropping of /h/ in the cluster *wh*, the occasional spelling of *h* in English and other languages when no sound is made, etc.), it is advisable to drill the presence and absence of /h/. In the drill that follows, /h/ and /∅/ are in contrast.

3.8a Presence and absence of English /h/
Comparison of pattern; read across:

	/h-/	/ø-/		
1.	hɪl	ɪl	hill	ill
2.	hiyl	iyl	heel	eel
3.	hɛn	ɛn	hen	n
4.	heyl	eyl	hail	ale
5.	hænd	ænd	hand	and
6.	hayv	ayv	hive	I've
7.	hɑt	ɑt	hot	Ott
8.	hɔl	ɔl	hall	all
9.	how	ow	hoe	owe
10.	həs	əs	Huss	us

The liquid consonants are sonorous sounds produced with a minimum of friction. These include the lateral /l/ and the retroflex /r/. The /l/ is described as a lateral because one side of the front part of the tongue is lifted to the roof of the mouth, the tip on the alveolus and the side along the inside of the upper row of teeth, sending the air column over the other side of the tongue. The back of the tongue is held down, giving the articulation a suggestion of the /ə/-sound, which is characteristic of English /l/ as compared to the similar sound of other languages. English /l/ is always voiced.

The retroflex /r/ is typical in American English. It is similar to the /l/ in having the back of the tongue relatively low in the mouth. The tip is curled high toward the back of the mouth, but not touching anywhere. This American variety has sometimes been called a growled /r/. Actually the /r/ is very much like a vowel, and when it follows /ə/ the effect is a /ə/ with retroflection (tongue tip curled back) added. It would be possible to represent the syllabic part of the word *fur* with an /ɚ/ symbol (which combines /ə/ with /r/) or with an /r̩/ to show syllabic quality. Certainly in a word like *bird* one distinguishes only three sounds: the initial *b*, the final *d*, and the *r*-colored schwa in between them. Nevertheless in this text we will use /ər/ and transcribe *purr* as /pər/, matching /pɪr-pɛr-pɑr-pɔr-pur/ for *peer* (or *pier*), *pear* (or *pair*), *par*, *pour* (or *pore*), *poor*. In all of these words the /r/ pulls the pronunciation toward the central position of /ə/, so we could write /pɪər-pɛər-pɑər-pɔər-puər/, but then we would lose the advantage of having a separate syllable represented by each vowel symbol. Anyway this centering tendency is part of the articulation of the /r/, and a student should get used to the normal effect /r/ has on any vowel it follows. It might be of interest to point out that in British English (and in other varieties, including some American dialects) the retroflex character of the /r/ has been lost (unless a vowel follows immediately) leaving only the centering glide, which is represented by /ə/, thus for the words cited earlier we should have /pɪ́ə-pɛ́ə-pɑ́ə-pɔ́ə-pʊ́ə/.

As a point of information it should be recognized that some dialects of American English do not have the vowel /ʊ/ before /r/, so that *poor* is not distinguished from *pore, sure* from *shore, tour* from *tore,* etc. Interestingly there is another pattern that distinguishes two kinds of /ʊr/ verbs; while some speakers allow /ɔr/ for any of these words, others differentiate a pattern that allows /ər/, especially in informal styles, after a palatal sound. Thus *sure, pure, cure,* etc. may become /ər/, while *poor, boor, Moor,* etc. will not. (Note that the spelling usually reflects these differences.) One possible solution would be to ignore the distinction between /ɔr/ and /ʊr/, pronouncing them both /ɔr/, as a substantial number of Americans do.

The retroflex American /r/ is often the most difficult sound for second-language students of English to master. Apparently it is not common among the world's languages, and there is a marked tendency to substitute a flap (which when it occurs in English is associated with the /t/—cf., *3.3b*). Also /r/ and /l/ are often confused with each other, which is not surprising given the similarity of their production, as described above. Listen carefully and try to imitate these two sounds accurately, since a poor pronunciation will immediately mark a speaker as foreign-influenced.

3.9 English /l/ and /r/
  Presentation of pattern; read down:

/l - l/	/r - r/		
lɪl	rɪr	Lil	rear
ləl	rɛr	lull	rare
lɑl	rɔr	loll	roar
leyl	rʊr	Lael	Ruhr
layl		Lyle	
loyl		loyal	
lowl		Lowell	

3.9 (continued)

Distribution of pattern; read across:

	/l-/	/-l/		
1a.	lɪm	mɪl	limb	mill
b.	leym	meyl	lame	mail, male
c.	lay	ayl	lie	aisle, isle, I'll
d.	layt	tayl	light	tile
e.	lown	nowl	loan	knoll
f.	lək	kəl	luck	cull
g.	luwp	puwl	loop	pool
h.	lɪps	spɪl	lips	spill

Distribution of pattern; read across:

	/r-/	/-r/		
2a.	rɪb	bɪr	rib	beer
b.	rɪch	chɪr	rich	cheer
c.	rɪj	jɪr	ridge	jeer
d.	rɛch	chɛr	wretch	chair
e.	rɛk	kɛr	wreck	care
f.	rɑb	bɑr	rob	bar
g.	rɑk	kɑr	rock	car
h.	rɑt	tɑr	rot	tar
i.	rəf	fər	rough	fur
j.	rəs	sər	Russ	sir
k.	rɔs	sɔr	Ross	sore

The last three are not ideal examples because in the case of /r/ after /ə/ there is a tendency for the vowel to rise (cf., /bəd/ and /bərd/, *bud* and *bird*), and in the case of /r/ after /ɔ/ it is possible that the best match would be /rowg - gɔr/ (*rogue - gore*), with /ow/ after /r/ the reverse of /ɔ/ before /r/.

Only rarely does the so-called "bright" /l/ (produced with the back of the tongue high in the mouth) appear in English, at least in the dialect assumed. To illustrate this contrast, specifically to show the student the variety of /l/ that is almost always inappropriate, the following exercise is included. The /l/ in the first column is dark (the usual /l/ of American English); the /l/ of the second column is bright.

This is one of the few contexts where bright /l/ appears, occurring between two /iy/ diphthongs.

3.9a English dark /l/ and bright /l/
Distribution of pattern; read across:

/l/	/l/		
1. riyl	ríyliy	real	really
2. miyl	míyliy	meal	mealy
3. siyl	síyliy	seal	Seely
4. iyl	íyliy	eel	Ely
5. niyl	níyliy	kneel	Neeley
6. hiyl	híyliy	heel	Healy
7. kiyl	kíyliy	keel	Keeley
8. piyl	píyliy	peel	pili

Bright /l/ also appears in words where the stressed /iy/ follows the /l/, as in /riylíys, biylíyv/ *(release, believe)*, etc. But it is common for the unstressed first /iy/ to change to /ə/, in which case dark /l/ appears: /rəlíys-bəlíyv/, etc. It takes /iy/ on both sides of the /l/ to keep it bright.

Another common example of bright /l/ in English is syllabic /l/ after /t/ or /d/, illustrated in exercise *3.3g*. Note the following contrast of dark /l/ in the first column, bright /l/ (when syllabic) in the second.

3.9b English bright syllabic /l̩/
Distribution of pattern; read across:

/l/	/l/		
1. biyl	bíytl̩	Beal	beatle
2. fiyl	fíytl̩	feel	fetal
3. niyl	níydl̩	kneel	needle
4. hwiyl	hwíydl̩	wheel	wheedle
5. biyl	bíydl̩	Beal	beadle

Additionally bright /l/ can be found before the consonant /y/, particularly if the following syllable is weak-stressed, as pronounced by many speakers. Thus /mɪl/ *mill* has dark /l/ but /mílyən/ has bright /l/. The following drill lists relevant contrasts.

3.9c English bright /l/ before palatal /y/
Distribution of pattern; read across:

1. feyl	féylyər	fail	failure
2. seyl	séylyənt	sale	salient
3. væl	vǽlyənt	Val	valiant
4. bɪl	bílyərd	bill	billiard
5. mɪl	mílyən	mill	million
6. bɪl	bílyən	bill	billion
7. trɪl	trílyən	trill	trillion
8. bɪl	bílyəs	bill	bilious

English /r/, as indicated in earlier discussion occurs (in the dialect represented by this manual) only after simple vowels, and after only six of the seven: /ɪ-ɛ-ə-ɑ-ɔ-ʊ/. The diphthongs are never followed directly by an /r/, though they frequently precede /ər/, which means an additional syllable is attached. This is heard as a centering glide toward /r/ after the /y/ or /w/ of the diphthong. Examples and contrasts are given in the following exercise.

3.9d English /-Vr/ and /-VSər/
Distribution of pattern; read across:

/r/	/ər/		
1. sɪr	síyər	seer (prophet)	seer (one who sees)
2. frɪr	fríyər	Freer (family name)	freer (more free)
3. prɛr	préyər	prayer (invocation to God)	prayer (one who prays)
4. pɛr	péyər	pear	payer (one who pays)
5. fɑr	fáyər	far	fire
6. bɑr	báyər	bar	buyer
7. ɑr	áwər	are	our, hour
8. tɑr	táwər	tar	tower
9. fɔr	fóyər	for	foyer
10. bɔr	bóyər	bore	Boyer
11. lɔr	lówər	lore	lower
12. mɔr	mówər	more	mower
13. mʊr	múwər	Moor	mooer
14. shʊr	shúwər	sure	shoer

An especially difficult problem arises when the weak-stressed syllable /-ər/ is added to a word that ends in /-r/, such as when the comparative ending *-er* is added to *near* to produce *nearer.* In this case the final /r/ of the shorter word is dropped off, or more accurately is realized as a kind of anticipatory retroflex coloring, and the vowel of the shorter word is attached to a centering glide that ends in the final /r/ of the longer word. Listen carefully and imitate as accurately as you can. It is especially important to avoid a flapped /r/ in both positions.

3.9e English /r/ plus /ər/
Distribution of pattern; read across:

/-r/	/-(r)ər/		
1. nɪr	nɪ́ər	near	nearer
2. dɪr	dɪ́ər	dear	dearer
3. mɪr	mɪ́ər	mere	mirror
4. ɛr	ɛ́ər	air	error
5. bɛr	bɛ́ər	bear	bearer
6. fɛr	fɛ́ər	fair	fairer
7. dhɛr	dhɛ́ər	there	there're
8. mɑr	mɑ́ər	mar	marrer
9. jɑr	jɑ́ər	jar	jarrer
10. bɔr	bɔ́ər	bore	borer
11. pɔr	pɔ́ər	pour	pourer
12. hɔr	hɔ́ər	whore	horror
13. pʊr	pʊ́ər	poor	poorer
14. shʊr	shʊ́ər	sure	surer
15. stər	stə́ər	stir	stirrer
16. pər	pə́ər	purr	purrer

A clear enunciation of the medial /r/ in the second column is a conspicuous overpronunciation that immediately marks a speaker as nonnative. In many of these forms, and especially in the last two (where the stem vowel is schwa), the acoustic effect is that the /r/ is held rather long.

The final two sounds of the consonant set are the semiconsonants /y/ and /w/. We have already treated their occurrence after a vowel, described as semivowels, where they join the vowel to form a diphthong (or complex vowel). Now we see them preceding a vowel where they have a basically consonantal function and are referred to as semiconsonants. They still are related to the vowels (/y/ to /i/ and /w/ to /u/) and are produced as a kind of onglide from the /i/ and /u/ position of the tongue, high in the front or back of the mouth. The following presentation exercise matches the semivowels and semiconsonants.

3.10 The semiconsonants and (semivowels) /y/ and /w/

Presentation of pattern; read down:

/y - y/	/w - w/		
yiy	wuw	ye	woo
yey	wow	yea	whoa, woe
yay	waw	yi!	wow
/w - y/			
wiy	yuw	we	you
wey	yow	weigh, way	yo
way	yaw	Wye, Y	yeow

Distribution of pattern; read across:

	/y-/	/w-/		
1.	yeyl	weyl	Yale	wail
2.	yayp	wayp	yipe	wipe
3.	yɛt	wɛt	yet	wet
4.	yɛl	wɛl	yell	well
5.	yɛs	wɛs	yes	Wes
6.	yɔr	wɔr	yore	wore
7.	yowk	wowk	yoke	woke
8.	yɑrd	wɑrd	yard	ward
9.	yɑrn	wɑrn	yarn	warn
10.	yɑn	wɑn	yon	wan

This concludes the presentation of the consonant sounds of American English. It is not a detailed description of English phonetics, but rather selects those features for treatment that are pedagogically significant, particularly from the point of view of an acceptable production of simple English words. The combination of these words into phrases and sentences entails other patterns which will be presented and discussed in some detail in later chapters. The remainder of the present chapter consists of a contextual presentation of pairs of consonant sounds that have been shown by experience to be subject to confusion by some students. It is not expected that any particular student will find all of these exercises necessary or even helpful, since students of different background languages have different problems, and nobody would have all these problems. However, all the comparisons *have* been problems for some student or other, and a full range of exercises is provided for students to select from as needed.

The consonant sounds were arranged in a chart early in this chapter. The listing in lines and rows represents groupings of common features (of place of articulation, type of articulation, etc.), and these groupings also represent acoustic features and affinities. As a generalization (which like most generalizations, doesn't always hold true) sounds in the same box or in adjacent boxes are most likely to be confused. However, the basis on which pairs of sounds are chosen for contrast is not placement in one or another box, but experience with actual students studying English as a second language.

The consonant contrasts are presented in minimal-pair sentences, with paraphrases suggested to be used as cues. These can be used for both recognition or production to practice and to test the mastery of particular sets of consonants. Some of the sentence pairs are more natural and therefore more useful pedagogically than others. Examples of this kind are extremely hard to improvise for some pairs, and the not-so-good sets are included in the hope they are better than the alternative of omitting contrast drills for some sounds.

3.11 English /p/ and /b/

pæk/bæk	1. Before we leave we must pack/back the car up. (load/reverse)
plɑt/blɑt	2. There's a plot/blot in his record. (conspiracy/blemish)
rǽpəd/rǽbəd	3. John is a rapid/rabid reader. (fast/fanatical)
dɪspə́rst/dɪsbə́rst	4. The secretary dispersed/disbursed the funds. (scattered/paid out)
rowp/rowb	5. The native wore nothing but a kind of rope/robe. (braided cord/loose garment)
rɪp/rɪb	6. You shouldn't rip/rib the other team. (tear into/tease)

It is perhaps worth pointing out that with /p, b/ and other stop consonants (/t, d, k, g/) it is in final position before pause that the contrast of voiced vs voiceless is most difficult to perceive, since unless strongly emphasized, stops are not released in this position. As will be pointed out in detail in Chapter 5, it is the length of the preceding vowel that identifies the consonant, a longer vowel preceding a voiced consonant.

3.12 English /t/ and /d/

tɑrt/dɑrt	1. He threw a tart/dart at her. (pastry/feathered pin)
tay/day	2. Tie/dye the sash around her waist. (make a knot/change the color)
tréytər/tréydər*	3. The traitor/trader was shot on sight. (betrayer/merchant)
sɛ́ntɪŋ/sɛ́ndɪŋ	4. His job is scenting/sending perfume. (adding fragrance/transmitting)
reyt/reyd	5. The new rate/raid was a surprise. (charge per unit/attack)
lɛt/lɛd	6. He let/led the blind student out of the house. (permitted/conducted)

3.13 English /tn̩/ and /dn̩/

rítn̩/rídn̩	1. He's written/ridden about the country. (produced books/traveled)
íytn̩/íydn̩	2. He must think he comes from Eton/Eden. (prestige school/paradise)
bítn̩/bídn̩	3. He was bitten/bidden too late. (wounded by teeth/invited)
hɑ́rtn̩d/hɑ́rdn̩d	4. John was heartened/hardened by the news. (encouraged/embittered)
sə́tn̩/sə́dn̩	5. I am distressed by the Sutton/sudden failure. (in the Sutton family/unforeseen)

---

*Recall that the contrast is lost in this pair of words unless exaggerated pronunciations are used. Cf., drill *3.3e.*

3.14 English /k/ and /g/

kowld/gowld	1. There's a lot of cold/gold in Alaska. (low temperature/yellow metal)
kowt/gowt	2. Bring your new coat/goat outside. (garment, animal)
píkiy/pígiy	3. He's a bit picky/piggy in his eating. (choosy/sloppy)
tǽkɪŋ/tǽgɪŋ	4. He's tacking/tagging the boxes. (nailing/labelling)
snæk/snæg	5. I have a snack/snag in my pocket. (light refreshment/torn place)
wɪk/wɪg	6. The wick/wig has to be trimmed. (lamp cord/hair piece)

3.15 English /p/ and /f/

pǽshən/fǽshən	1. What a display of passion/fashion. (emotion/style)
péyntəd/féyntəd	2. The girl painted/fainted every day. (made pictures/lost consciousness)
sə́pər/sə́fər	3. I'm sure she's going to supper/suffer. (evening meal/experience pain)
snípiy/snífiy	4. She's a little bit snippy/sniffy. (impertinent/scornful)
læp/læf	5. She has a tremendous lap/laugh. (upper legs when sitting/expression of mirth)
chiyp/chiyf	6. That's our cheap/chief medicine. (inexpensive/most important)

3.16 English /b/ and /v/

bowt/vowt	1. We'll need a bigger boat/vote to win the race. (water vehicle/political support)
bawd/vawd	2. He bowed/vowed to acknowledge her authority. (bent at the waist/solemnly promised)

3.16 (continued)

lə́bər/lə́vər	3. He's a landlubber/land lover. (clumsy on shipboard/fond of the land)
mɑ́rbəl/mɑ́rvəl	4. The marble/marvel of the palace is out of this world. (stone/wonder)
kərb/kərv	5. The motorcycle ran off the curb/curve. (edge of sidewalk/bend in the road)
ɛb/ɛv	6. Did you see Eb/Ev? (Ebenezer/Everett)

3.17 English /f/ and /v/

fæst/væst	1. He directs a fast/vast airline. (rapid/extensive)
fɛ́riy/vɛ́riy	2. We can ferry/vary the distance. (go by boat/change)
sə́rfəs/sə́rvəs	3. The surface/service is pretty rough here. (outside area/manner in which waited on)
ráyfəl/ráyvəl	4. He took his rifle/rival to the match. (gun/competitor)
fayf/fayv	5. He played the fife/five. (piccolo/card after four)
sərf/sərv	6. What's his surf/serve like? (sea swell/delivery stroke)

3.18 English /t/ and /th/

tiym/thiym	1. My team/theme won first place. (players/written assignment)
tay/thay	2. The axe sliced into his tie/thigh. (cravat/upper leg)
bǽtləs/bǽthləs	3. The school team went batless/bathless. (without clubs/without bathing)
rìytɔ́t/rìythɔ́t	4. We retaught/rethought the answer. (gave another lesson/considered again)

3.18 (continued)

dɛt/dɛth	5. They couldn't forget his debt/death. (amount owed/demise)
fɔrt/fɔrth	6. He left the fort/fourth. (military fortification/day after the third)

3.19 English /d/ and /dh/

dey/dhey	1. Day/they came early on the 25th of December. (dawn/the people)
diyz/dhiyz	2. Dee's/these clothes are dirty. (belonging to Dee/the ones right here)
fádər/fádhər	3. His fodder/father is in the barn. (cattle food/male parent)
wə́rdiy/wə́rdhiy	4. That's a wordy/worthy statement. (verbose/meritorious)
briyd/briydh	5. How do rabbits breed/breathe so fast? (procreate/inhale and exhale)
lowd/lowdh	6. They really load/loathe that old washer. (insert clothes/despise)

3.20 English /th/ and /dh/

thay/dhay	1. The word thigh/thy is not used much today. (upper leg bone/possessive of *thou*)
thísəl/dhísəl	2. Thistle/this'll be gone! (prickly plant/the one here will)
íythər/íydhər	3. She really doesn't want ether/either. (anaesthesia/one or the other)
lǽthər/lǽdhər	4. He makes *some* lather/lather! (carpenter installing base for plaster/soap froth)
tiyth/tiydh	5. My Jack is going to teeth/teethe. (my money goes for dental bills/my son is starting to grow incisors)
mawth/mawdh	6. I wanna mouth/mouthe. (an oral opening/to declaim)

3.21 English /s/ and /th/

sɔ/thɔ	1. We'll have to saw/thaw this ice. (cut/melt)
sɔt/thɔt	2. I never sought/thought to do it. (actively tried/mentally considered)
féyslǝs/féythlǝs	3. I never met the faceless/faithless informer. (unidentified/disloyal)
ǝnsíngkǝbǝl/ ǝnthíngkǝbǝl	4. His reasoning is unsinkable/ unthinkable. (not to be disproved/not to be considered)
pæs/pæth	5. They came by the mountain pass/path. (break between two peaks/foot trail)
mæs/mæth	6. This new mass/math is more than I can take. (religious rite/science of numbers)

3.22 English /z/ and /dh/

zówiy/dhówiy	1. Zoie/though he came in later. (little Zorabelle/even if he)
zɛn/dhɛn	2. Zen/then came the next day. (Mahayana Buddhism/at that point)
klówzɪng/klówdhɪng	3. They should be closing/clothing this country. (restricting entry/providing garments)
máwzǝr/máwdhǝr	4. She's a real mouser/mouther. (mice hunter/actress who exaggerates bombastically)
tayz/taydh	5. He offered his ties/tithe. (cravats/ten percent contribution)
tiyz/tiydh	6. I guess every baby has to tease/teethe. (harass/grow dental appendages)

3.23 English /s/ and /z/

siy/ziy	1. Is zinc spelled with a C/Z? (Yes, *c* as in *cent*/Yes, *z* as in *zebra*)

3.23 (continued)

sĭnger/zĭngər	2. She's a real singer/zinger. (vocal musician/zestful person)
prɛ́sədənt/ /prɛ́zədənt	3. We should follow the precedent/president. (established standard/chief executive)
réysər/réyzər	4. His racer/razor is real sharp. (speedy car/shaving device)
reys/reyz	5. Joe wants to race/raise horses. (compete in speed contest/breed and grow)
spays/spayz	6. There may be spice/spies on this island. (aromatic herbs/secret agents)

3.24 English /ch/ and /sh/

chɪn/shɪn	1. He got a bad cut on his chin/shin. (jaw/lower leg)
chɛ́riy/shɛ́riy	2. We'll have cherry/sherry cobbler for dinner. (fruit pie/iced wine)
wɑ́chɪng/wɑ́shɪng	3. He's watching/washing my car. (guarding/cleaning)
dɪ́chəs/dɪ́shəs	4. Did you clean the ditches/dishes? (irrigation channels/vessels for food)
bæch/bæsh	5. That was quite a batch/bash last night! (quantity/party)
wɪch/wɪsh	6. If I had my witch/wish, I'd show you! (sorceress/desire)

3.25 English /j/ and /zh/

líyjən/líyzhən	1. I'm really distressed by the legion/lesion. (military unit/injury)
vә́rjən/vә́rzhən	2. He told another virgin/version. (maiden/account)
plɛ́jər/plɛ́zhər	3. The club is responsible for this pledger/pleasure. (one who guarantees/joy)

3.26 English /ch/ and /j/

chíriŋ/jíriŋ	1. The large audience was cheering/jeering. (shouting encouragement/shouting derisively)
chowks/jowks	2. Don't laugh if he chokes/jokes. (strangles/tells funny stories)
lə́nchıŋ/lə́njıŋ	3. He was lunching/lunging at Colonel Sanders. (eating noon meal/diving)
bríchəz/bríjəz	4. He burned his britches/bridges behind him. (trousers/structures across waterway)
ɛch/ɛj	5. How many plates do you have to etch/edge? (engrave/furnish a border)
sınch/sınj	6. He hadn't planned to cinch/singe the saddle. (fasten/burn)

3.27 English /s/ and /sh/

sɑk/shɑk	1. Cassius got the sock/shock of his career. (fist blow/unpleasant surprise)
sɛl/shɛl	2. Ann can't sell/shell the corn. (trade for money/husk)
fǽsən/fǽshən	3. We'll have to fasten/fashion this dress better. (attach/style)
klǽsəz/klǽshəz	4. There were classes/clashes all during the strike. (students with teacher/violent confrontations)
liys/liysh	5. The studio has the lion on a lease/leash. (rental contract/rope)
pɛ́rıs/pɛ́rısh	6. This is not the Paris/parish I used to know. (capital of France/church district)

3.28 English /z/ and /zh/

ɛ̀nklówzər/ ɛ̀nklówzhər	1. The encloser/enclosure was very small. (person who included something in a letter/fenced area)
síyzər/síyzhər	2. The trouble started with this Caesar/seizure. (Roman emperor/capture)

3.28 (continued)

ruwz/ruwzh	3. The ruse/rouge just didn't work. (stratagem/cosmetic for cheeks)
beyz/beyzh	4. That reminds me of the bays/beige. (sea inlets/the tan one)
kɔ̀rtɛ́z/kɔ̀rtɛ́zh	5. This Cortez/cortège was unusually slow that day. (Spanish explorer/ceremonial procession)

3.29 English /sh/ and /zh/

əlûwshən/əlûwzhen	1. After all that, it was just an Aleutian/allusion. (native of islands off Alaska/indirect reference)
ǽshər/ǽzhər	2. My favorite is Asher/azure. (son of Jacob/light blue)
trɛ́shər/trɛ́zhər	3. The heraldic tressure/treasure was impressive. (ornamental border on shield/collection of valuables)
dəlûwshən/ dəlûwzhən	4. It's the dilution/delusion that bothers me. (weakening/deception)

3.30 English /h/ and /∅/

hiyt/iyt	1. Did you heat/eat the soup? (warm/consume)
heyt/eyt	2. I hate/ate hominy. (despise/consumed)
hâltər/âltər	3. He held back because of the halter/altar. (horse's headstall/worship table)
hiyl/iyl	4. He slipped on his heel/eel. (back of foot/snakelike fish)
əphíyvəlz/əpíyvəlz	5. This legislation will bring upheavals/up evils. (violent disturbances/wicked consequences)
ənhârmd/ənârmd	6. The victims were unharmed/unarmed. (not hurt/without weapons)

3.31 English /r/ and /t/

ræliy/tæliy	1. The rally/tally shows we're successful. (political meeting/reckoning)
ruwm/tuwm	2. He's gone to his room/tomb. (chamber/burial vault)
wíriy/wítiy	3. He's very weary/witty after four years in college. (tired/clever)
híriŋ/hítiŋ	4. His hearing/hitting has gone bad. (aural perception/baseball skill)
kɑr/kɑt	5. His old car/cot finally fell to pieces. (automobile/narrow bed)
hɪr/hɪt	6. Was he really here/hit? (in this place/struck a blow)

3.32 English /r/ and /d/

rəsíyvd/dəsíyvd	1. He was received/deceived by the king. (seen and welcomed/tricked)
ríysənt/díysənt	2. He had a recent/decent burial. (not long past/respectable)
bəréy/bədéy	3. She got a new beret/bidet. (soft flat cap/sitz bath)
dáwriyz/dáwdiyz	4. These dowries/dowdies are a national shame. (marriage gifts/frumpish women)
hɛr/hɛd	5. He got his hair/head cut. (purposely trimmed/accidentally gashed)
bɪr/bɪd	6. His offer won the beer/bid. (alcoholic beverage/competition)

3.33 English /r/ and /l/

ræm/læm	1. The ram/lamb went to market. (male sheep/young sheep)
rɔŋ/lɔŋ	2. That's the wrong/long way home. (mistaken/lengthy)
páyrəts/páyləts	3. Pirates/pilots have affected air safety. (hijackers/licensed plane operators)

3.33 (continued)

kərɛ́kt/kəlɛ́kt	4. Now, please correct/collect the papers. (mark errors/gather)
wɑr/wɑl	5. A great war/wall divides the nation. (armed conflict/fence of stone)
shɛr/shɛl	6. Mom told me to share/shell these walnuts. (divide and apportion/remove covering)

3.34 English /r/ and /n/

rowm/nowm	1. He was born in Rome/Nome. (Italy/Alaska)
rɛst/nɛst	2. The little bird went to his rest/nest. (repose/habitation)
tɛ́rər/tɛ́nər	3. Her youngest son is a terror/tenor. (intolerable nuisance/high male voice)
spáyrəl/spáynəl	4. He drew a spiral/spinal column. (winding curve/backbone)
pɛr/pɛn	5. I just bought a pair/pen of rabbits. (two/enclosure)
dhɛr/dhɛn	6. There/then we saw the king come out. (at that place/at that time)

3.35 English /l/ and /n/

luwd/nuwd	1. He's opposed to lewd/nude pictures. (obscene/naked)
lówshən/nówshən	2. Where did you ever get that lotion/notion? (medicated liquid/strange idea)
wílɪng/wínɪng	3. She always had a willing/winning smile. (helpful/attractive)
féylɪng/féynɪng	4. Everybody realizes he's failing/feigning. (getting weaker/pretending)
payl/payn	5. He climbed the tall pile/pine. (heap/evergreen)
bowl/bown	6. What did you do with the dog's bowl/bone? (dish/piece of a skeleton)

3.36 English /l/ and /∅/

bowl/bow	1. Don't drop that bowl/bow. (concave container/archer's weapon)
rowld/rowd	2. He rolled/rode the cart down the hill. (moved/was carried by)
duwl/duw	3. The duel/dew is in the meadow. (grudge fight/condensed moisture)
yuwl/yuw	4. This is the Yule/ewe season. (Christmas/female sheep)
stuwl/stuw	5. The stool/stew was in the kitchen. (backless seat/meat and vegetables)

3.37 English /m/ and /n/

meyl/neyl	1. He brought me the mail/nail. (letters/metal fastener)
riymít/riynít	2. She promised to remit/reknit the sweater. (send/repair)
jímiy/jíniy	3. Have you seen Jimmy/Ginny? (James/Virginia)
dəm/dən	4. Is he really dumb/done? (unintelligent/finished)
klæm/klæn	5. We had the clam/clan for dinner. (bivalve mollusk/relatives)

3.38 English /m/ and /ng/

hǽmɪŋ/hǽŋɪŋ	1. He's really hamming/hanging it up. (overacting his role/suspending it)
hǽmər/hǽŋər	2. Have you got a hammer/hanger I can borrow? (tool for pounding/wire loop for clothes)
rɪm/rɪŋ	3. He broke his rim/ring. (car wheel/finger jewelry)
strəm/strəŋ	4. I hope they strum/strung the guitar. (play idly/attached strings)
bɑm/bɑŋ	5. We heard a loud bomb/bong. (explosion/deep reverberation)

3.39 English /n/ and /ng/

sínər/síngər	1. She's a well-known sinner/singer. (transgressor/musician)
hǽnòwvər/ /hǽngòwvər	2. He has a real Hanover/hangover headache. (capital of Lower Saxony/caused by drunkenness)
wínər/wíngər	3. He's the best winner/winger on the team. (victory gainer/player positioned to one side)
ræn/ræng	4. They ran/rang the bells all over town. (carried/sounded)
bæn/bæng	5. If they could just ban/bang the drum. (prohibit/beat)
rɔn/rɔng	6. Everybody knows that's Ron/wrong. (Ronald/improper)

3.40 English /y/ and /j/

yɛ́low/jɛ́low	1. That yellow/Jello dessert looks good. (lemon-colored/gelatin)
yuw/juw	2. There's a ewe/Jew by the front gate. (female sheep/Hebrew)
yowk/jowk	3. He let the yolk/joke fall flat. (egg yellow/funny story)
yɪr/jɪr	4. I thought that year/jeer would never end. (twelve months/derisive outburst)
yɛs/jɛs	5. I said, "Yes/Jess, I'll go." (it's agreed/Jesse)
mɛ́yər/mɛ́yjər	6. I'll have to ask the mayor/major. (city official/army officer)

3.41 English /y/ and /ø/

yɪrz/ɪrz	1. The years/ears have been long. (annual measures/hearing organs)
yɛg/ɛg	2. This yegg/egg is dangerous. (safecracker/ovum)
yiyst/iyst	3. The secret's in the yeast/east. (leavening agent/direction of sunrise)

3.41 (continued)

yərnd/ərnd	4. He yearned/earned too much for his family. (longed for/received as compensation)
yûwzəz/ûwzəz	5. My dune buggy uses/oozes oil. (consumes/leaks slowly)

3.42 English /w/ and /v/

wərs/vərs	1. Are you sure this poem is worse/verse? (less good/poetic form)
wayn/vayn	2. Is this wine/vine from your vineyard? (fermented grape juice/grape plant)
waylz/vaylz	3. Beware the druggist with his wiles/vials. (tricks/small bottles)
wĭmən/vĭmən	4. The girls have plenty of women/vim and vigor. (females/energy and)
wɛts/vɛts	5. The wets/vets influenced the election. (those opposing prohibition/military veterans)
wɛst/vɛst	6. You'll find it in the west/vest. (direction of sunset/sleeveless jacket)

3.43 English /w/ and /g/

wɔkt/gɔkt	1. Gus walked/gawked all the way down the street. (moved on foot/stared awkwardly)
wʊd/gʊd	2. This is a wood/good stove. (burns tree trunks/excellent)
wɛst/gɛst	3. The west/guest house is ready. (direction of sunset/visitors')
wĭgəld/gĭgəld	4. The girl wiggled/giggled through her dance. (moved side to side/laughed nervously)
wow/gow	5. The dude shouted "whoa/go" to the horse. (stop/move ahead)
riywârdəd/riygârdəd	6. He was rewarded/regarded as a hero. (presented a gift/considered)

3.44 English /w/ and /r/

wayld/rayld	1. That rhino is really wild/riled. (not tame/irritated)
weyvd/reyvd	2. The crowd waved/raved enthusiastically. (signaled a greeting/praised extravagantly)
wuwm/ruwm	3. He wished he were back in his mother's womb/room. (uterus/chamber)
wɪrd/rɪrd	4. His children are weird/reared by any standard. (bizarre/raised)
wiydz/riydz	5. Chop all the weeds/reeds out of this plot. (undesirable plants/stem-jointed grass)
rìywə́n/rìyrə́n	6. The race was re-won/rerun on video tape. (again achieved victory/presented again)

Some of the sentence pairs in the foregoing lists are better than others. A good pair presents two sentences in which two interpretations are governed by a single pair of similar sounds to focus on a crucial discrimination in the sound system. But more than just possible, the contrasted sentences should both be reasonable and realistic, hopefully sharing part of the same semantic range, and equally plausible. A good example is "Where's the dog's bone/bowl," contrasting /n/ and /l/. It is possible to readily associate both bones and bowls with a canine pet, and the two interpretations are in balance.

Sometimes it is extremely hard to contrive sentences that illustrate a contrast between two sounds and still are natural, plausible, and semantically in balance. This is especially true of the low frequency sounds like /zh/ and /th/. One might ask, if good sentences are so hard to devise, why not forget the contrast on the grounds that the functional load it carries cannot be very great. The answer is that we're not really working on sound pairs, but on individual sounds. The contrast in minimal-pair sentences is merely a device to provide practice in context. Actually, in real communication situations the context will invariably force a correct interpretation. When the Japanese airline stewardess says "I hope you have a present fright," her passengers may smile, but they know what she means to say. The point of pronunciation practice is to learn to accurately identify and produce speech sounds, not to solve minimal-pair confusions. Hopefully the practice of a focused exercise will have a carryover effect and will improve pronunciation in a general way—to improve comprehension and to minimize accent.

A couple of problems may arise. One is that there will be dialect mismatches that invalidate specific pairs of words as minimal. For some speakers of American English *ward* and *yard* are a rhyming minimal pair: /wɑrd ~ yɑrd/; for others there is a difference in the vowels: /wɔrd ~ yɑrd/. If some of the pairs presented in the exercises of this book don't work for a particular sub-dialect, they should be skipped. There should be plenty that do work. And of course the user can contrive additional pairs of sentences that illustrate the contrasts present in his own dialect.

The other problem is in the paraphrase (or expansion or rejoinder) suggested to facilitate identification for accurate comprehension or as a cue to the intended oral production. Ideally the paraphrase should be a simpler word, but this is often difficult to arrange. In fact some words almost defy a brief and accurate paraphrase of any kind: how do you paraphrase "room" or "run?" Is it fair to paraphrase one probably unknown word (like "weird") with another that is even less likely to be known (like "bizarre")? The answer is that the words are simply to be used as keys for visual association. Whereas "cinch" and "singe" are similar sounding and therefore subject to confusion, "fasten" and "burn" are easy to tell apart. It is not intended that these exercises be used for vocabulary building.

Finally, it bears repeating to say that not all these exercises should be used for any class—only those that are problems for particular students. But how does a teacher (or student) determine which are appropriate and useful? Observation and experience can help, but the problem can be really complex in a class of students who have various background languages. One suggestion is to consult appropriate contrastive analyses or summaries of such analyses. One can be found in a recent book by Don L. F. Nilsen and Alleen Pace Nilsen, *Pronunciation Contrasts in English* (New York: Simon & Schuster (Regents), 1971), which lists problems by background language.

Chapter 4
ENGLISH STRESS AND INTONATION PATTERNS

In Chapter 1 we looked at the features of stress and pitch and examined a few simple intonation patterns—some that apply to words, like /əbówd/ *(abode)*, and to very simple phrases, like /əbówt/ *(a boat)*. We found that English words can be described with three levels of stress: strong, medial, and weak, marked /ˊ ˋ ˇ/ (or in the case of weak stress, usually "marked" by being unmarked), all illustrated in a word like /dɑ́mənèyt/ *(dominate)*. But in real communication, words don't usually come one at a time, but in strings or sequences that combine to produce phrases and sentences. When sentences are analyzed, it's necessary to have a more complex analytical framework, and more contrasts appear.

An intonation phrase includes all the suprasegmental features of stress, pitch, and transition associated with a string of words (usually a syntactic phrase) pronounced as a unit. A useful generalization about intonation phrases is that each has only one strong stress. If two (or more) words, each carrying its lexical strong stress, are combined in a single intonation phrase, only one strong stress will be kept; the other(s) will be "demoted" or reduced to the level of stress usually called *secondary*. Secondary fits between *strong* and *medial*, so we now work with four levels of stress, as follows:

/ˊ/	strong
/ˆ/	secondary
/ˋ/	medial
/ˇ/ or / /	weak

If we combine the words *a* and *dog*, we get /ə dɔ́g/; *a* is a word that typically occurs with weak stress in phrases, though pronounced alone, in what we refer to as a "citation form," it carries strong stress

4.1 Simple intonation phrases—secondary plus strong
Build-up of pattern; read across:

1. /rɛ́d/	/hɛ́n/	/rɛ́d hɛ́n/		red	hen	red hen	
2. /brâwn/	/dɔ́g/	/brâwn dɔ́g/		brown	dog	brown dog	
3. /grêy/	/kǽt/	/grêy kǽt/		gray	cat	gray cat	
4. /tǽn/	/hɔ́rs/	/tǽn hɔ́rs/		tan	horse	tan horse	
5. /grîyn/	/tríy/	/grîyn tríy/		green	tree	green tree	
6. /blúw/	/skây/	/blûw skây/		blue	sky	blue sky	
7. /núw/	/kâr/	/núw kâr/		new	car	new car	
8. /ówld/	/hǽt/	/ôwld hǽt/		old	hat	old hat	
9. /gʊ́d/	/bóy/	/gûd bóy/		good	boy	good boy	
10. /náys/	/gə́rl/	/nâys gə́rl/		nice	girl	nice girl	
11. /ey/	/fâyn/	/déy/	/ə fâyn déy/	a	fine	day	a fine day
12. /ey/	/káynd/	/mǽn/	/ə kâynd mǽn/	a	kind	man	a kind man
13. /ey/	/gʊ́d/	/díyd/	/ə gûd díyd/	a	good	deed	a good deed
14. /dhíy/	/fə́rst/	/rów/	/dhə fə̂rst rów/	the	first	row	the first row
15. /dhíy/	/lǽst/	/wíyk/	/dhə lǽst wíyk/	the	last	week	the last week
16. /dhíy/	/bɛ́st/	/plǽn/	/dhə bɛ̂st plǽn/	the	best	plan	the best plan
17. /sə́m/	/mɔ́r/	/mɪ́lk/	/səm mɔ̂r mɪ́lk/	some	more	milk	some more milk
18. /sə́m/	/ówld/	/shúwz/	/səm ôwld shúwz/	some	old	shoes	some old shoes

(as do all words in citation form). In fact we may change the weak-stressed vowel from /ə̆/ to /éy/, though /ə̂/ is possible as a citation form. Thus *a* and *dog* put together in an intonation phrase produces /ə dɔ́g/, a weak-stressed followed by a strong-stressed syllable. But if we combine *one* and *dog,* two words that each carry a strong stress (/wə̂n/ and /dɔ́g/), one of the two must be reduced to secondary. It *may* be either, but normally, unless there is some reason to do otherwise, such as contrastive emphasis, the last will be kept strong and the earlier word(s) will be reduced to secondary. Thus *one* and *dog* combine as /wə̂n dɔ́g/.

In exercise 4.1 you are asked to combine two or more words given in citation form (each with a strong stress) into a single intonation phrase. This will require a change from strong to secondary (or weak) stress in the first word(s). Listen to the individual words and combine them into a phrase.

Two pitch patterns are possible, both of which are quite usual and normal in English for a phrase consisting of adjective plus noun. For the three-syllable phrases cited above, the first pattern is a sequence of levels 1231 and the second is 1321. The following exercise illustrates these two patterns. See if you can listen to each and imitate it carefully. Then listen to one and produce the other. The sequence of stresses is the same in both patterns: weak plus secondary plus strong.

4.1a Simple intonation phrases—pitch patterns
   Comparison of pattern; read across:

1. ə fâyn déy	ə fâyn déy	a fine day
2. ə kâynd mǽn	ə kâynd mǽn	a kind man
3. ə gûd dı́yd	ə gûd dı́yd	a good deed
4. dhə fə̂rst rów	dhə fə̂rst rów	the first row
5. dhə lǽst wı́yk	dhə lǽst wı́yk	the last week
6. dhə bɛ̂st plǽn	dhə bɛ̂st plǽn	the best plan
7. səm mɔ̂r ráys	səm mɔ̂r ráys	some more rice
8. hər ôwld shûwz	hər ôwld shûwz	her old shoes
9. hɪz nûw kár	hɪz nûw kár	his new car
10. hɪz rɛ̂d dɔ́g	hɪz rɛ̂d dɔ́g	his red dog

It is very important to note that the second pattern in the above drill has a secondary stress on the adjective just as the first pattern does. That is to say, in both patterns the heaviest stressed word is the noun in final position. This is not the pattern of contrastive stress that one would use in a sentence like "Not the black dog, the *red* dog." (Contrastive stress patterns will be presented and drilled later in this chapter.)

The pattern described above for adjective-noun phrases can be contrasted with the pattern of strong plus medial stress introduced in Section *1.4*. This contrast of secondary-strong versus strong-medial is one of the most difficult to master for many second-language students of English. Yet it is very common and carries a lot of information which must not be lost if the student is to participate effectively as a listener or as a speaker of English.

The pattern strong plus medial identifies what has been called a compound noun or construct in English. Syntactically it is a noun made up of two stems. For example the terms *blâck bóard* (a phrase made up of adjective plus noun) indicates a board which is black, and any board which is black can be referred to as a *blâck bóard*. The meaning of the phrase is the sum of the meanings of the words that make up the phrase. The word *bláckbòard* refers to something quite different which is neither a board nor is it necessarily black. It is usually a green plastered surface used in schoolrooms on which the teacher displays words or figures by writing or drawing with chalk. A *bláckbòard* is a compound lexical unit, whose meaning is not the sum of its parts.

Notice that *blâck bóard* (the adjective-noun phrase) is written as two words while the word *bláckbòard* (the compound noun) is written as one word. It would be nice if all contrasting sets in this pattern had this same consistent spelling representation, but unfortunately this is only partially true. Adjective-noun phrases are usually two words, but though some compound nouns are written as a single word, others are written as two words. The latter spelling is usual when the adjective-noun components of the compound noun are more than one syllable. Thus a *yêllow jácket* is an article of clothing which is yellow. But a *yéllow jàcket* is a kind of wasp with a painful sting. They are not distinguished in normal English spelling. Perhaps one should say "modifier" plus noun instead of adjective plus noun, since sometimes one noun modifies another as in the case of *gôld rîng* or *stône wâll*. The pattern of secondary plus strong stress in a noun phrase is a fairly reliable indication that the word under secondary stress is in a subordinate or modifying relation to the word under strong stress.

In the following exercise be sure that you accurately and carefully distinguish the phrases from the compound nouns. Note that the sequence of pitches as well as the stress contrasts helps to differentiate the two patterns.

4.2 Modifier-noun phrase versus compound noun
   Comparison of pattern; read across:

1. blǽk bɔ́rd	blǽkbɔ̀rd	black board	blackboard
2. kôwld krîym	kôwldkrìym	cold cream	cold cream
3. wîyk ɛ̂nd	wîykɛ̀nd	weak end	weekend
4. blûw bɔ̂rd	blûwbɔ̀rd	blue bird	bluebird
5. rɛ̂d kǽp	rɛ̂dkæ̀p	red cap	redcap
6. hɛ̂r brɔ̂sh	hɛ̂rbrɔ̀sh	hair brush	hairbrush
7. grîyn hɔ́ws	grîynhɔ̀ws	green house	greenhouse
8. frîy wêy	frîywèy	free way	freeway
9. shɔ̂rt stɑ̂p	shɔ̂rtstɑ̀p	short stop	shortstop
10. blûw bʊ̂k	blûwbʊ̀k	blue book	bluebook
11. wâyt hɑ́ws	wâythɑ̀ws	white house	White House
12. tôy stɔ́r	tôystɔ̀r	toy store	toy store
13. pôwst ɔ́fəs	pôwstɔ̀fəs	post office	post office
14. gôwld fîsh	gôwldfìsh	gold fish	goldfish
15. hɛ̂d dɑ́ktər	hɛ̂ddɑ̀ktər	head doctor	head doctor
16. îngglɪsh tîychər	înggIɪshtìychər	English teacher	English teacher

Not all combinations of modifier plus noun can be reinterpreted as compound nouns, and not all compound nouns have equivalent modifier-noun phrases. This is a major problem for the learner of English, and there are no easy cues that can reliably serve to differentiate the two patterns. The following exercise lists a few typical examples of each pattern.

4.2a Modifier-noun phrases and compound nouns
Comparison of pattern; read across:

1. ǽpəl páy	ǽpəltrìy	apple pie	apple tree
2. páyn bɑ́kx	páynkòwn	pine box	pine cone
3. hǎy práysəz	háyskùwl	high prices	high school
4. frúwt kɑ́kteyl	frúwt jùws	fruit cocktail	fruit juice
5. swíyt gə́rl	swíyt-hɑ̀rt	sweet girl	sweetheart
6. stówn wɔ́l	stównkə̀tər	stone wall	stone cutter
7. lívɪŋ wéyj	lívɪŋrùwm	living wage	living room
8. pɔ́rɪŋ réyn	pɔ́rɪŋspàwt	pouring rain	pouring spout
9. sɛ́tɪŋ sə́n	sɛ́tɪŋhɛ̀n	setting sun	setting hen
10. slíypɪŋ méydn̩	slíypɪŋpɪ̀lz	sleeping maiden	sleeping pills
11. wínɪŋ tíym	wínɪŋ strìyk	winning team	winning streak
12. vówtɪŋ pə́blɪk	vówtɪŋməshìyn	voting public	voting machine
13. fláyɪŋ sɔ́sər	fláyɪŋməshìyn	flying saucer	flying machine
14. shúwtɪŋ stɑ́r	shúwtɪŋmæ̀ch	shooting star	shooting match

Often the choice of /´`/ versus /ˆ´/ seems arbitrary, as in the case of *Hĺll Strèet* versus *Hîll Ávenue*. It is difficult to see why *Hill Street* is pronounced with the /´`/ pattern but *Hill Avenue* with the /ˆ´/. Or why should *frûit júìce* be /´`/ but *frûit côcktail* be /ˆ´/? In some forms a change seems to be taking place, and both patterns are acceptable, as in *îce creàm* and *íce créam,* or *bóy scòut* and *bôy scoût.* Also, speakers of different dialects of English, though they agree that both patterns occur, may not select the same pattern for all combinations; thus some speakers say *swéet potàtoes* and others say *swêet potátoes.* All of these factors are unfortunate complications for the second-language student of English.

There are regularities of interpretation, however, that can be helpful. These can be seen in the kinds of paraphrase that equate with each pattern. For example *a sléeping mâiden* is "a maiden who is sleeping," but *a sléeping pìll* is "a pill for sleeping; *a sêtting sún* is "a sun that is setting," but *a sétting hèn* is "a hen for setting on eggs (to hatch them)." In the following exercise identify the correct intonation pattern by the contrasts in meaning associated with each pattern.

4.2b Phrases and compounds with -ing- words
Comparison of pattern; read across and associate meanings:

1a.	smôwkıng rûwm	smoking room	a room on fire (that is smoking)
b.	smôwkıngrùwm	smoking room	a room where one may smoke (for smoking)
2a.	dǽntsıng gârl	dancing girl	a girl who is dancing
b.	dǽntsınggàrl	dancing girl	a girl who dances professionally
3a.	hântıng dɔ́g	hunting dog	a dog that is hunting
b.	hấntıngdɔ̀g	hunting dog	a dog used for hunting
4a.	smôwkıng jǽkət	smoking jacket	a jacket on fire (that is smoking)
b.	smôwkıngjæ̀kət	smoking jacket	a jacket commonly worn while smoking or lounging
5a.	rêysıng kâr	racing car	a car that is speeding or racing
b.	rêysıngkàr	racing car	a car used for formal racing
6a.	râkıng chɛ̂r	rocking chair	a chair that is rocking
b.	râkıngchɛ̀r	rocking chair	a chair built and used for rocking
7a.	grôwıng péyn	growing pain	a pain increasing in intensity
b.	grôwıngpèyn	growing pain	a pain associated with rapid growth (during adolescence)
8a.	diybêytıng tíym	debating team	a team that is debating or arguing
b.	diybêytıngtìym	debating team	a team organized for formal debate
9a.	sîngıng vɔ́ys	singing voice	a voice that is singing
b.	síngıngvɔ̀ys	singing voice	a voice appropriate for singing
10a.	tûrıng kə́mpəniy	touring company	a company (of actors) on tour
b.	tûrıngkə̀mpəniy	touring company	a company that arranges tours
11a.	wípıng bóy	whipping boy	a boy who is whipping
b.	wípıngbòy	whipping boy	a boy punished for another (scapegoat)
12a.	chîrıng sɛ́kshən	cheering section	a section (of people) who are cheering
b.	chîrıngsɛ̀kshən	cheering section	a group (of students) organized to encourage athletic teams

Exercise 4.2b shows pairs for which both members can be meaningful, though in some cases one interpretation is more likely than the other (e.g., rócking chàir over rócking cháir). There are hundreds of similar examples where only one interpretation is at all likely. Thus wálking stìck (a staff or cane carried in the hand) is normal and expected, but wâlking stíck is very unlikely because sticks don't ordinarily walk. Similarly dárning nèedle (a large-eyed needle used for darning—or a dragonfly), but not dârning neédle, because needles don't darn—people do. Several years ago a Costa Rican colleague who had not mastered English stress and intonation patterns used to take his leave on Friday afternoon with a cheery "Goodbye. Have a nice week end." Once he asked why his American friends laughed and was told he should say wéekènd because wêek énd suggested the humorous reinterpretation wêak énd (debilitated posterior). He was not really misunderstood, but his communication was inefficient because the literal meanings signalled by his intonation were distracting.

4.2c Contrast of modifier-noun phrase and noun compound—minimal-pair exercise

Comparison of pattern: select the appropriate paraphrase or identification clue:

/ˆ ´/ or /´ ˆ/

1. Where's the *German teacher?* (teacher from Germany/teacher of German)
2. Is he really a grand father/grandfather? (one generation/two generations)
3. So John's a fine clerk! (reliable salesman/one who collects fines)
4. Mario went to the big house. (large residence/penitentiary)
5. His father runs the post office. (he's a general/he's a postmaster)
6. Elmer has a toy store. (he's a child with a toy/he's a businessman)
7. Put the cold cream away. (in the refrigerator/in the bedroom)
8. Scott is the clinic's head doctor. (supervising physician/psychiatrist)
9. Where's your gold fish/goldfish? (in the drawer/in the pond)
10. We need a short stop/shortstop. (a break in our trip/a ball player)
11. He works in the green house/greenhouse. (as a cook/as a gardener)
12. Is there a free way/freeway to get there? (means without paying/limited access highway)

English Stress and Intonation Patterns 83

So far we have assumed three pitch levels, which can be referred to as high, mid, and low. These have been associated with stress patterns and have been charted in various word and simple phrase patterns as follows:

fáther   dóminant   fíne   helló   becóming   áfternoon   cónjugate   cónjugation
áfter   fláttering góod a bóok a péncil   at the stóre únderwear únderstánding

Introducing more than one primary stress into a phrase will produce a secondary stress:

a fine day   a good morning   a good recipe   a good afternoon   a big celebration
a good book   a fine teacher   an old colony   a firm guarantee   a new understanding

These can also be interpreted in other ways, such as:

a fine day   a good morning   a good recipe   a good afternoon   a big celebration
a good book   a fine teacher   an old colony   a firm guarantee   a new understanding

In these patterns the four levels of stress are represented by a dot and three lines of increasing length for heavier stress, as follows:

	with transcription or spelling	on graph
strong	/´/	——
secondary	/ˆ/	—
medial	/ˋ/	-
weak	/˘/ or / /	•

Pitch is shown on the graphs by position relative to the reference lines, with higher lines for higher pitches:

	pitch level		on graph
high	/3/		
mid	/2/		
low	/1/		

The graph thus indicates both stress and pitch, which can occur in patterns independent of each other, though there are general correlations.

English has a pattern of contrastive stress, which is often signaled by a pitch higher than level /3/. This is designated level /4/ and is referred to as extra high, since it is above the levels of "normal" speech. Pitch level /4/ is used for several purposes, one of which is to emphasize information that may not have been heard. In the following drill the first speaker is asked to repeat the information he offers. The strong-stressed syllable originally on level /3/ is lifted to level /4/.

4.3 Contrastive stress—emphasis
Comparison of pattern; read across with two voices:

1. I'm going later.	When?	Later!
2. I'm going home.	Where?	Home!
3. She's speaking softly.	How?	Softly!
4. He's bringing John.	Who?	John!
5. He lost Mary's.	Whose?	Mary's!
6. He found a dollar.	What?	A dollar!
7. She brought the brown one.	Which?	The brown one!
8. She hit him.	Why?	Because!

This pattern is common but not obligatory. It is especially likely if the person queried is excited, annoyed, or angry, or if the communicants are some distance apart and are speaking in loud voices.

Contrastive stress is regularly used to correct false information or to contradict. In the following exercise the second speaker corrects the first one.

4.3a Contrastive stress—correction
Comparison of pattern; read across with two voices:

1. A dead cat?	No,	a red cat.
2. A new coat?	No,	a blue coat.
3. A bay horse?	No,	a gray horse.
4. A clean shirt?	No,	a green shirt.
5. A sack dress?	No,	a black dress.
6. An old tie?	No,	a gold tie.
7. A light shade?	No,	a bright shade.
8. The worst book?	No,	the first book.
9. The last bus?	No,	the fast bus.
10. The wood chair?	No,	the good chair.

If the response were in any respect emphasized, the "no" would also be lifted to pitch level /4/.

4.3b Contrastive stress—contradiction
Comparison of pattern; read across:

1. Not the first week,   the third.
2. Not the fourth term,   the sixth.
3. Not the tenth time,   the fifth.
4. Not the eighth seat,   the twelfth.
5. Not the last row,   the first.
6. Not the new car,   the old one.
7. Not the red book,   the green one.
8. Not the next street,   the last one.
9. Not the gold ring,   the brass one.
10. Not the dark cloth,   the light one.

The above two drills of course are not the only patterns that can be used, but they are expressive and common. It would be too great an assignment to present all possible patterns. Hopefully, listening to and drilling a few will encourage an awareness that will enable students to adjust their use of English patterns and standards to prevailing norms.

Annoyance or disapproval can be communicated through contrastive stress, as the following exercise illustrates.

4.3c Contrastive stress—annoyance
Comparison of pattern; read across with two voices, one for the questions and one for the answers:

1. Where are you going?   To Paris.   Why are you going to Paris?
2. When are you leaving?   Tomorrow.   Why are you leaving tomorrow?
3. Who are you taking with you?   Andrew.   Why are you taking Andrew?
4. How are you going?   By plane.   Why are you going by plane?
5. What airline are you going on?   PanAm.   Why are you going on PanAm?
6. What time of day are you leaving?   At noon.   Why are you leaving at noon?
7. What seat do you have?   One on the aisle.   Why are you sitting on the aisle?
8. Which airport are you landing at?   Orly.   Why are you landing at Orly?
9. Where are you staying?   At a hotel.   Why are you staying at a hotel?
10. How long are you staying?   A month.   Why are you staying a month?

It may be noted in passing that a series of questions like those in column three above would likely be considered an unjustifiable impertinence, to which the answer "It's none of your business" would probably be thought, if not offered aloud.

One of the characteristics of contrastive stress is the pitch drop immediately following the occurrence of a pitch /4/. The drop is shown in all the above exercise sentences, but is not too noticeable, since pitch /4/ is on the last or almost the last syllable. But the drop to level /1/ can occur early in a sentence with a considerable string of material on level /1/, as illustrated in the following sentence:

He's not the only man I met at the inauguration.

The exercise below shows this pattern in context.

4.3d Contrastive stress—correction with early downshift
Comparison of pattern; read across with two voices:

1. Why didn't you go to the store this morning?
   I did go to the store this morning.
2. Why didn't you do your homework last night?
   I did do my homework last night.
3. Why didn't you park in the driveway when you came home?
   I did park in the driveway when I came home.
4. Why didn't you go straight to your bedroom?
   I did go straight to my bedroom.
5. Why didn't you get up at seven, when your dad got up?
   I did get up at seven when my dad got up.
6. Why didn't you finish the novel I gave you to read?
   I did finish the novel you gave me to read.
7. Why didn't you put it back on the shelf in the library?
   I did put it back on the shelf in the library.
8. Why didn't you write the book report you were assigned to do?
   I did write the book report I was assigned to do.
9. Why didn't you practice the piano while I was out?
   I did practice the piano while you were out.
10. Why didn't you get your room straightened up this morning?
    I did get my room straightened up this morning.

88 Patterns of English Pronunciation

In some sentences contrast is built in by the occurrence of antonyms or opposites in the same context. When the antonyms are made by a negative prefix on one form (and that form comes second), contrastive stress is placed on the prefix, even though it does not normally come there. This is illustrated in the next drill.

4.3e Contrastive stress—antonyms in the same context
Comparison of pattern; read across with two voices:

1. Does the plane have disadvantages? — Well, it has both advantages and disadvantages.
2. Was the landlord unfriendly? — Well, he was neither friendly nor unfriendly.
3. Was the bellboy discourteous? — Well, he was both courteous and discourteous.
4. Was your request for a bank loan disapppoved? — Well, it was neither approved nor disapproved.
5. Is there much intolerance in the schools? — Well, there's both tolerance and intolerance.
6. Was this your unlucky day? — Well, it was neither lucky nor unlucky.
7. Were the questions immodest? — Well, they were both modest and immodest.
8. Was the old strategy deemphasized? — Well, it was neither emphasized nor deemphasized.
9. Are your friends nonresidents? — Well, they're both residents and nonresidents.
10. Was the apartment left unclean? — Well, it was neither clean nor unclean.
11. Were the witnesses irrational? — Well, they were both rational and irrational.
12. Was the automobile salesman dishonest? — Well, he was neither honest nor dishonest.

The variations on contrastive stress patterns in English are innumerable, and it is not feasible to attempt anything approaching an exhaustive inventory. But a few generalizations can be made: (1) contrastive stress is normally signaled by pitch, (2) level /4/ is the cue that directs special attention to an item (word or syllable), (3) after an occurrence of level /4/ there is typically a drop to level /1/, and the voice remains on level /1/ for the remainder of the intonation phrase, (4) in sentences that repeat information already in the context, except for a single new item, that new item may be given emphasis by contrastive stress, especially if the pattern called for is not the neutral, uncolored interpretation This last generalization can be illustrated by reading series of numbers.

4.3f Contrastive stress—novel information in series of numbers
Illustration of pattern; read down:

41. forty-one	21. twenty-one	
42. forty-two	31.	thirty-one
43. forty-three	41.	forty-one
44. forty-four	51.	fifty-one
45. forty-five	61.	sixty-one
46. forty-six	71.	seventy-one
47. forty-seven	81	eighty-one
48. forty-eight	91.	ninety-one
49. forty-nine		

104. one hundred and four	
204.	two hundred and four
304.	three hundred and four
404.	four hundred and four
504.	five hundred and four
604.	six hundred and four
704.	seven hundred and four
804.	eight hundred and four
904.	nine hundred and four
1004.	ten hundred and four

The operation of the sequence can become quite complex in a mixed series:

90   Patterns of English Pronunciation

23. twenty-three
24. twenty-four
34.   thirty-four
44.   forty-four
45.   forty-five
46.   forty-six
47.   forty-seven
57.   fifty-seven
67.   sixty-seven
68.   sixty-eight
69.   sixty-nine
79.   seventy-nine
89.   eighty-nine
99.   ninety-nine

It may be that the rise to level /4/ applies only to the first item after a pattern switch, and that following items in the same pattern have only level /3/ as a peak.

Once again it seems advisable to warn the student that these patterns, while strong and typical, are not completely obligatory. There are variations possible, and the system is not as rigid as this brief presentation may imply.

For various reasons, including some variant pronunciations, students often have trouble distinguishing the teens from the tens in the English number system. The following drill is designed to help keep these separate.

4.3g Stress patterns on the teens and the tens

Comparison of pattern; read across with two voices:

	A		B				A	
1.	Thirteen	How many did you say?	Thirty?	No, thirteen.	Thirteen years
2.	Fourteen	How many did you say?	Forty?	No, fourteen.	Fourteen year
3.	Fifteen	How many did you say?	Fifty?	No, fifteen.	Fifteen years.
4.	Sixteen	How many did you say?	Sixty?	No, sixteen.	Sixteen years.
5.	Seventeen	How many did you say?	Seventy?	No, seventeen.	Seventeen yea
6.	Eighteen	How many did you say?	Eighty?	No, eighteen.	Eighteen year
7.	Nineteen	How many did you say?	Ninety?	No, nineteen.	Nineteen year

English Stress and Intonation Patterns 91

In the context assumed for the above drill speaker A gives a number. Speaker B is not sure he heard right, so uses an echo question to ask for a verification. Speaker A then gives a correction (using a contrastive pattern) and then puts the number word in a phrase which conditions a shift in the stress. Note how the context determines the intonation (e.g., the stress and pitch) pattern. If the mishearing had been within the teens, the contrastive correction would have been on the first syllable:

Thirteen   How many did you say?   Fourteen?   No, thirteen.   Thirteen years.

The contrastive-stress patterns in English can be used to highlight almost any word or syllable in a sentence. Highlighting, by means of the application of a pitch-stress focus, particularly with pitch level /4/ and a shift (if necessary) of strong stress, is very frequently used to emphasize an item the speaker thinks is particularly important, or that carries new and contrasting information. This "manipulation" of pitch and stress may seem complex, but is in effect basically simple, and it gives the language an enormous flexibility of expression. This is illustrated in the following exercise, which consists of questions eliciting selective repeated information.

4.3h Contrastive stress—selective questions
  Comparison of pattern; read across with two voices:
I tôok my sĭster to the môvies yêsterday.

When did you take your sister to the movies?

I took her to the movies yesterday.

Who did you take to the movies yesterday?

I took my sister to the movies yesterday.

4.3h (continued)

Whose sister did you take to the movies yesterday?

I took my sister to the movies yesterday.

Weren't you going to take your sister to the movies yesterday?

I took my sister to the movies yesterday.

Where did you take your sister yesterday?

I took my sister to the movies yesterday.

Why didn't you take your sister to the movies yesterday?

I did take my sister to the movies yesterday.

This exercise shows the successive highlighting of different elements (or pieces of information) in the answers, as each element is solicited in the series of questions. In each answer the crucial item is pronounced with strong stress on pitch level /4/ after which there is a drop to level /1/ for the completion of the sentence. Note that a special intonation pattern is present in the questions, an "echo" pattern pronounced on level /3/ that signals "I didn't quite get all of what you said; could you repeat for me please?" (except for the last question which queries "why" and does not ask that information once given be repeated).

It is worth noting that the echo question could ask for more than one piece of information. In this case two (or more) question words (but only one fronted to the beginning of the question) would appear, and both requested pieces of information would be highlighted in the answer:

Whose sister did you take where yesterday?

I took my sister to the movies yesterday.

It would of course not be incorrect in all the answers above to give, as a word or phrase, just the item of information asked for, instead of repeating the whole sentence. Even so the phrase or single-word answers given in response to an echo question request would be lifted to level /4/. The longer answers are not unnatural, especially if the speaker wishes to express irritation with the questions.

In the next chapter we will discuss the inventory and distribution of weak-stressed vowels. In anticipation of some of the problems expected in that discussion, I'd like to present an exercise that contrasts medial and weak stress. The exercise involves two- and three-syllable words. The first pattern is strong-medial, the second is strong-weak. The selection of items in each list is lexically determined—I have not been able to identify any defining criteria that indicate why a particular word is in one list and not the other. It seems to be a combination of time since the word was introduced into the language plus its phonetic form. In any case, speculation on origins doesn't help the second-language learner of English. The pronunciation has to be learned along with the form.

4.4 Three stress levels—medial and weak contrasted

Presentation and comparison of pattern; read down, then across:

méylmæ̀n	pówstmən	mailman	postman
frágmæ̀n	hɔ́rsmən	frogman	horseman
bráshmæ̀n	búshmən	brushman	bushman
trǽshmæ̀n	fréshmən	trashman	freshman
áysmæ̀n	ɛ́rmən	iceman	airman
lɔ́wmæ̀n	fáyərmən	lawman	fireman
tǽksmæ̀n	wə́rkmən	taxman	workman
sǽndmæ̀n	chɛ́rmən	sandman	chairman
stɔ́rmæ̀n	fɔ́rmən	storeman	foreman
yárdmæ̀n	krúwmən	yardman	crewman
shíypmæ̀n	hə́rdzmən	sheepman	herdsman
mínətmæ̀n	físhərmən	minuteman	fisherman
sə́rvəsmæ̀n	nówbəlmən	serviceman	nobleman
bówgiymæ̀n	gɛ́ntəlmən	bogeyman	gentleman
mídəlmæ̀n	káwnsəlmən	middleman	councilman
gərájmæ̀n	pəlíysmən	garageman	policeman

It is noted that these derivational nouns are very similar in composition, both patterns consisting of two items, the second of which is *-man*. Most important, for the discussion in Chapter 5, the vowel of *-man* is /æ/ when medial stress occurs, but /ə/ when weak stressed.

Chapter 5
ENGLISH VOWEL PATTERNS

In Chapter 2 an inventory of stressed vowels and diphthongs was given along with exercises for pairs that are similar and thus likely to be confused by second-language students of English. Vowels in weak-stressed syllables have been cited, especially in the stress contrasts of Chapters 1 and 4, but have not been systematically discussed. It is time now to formally present the English weak-stressed vowel system, which has patterns that are very distinctive and characteristic of English and very different from the vowel systems of many other languages.

I speak of a "weak-stressed vowel system" as if weak-stressed vowels differed from vowels with a higher stress (strong, secondary, or medial) in ways other than by stress alone. This may be justified—weak-stressed vowels are very different, but most transcriptions of English nevertheless use some of the same vowel symbols employed to represent strong-stressed vowels. The weak-stressed vowels are sufficiently dissimilar from their strong-stressed counterparts that analysts and authors of pronunciation books and dictionaries have not always agreed on how to interpret certain weak-stressed vowels—for example, is the second syllable of *victim* best represented by /ɪ/ or /ə/: /vɪ́ktɪm/ or /vɪ́ktəm/? To further complicate matters, some weak-stressed vowels in some words may take alternate pronunciations, such as the first syllable of *regard*, which may be either /riygârd/ or /rəgârd/. To clarify these problems is one of the purposes of the present chapter.

There are five vowels (and diphthongs) in the weak-stressed pattern. These are illustrated on the grid presented in Chapter 2, as follows:

iy		uw
I	ə	
		ow

No other vowel or diphthong than the above occurs under weak stress in the dialect of English assumed for this text.

The weak-stressed vowel par excellence in English is the /ə/, usually referred to as the "schwa." It occurs very extensively and, as we shall see in Chapter 7, is regularly substituted for other vowels in related words that show stress alternations. The weak-stressed schwa is produced much higher in the mouth than its strong-stressed counterpart. In fact, it could be analyzed as follows, with /ə̌/ represented substantially higher than /ə̂/.

	ə̌	
	ə̂	

Thus a difference may be heard in the vowels of words like /əbə́v/ *(above)*, /səkə́m/ *(succumb)*, /pə́pət/ *(puppet)*, /yə́kə/ *(yucca)*, but I will take the position that it is a difference that can be assigned to stress rather than one involving different vowels.

The schwa (under weak stress) is the main exception to the generalization that simple vowels in English occur in closed syllables (with a consonant following in the same syllable). Schwa *can* occur finally, in words like /sṓwfə, víĺə, ḗyzhə/ *(sofa, villa, Asia)*, etc. Schwa is a potential weak-stress alternate for every other vowel; consequently there is no typical spelling for this very commonly occurring vowel. The following lists show numerous possibilities:

ǽtləs	dǽləs	atlas	Dallas
mṓwzəs	də́ləs	Moses	Dulles
thíysəs	dḗnəs	thesis	Dennis
thə́rməs	íynəs	thermos	Enos
máynəs	rúwfəs	minus	Rufus
	glǽdəs		Gladys

pǽləs	pə́rchəs	kə́mpəs	palace	purchase	compass
hárnəs			harness		
práməs	sə́rvəs	kǽshəs	promise	service	Cassius
pə́rpəs	pɔ́rpəs		purpose	porpoise	
léțəs	nə́rvəs	kɔ́shəs	lettuce	nervous	cautious

Each of these two-syllable words has in common a stressed first syllable and a second syllable ending in /-əs/, but there are at least eighteen different spellings. This indicates the generality and, in terms of spelling, the neutrality of schwa.

The following exercise contrasts schwa in strong- and weak-stressed syllables. Note that when weak, the syllable with schwa is extremely short and pronounced very lightly. Also, the tongue is positioned higher, which gives the schwa a somewhat different sound. Listen carefully and imitate the difference.

5.1 Schwa in strong-stressed and weak-stressed syllables
Comparison of pattern; read across:

	/ə́/	/ə̆/		
1a.	pə́s	ówpəs	pus	opus
b.	bə́s	nímbəs	bus	nimbus
c.	mə́s	hyúwməs	muss	humus
d.	gə́s	bówgəs	Gus	bogus
e.	fə́s	táyfəs	fuss	typhus
f.	kə́s	fówkəs	cuss	focus
g.	rə́s	sáyrəs	Russ	Cyrus
h.	trə́s	sítrəs	truss	citrus
i.	də́st	sǽdəst	dust	saddest
j.	gə́st	ɔ́gəst	gust	August
k.	mə́st	slíməst	must	slimmest
l.	jə́st	séyjəst	just	sagest
m.	rə́st	shúrəst	rust	surest
n.	lə́st	fúləst	lust	fullest
o.	fə́n	ɛ́lfən	fun	elfin
p.	sə́n	nɛ́lsən	son	Nelson
q.	pə́n	ráypən	pun	ripen
r.	gə́n	wǽgən	gun	wagon
s.	nə́m	dɛ́nəm	numb	denim
2a.	sə́p	səpɔ́rt	sup	support
b.	sə́k	səkə́m	suck	succumb
c.	bə́g	bəgǽs	bug	bagasse
d.	də́st	dəstə́rb	dust	disturb
e.	pə́t	pətíyt	putt	petite

When schwa occurs before /r/, it is pronounced with the tongue curled back toward the roof of the mouth, which has the effect of raising the vowel—whether under weak or strong stress. Two-syllable words like /mə́rmər, bə́rbər/ *(murmur, Berber)* illustrate the acoustic similarity of /ə́r/ and /ə̆r/.

5.1a Schwa plus /r/ in strong-stressed and weak-stressed syllables

Comparison of pattern; read across:

	/ə́r/	/ər/		
1.	bə́r	rə́bər	burr	rubber
2.	kə́r	bǽkər	cur	backer
3.	pə́r	zípər	purr	zipper
4.	fə́r	dífər	fir	differ
5.	mə́r	hǽmər	myrrh	hammer
6.	sə́r	sɔ́sər	sir	saucer
7.	blə́r	gǽmblər	blur	gambler
8.	slə́r	wíslər	slur	whistler

In these examples it is impossible to separately distinguish /ə/ from /r/. We could say we have a single sound—an r-colored schwa.

This means that the vowel /ə/ will sound noticeably different when followed by /r/. The following exercise illustrates the difference.

5.1b Schwa compared to schwa plus /r/

Comparison of pattern; read across:

	/ə́/	/ə́r/		
1.	bə́d	bə́rd	bud	bird
2.	θə́d	θə́rd	thud	third
3.	fə́n	fə́rn	fun	fern
4.	bə́n	bə́rn	bun	burn
5.	kə́b	kə́rb	cub	curb
6.	kə́l	kə́rl	cull	curl
7.	gə́l	gə́rl	gull	girl
8.	θə́m	θə́rm	thumb	therm
9.	pə́t	pə́rt	putt	pert
10.	bə́t	bə́rt	but	Bert
11.	pə́s	pə́rs	pus	purse
12.	kə́s	kə́rs	cuss	curse
13.	fə́z	fə́rz	fuzz	firs
14.	bə́st	bə́rst	bust	burst
15.	fə́st	fə́rst	fussed	first

In some three-syllable words, typically with the stress pattern /ˊ ˇˇ/ and with /ər/ in the middle syllable, the schwa in that syllable may drop, leaving a kind of contracted pronunciation. This illustrates the very short pronunciation of schwa and the integration of /r/ into adjacent syllables. In the following exercise the adjective is shown in alternate pronunciations, one fuller and one reduced. The corresponding adverb is invariably reduced.

5.1c Weak-stressed schwa plus /r/
Comparison of pattern; read across:

	/ə̆r/	~	/r/	/r/		
1.	líbərəl		líbrəl	líbrəliy	liberal	liberally
2.	jénərəl		jénrəl	jénrəliy	general	generally
3.	témpərəl		témprəl	témprəliy	temporal	temporally
4.	kɔ́rpərəl		kɔ́rprəl	kɔ́rprəliy	corporal	corporally
5.	nǽchərəl		nǽchrəl	nǽchrəliy	natural	naturally
6.	pǽstərəl		pǽstrəl	pǽstrəliy	pastoral	pastorally
7.	vísərəl		vísrəl	vísrəliy	visceral	viscerally
8.	strə́kchərəl		strə́kchrəl	strə́kchrəliy	structural	structurally

The adjective *literal* fits in this pattern and illustrates the variants of the sound /t/, with a flap /t/ between vowels in /lítərəl/ and an aspirated /t/ released directly into the /r/ in /lítrəl/ and /lítrəliy/. A number of nouns also fit the first pattern (but of course do not have "adverb" equivalents): *mineral, funeral, mackerel, numeral.*

While schwa is the most general and most frequently occurring weak-stressed vowel in English, there are four others, as indicated earlier. These are /ɪ, iy, ow, uw/. Weak-stressed /ɪ/ (as strong-stressed /ɪ/) occurs in closed syllables (before a consonant), and in general /ɪ/ under weak stress occurs before palatal and velar consonants in final syllables: /-sh, -ch, -j, -k, -g, -ng/, as in /sélfɪsh, sǽnwɪch, kérɪj, pə́blɪk, vérɪg, kə́mɪng/ *(selfish, sandwich, carriage, public, Varig, coming).* Weak-stressed /ɪ/ can occur elsewhere (in syllables before the strong-stressed syllable of a word) but in this position is often substituted by schwa: /ɪndíyd ~ əndíyd/ *(indeed).*

The other three are diphthongs, all of which can occur in open (and therefore final) syllables. As in the case of schwa, the strong-stressed and weak-stressed vowels are not quite identical in sound, but with /ɪ, iy, ow, uw/ the difference is less conspicuous.

The following forms illustrate the contrast in a single word. Listen and imitate carefully.

5.2 Contrast of strong-stressed and weak-stressed vowels other than schwa
   Presentation of pattern; read across:

/ɪ/	krítɪk	síngɪng	critic	singing
/iy/	míytiy	níydiy	meaty	needy
/ow/	ówbow	kówkow	oboe	cocoa
/uw/	chúw chuw	kúwkuw	choo choo	cuckoo

In general the variants are recognizably similar.

In the following exercise, equivalent strong- and weak-stressed vowels are compared. Notice that the weak-stressed vowels tend to be pronounced with the tongue moved somewhat toward the center of the mouth (in the direction of /ə/). And also notice, of course, that weak-stressed syllables are very short.

5.2a Strong-stressed and weak-stressed /ɪ/
   Comparison of pattern; read across:

	/ɪ́/	/ɪ̆/		
1.	fɪ́sh	sélfɪsh	fish	selfish
2.	dɪ́sh	rǽdɪsh	dish	radish
3.	rɪ́ch	óstrɪch	rich	ostrich
4.	wɪ́ch	sǽnwɪch	witch	sandwich
5.	rɪ́j	pórɪj	ridge	porridge
6.	rɪ́j	mérɪj	ridge	marriage
7.	lɪ́k	pə́blɪk	lick	public
8.	tɪ́k	ǽtɪk	tick	attic
9.	sɪ́ng	réysɪng	sing	racing
10.	zɪ́ng	tíyzɪng	zing	teasing

The limitation of weak-stressed /ɪ/ to occurrence before certain consonants as illustrated above may not apply to all dialects of American English. Some speakers may use /ɪ/ in the weak-stressed (second) syllables of words like *passive, active, worship, tulip, tariff, pilgrim,* etc. For most speakers, schwa appears exclusively in these syllables, and for many more, as a very common alternate.

5.2b Strong-stressed and weak-stressed /iy/
Comparison of pattern; read across:

	/íy/	/ĭy/		
1.	tíy	pártiy	tea	party
2.	níy	mέniy	knee	many
3.	síy	sísiy	see	sissy
4.	zíy	bíziy	Z	busy
5.	bíy	ǽbiy	bee	abbey
6.	píy	hǽpiy	pea	happy
7.	kíy	lǎkiy	key	lucky
8.	fíy	líyfiy	fee	leafy
9.	víy	hέviy	V	heavy
10.	ríy	sɔ́riy	Rhee	sorry

Additionally, weak-stressed /iy/ appears as an alternate in syllables before the strong stress in a word, as in /riygárd/ *(regard)*. These will be the subject of a separate exercise to appear later.

5.2c Strong-stressed and weak-stressed /ow/
Comparison of pattern; read across:

	/ów/	/ŏw/		
1.	lów	pílow	low	pillow
2.	nów	mínow	know	minnow
3.	dów	wíndow	dough	window
4.	tów	ǽltow	toe	alto
5.	rów	έrow	row	arrow
6.	pów	hípow	Poe	hippo
7.	sów	ɔ́lsow	so	also
8.	bów	έlbow	bow	elbow
9.	jów	bǽnjow	Joe	banjo
10.	gów	tǽnggo	go	tango

As a generalization, weak-stressed /ow/ follows consonants other than palatals (/sh, zh, ch, j, y/) with some exceptions, like *Groucho*. The palatal consonants are usually, though also not exclusively, followed by /uw/, as shown below. It may be worth noting that the weak-stressed syllable with /ow/ is much shorter after a single consonant than after a sequence: cf., *motto* and *elbow*, a difference which might suggest that the /ow/ in *elbow* is actually medially stressed, as is the /ow/ in *rainbow*.

5.2d Strong-stressed and weak-stressed /uw/
Comparison of pattern; read across:

	/úw/	/ŭw/		
1.	shúw	íshuw	shoe	issue
2.	chúw	vә́rchuw	chew	virtue
3.	júw	ǽnjuw	Jew	Anjou
4.	yúw	vǽlyuw	you	value
5.	lúw	zúwluw	Lou	Zulu
6.	múw	íymuw	moo	emu
7.	kúw	kúwkuw	coo	cuckoo

It can be noted that from a phonetic point of view the weak-stressed vowels show a considerable range of pronunciation values. This range extends to the central area occupied by schwa, so that, in some contexts at least, there is a measure of overlap between each of the weak vowels /ɪ, iy, ow, uw/ and /ə/. Individual speakers may vary in their preferences and habits, but the alternative pronunciation (in the examples cited) are all acceptable. However, the distinct vowel (as opposed to schwa) will be preferred if there is any suggestion of raising the stress toward medial. The following exercises present variant pronunciations that illustrate this overlap.

5.2e Weak-stressed vowel overlap with schwa
Comparison of pattern; read across:

	/ɪ̆/	~	/ə̆/	
1a.	ɪndíyd		əndíyd	indeed
b.	ɪnépt		ənépt	inept
c.	ɪmprés		əmprés	impress
d.	ɪmpówz		əmpówz	impose
e.	ɪlíygəl		əlíygəl	illegal
f.	mɪstéyk		məstéyk	mistake
g.	dɪsláyk		dəsláyk	dislike
h.	dɪstə́rb		dəstə́rb	disturb
i.	dɪsént		dəsént	dissent
j.	rɪskéy		rəskéy	risqué

5.2e (continued)

	/iy/	~	/ə/	
2a.	riygárd		rəgárd	regard
b.	diyláyt		dəláyt	delight
c.	biykə́m		bəkə́m	become
d.	biylów		bəlów	below
e.	iylɛ́kt		əlɛ́kt	elect
f.	iylɛ́vən		əlɛ́vən	eleven
g.	diytéyn		dətéyn	detain
h.	diyzə́rt		dəzə́rt	desert
i.	priyzə́rv		prəzə́rv	preserve
j.	priydíkt		prədíkt	predict

	/ow/	~	/ə/	
3a.	prowmówt		prəmówt	promote
b.	prowkléym		prəkléym	proclaim
c.	prowsíyd		prəsíyd	proceed
d.	prowgrɛ́s		prəgrɛ́s	progress
e.	prowdúws		prədúws	produce
f.	prownáwnts		prənáwnts	pronounce
g.	rowmǽnts		rəmǽnts	romance
h.	rowtéyshən		rətéyshən	rotation
i.	sowlísət		səlísət	solicit
j.	towlíydow		təlíydow	Toledo

	/uw/	~	/ə(w)/	
4a.	rɛ́gyuwlər		rɛ́gyələr	regular
b.	sírkyuwlèyt		sírkyəlèyt	circulate
c.	nɛ́byuwləs		nɛ́byələs	nebulous
d.	síŋggyuwlər		síŋggyələr	singular
e.	fɔ́rmyuwlèyt		fɔ́rmyəlèyt	formulate
f.	mǽnyuwəl		mǽnyəwəl ~ mǽnyəl	manual
g.	ríchuwəl		ríchəwəl	ritual
h.	ǽkchuwəl		ǽkchəwəl	actual
i.	vízhuwəl		vízhəwəl	visual
j.	yúwzhuwəl		yúwzhəwəl	usual
k.	sɛ́kshuwəl		sɛ́kshəwəl	sexual

One pattern of alternation between /ĭ/ and /ə̆/ is worth special mention because it is so characteristic of spoken English: the *-ing* ending of verbs. Before the velar nasal the weak-stressed vowel of this ending is /ĭ/, but when the alveolar final /n/ is substituted in informal conversational style, the vowel regularly changes to schwa. Thus the /-ɪng/ forms are associated with formal style, the /-ən/ with informal.

5.2f The *-ing* ending in formal and informal style
Comparison of pattern; read across:

	formal	*informal*		
1.	bíyɪng	bíyən	being	bein'
2.	séyɪng	séyən	saying	sayin'
3.	báyɪng	báyən	buying	buyin'
4.	báwɪng	báwən	bowing	bowin'
5.	gówɪng	gówən	going	goin'
6.	chúwɪng	chúwən	chewing	chewin'
7.	sítɪng	sítn̩	sitting	sittin'
8.	rə́bɪng	rə́bən	rubbing	rubbin '
9.	pǽsɪng	pǽsən	passing	passin'
10.	hǽvɪng	hǽvən	having	havin'
11.	síngɪng	síngən	singing	singin'
12.	púlɪng	púlən	pulling	pullin'
13.	kɛ́rɪng	kɛ́rən	caring	carin'

Note that the /t/ in the verb *sit* is pronounced as a flap in *sitting* but is released as a glottal stop before the ending in *sittin'*, where the last syllable is realized as a syllabic /n̩/. These are regular pronunciations for the two contexts.

The idea of a phonetic range of pronunciations that produces overlaps extends to other vowels, though normally a stress contrast accompanies the vowel contrast. The alternate forms in the drill below are all acceptable in English, though they are usually perceived as marking differences in dialect, register, or level of formality. A student of English should be prepared to accept and interpret these kinds of variation.

5.2g Vowel reductions associated with weak stress
Presentation and comparison of pattern; read across:

		/ˆ/	/˘/	
/ɛ/	1a.	ɛ̂ndûr	əndûr	endure
	b.	mɛ̂nâzh	mənâzh	menage
	c.	ɛ̂kstɛ̂nd	əkstɛ̂nd	extend
	d.	ɛ̂kstrîym	əkstrîym	extreme
	e.	ɛ̂nklôwz	əngklôwz	enclose
/æ/	2a.	æ̂bstêyn	əbstêyn	abstain
	b.	æ̂bstrǽkt	əbstrǽkt	abstract
	c.	æ̂dvə́rbiyəl	ədvə́rbiyəl	adverbial
	d.	æ̂dvǽntij	ədvǽntij	advantage
	e.	æ̂ktîvətiy	əktîvətɪy	activity
/ɑ/	3a.	ɑ̂bzə́rv	əbzə́rv	observe
	b.	ɑ̂bjɛ̂kt	əbjɛ̂kt	object
	c.	ɑ̂ktôwbər	əktôwbər	October
	d.	ɑ̂bskyûr	əbskyûr	obscure
	e.	ɑ̂bstrə́kt	əbstrə́kt	obstruct
/ɔ/	4a.	ɔ̂stîr	əstîr	austere
	b.	ɔ̂gə́stə	əgə́stə	Augusta
	c.	ɔ̂dǽsətiy	ədǽsətiy	audacity
	d.	ɔ̂spîshəs	əspîshəs	auspicious
	e.	ɔ̂strêylyə	əstrêylyə	Australia
/ay/	5a.	mâynûwt	mənûwt	minute
	b.	ǽjàyl	ǽgəl	agile
	c.	fə́rtàyl	fə́rtəl	fertile
	d.	vîràyl	vîrəl	virile
	e.	stɛ̂ràyl	stɛ̂rəl	sterile

There are a few additional patterns of occurrence for weak-stressed vowels, such as those shown in the alternate forms /shɪkɔ́gow ~ shɪkɑ́gə/ *(Chicago)*, /wîndow ~ wîndə/ *(window)*, /məzə́riy ~ məzə́rə/ *(Missouri)*, /sìnsənǽtiy ~ sìnsənǽtə/ *(Cincinnati)*, /âyəwêy ~ âyəwə/ *(Iowa)*, but these are relatively unimportant regional or social variants, some of which may be considered slightly substandard. The point of even mentioning them is to observe that language (and especially pronunciation) is a living, changing process, and students undertaking to learn a language for purposes of live, face-to-face communication must be prepared to adapt their expectations, especially as listeners, to ranges of variance within patterns. Otherwise they may be perplexed or even lost.

An important distributional pattern that affects vowels is seen when an /r/ follows a vowel in the same syllable. In discussing /r/ as a consonant in Chapter 3, it was pointed out that the consonant /r/ can occur only after a simple vowel and then only after six of the seven: /I-ɛ-ə-ɑ-ɔ-U/. This is true for the dialect assumed as the basis of the presentation in this book, but other dialects may vary. Some would say /r/ can come after only five simple vowels (subtracting /U/, whose occurrences would join /ɔ/). Others would say all seven simple vowels (dividing the occurrences after /ɛ/ into /ɛ/ and /æ/). Still other dialects might claim diphthongs may directly precede /r/, that the vowel in *beer* is properly identified as the vowel of *bead* rather than (as assumed in this book) the vowel of *bid*. Or alternatively that the /iy-I/ contrast in *bead-bid* is just neutralized before /r/ and that in effect *beer* has an intermediate vowel that is actually neither /iy/ nor /I/. (Implications of the patterns assumed for this text were presented and discussed in Chapter 3 with examples such as the contrast *pear-payer*.)

And of course there is the solution to be found in the so-called r-less dialects (New England and Southern American and Standard British), where /r/ in a syllable after a vowel merely drops, or more accurately is replaced by a centering glide, with no perceptible r-coloring involved in the pronunciation. This centering glide is sometimes transcribed as /ə/ or (to show it is nonsyllabic) as /ɚ/ or as /h/, so that beer is written as /bɪ̆ə/ or /bɪ̆ɚ/ or bɪh/.

Other special problems involve the consonant /r/: the fact that it may drop when medial in words like *nearer, error, horror* (Chapter 3) and in special patterns of consonant clusters at the beginnings of syllables (Chapter 6). Even in general American English there are various instances of an /r/ dropping to produce an informal equivalent of a standard form, such as /kəs-bəst-fəst-hɔs/ from /kərs-bərst-fərst-hɔrs/ *(cuss, bust, fust, hoss* from *curse, burst, first, horse)*. This cannot be considered a general pattern of the language (the dictionary marks these forms as "illiterate usage"), though it is interesting to see that *cuss* has enlarged its semantic area to include the meaning "queer or perverse person or animal," a meaning not associated with *curse*. This is perhaps enough data to show that /r/ is a very complicated sound to describe in English, and no one should be surprised if there is disagreement on pronunciation patterns among speakers of English.

The pattern assumed in this presentation is:

	ər	
ɪr		ʊr
ɛr		
		ɔr
	ɑr	

ɪr	pɪr	peer, pier
ɛr	pɛr	pear, pair, pare
ər	pər	purr
ɑr	pɑr	par
ɔr	pɔr	pore, pour
ʊr	pʊr	poor

One immediate problem of /r/ is its perception when it comes after a vowel in the same syllable, where the /r/ may not be heard as a distinctive sound, but only as an effect on the quality of the vowel. The first exercise below contrasts the absence and the presence of /r/. You will note that /r/ is easier to distinguish after some vowels than after others.

5.3 Presence of postvocalic /r/

Presentation of pattern; select the appropriate paraphrase:

gɑd/gɑrd   1a. That's a statue of a Roman god/guard. (deity/sentinel)

kɑt/kɑrt   b. He stumbled over the cot/cart. (narrow bed/light vehicle)

5.3 (continued)

shak/shark
c. The shock/shark just about finished him. (electrical charge/man-eating fish)

hápɪŋ/hárpɪŋ
d. She kept hopping/harping about that dirty garage. (leaping/complaining)

shɛd/shɛrd
e. He shed/shared his old coat. (removed/offered use)

blɛd/blɛrd
f. The bugler bled/blared as the battle ended. (lost blood/trumpeted)

flɛd/flɛrd
g. The speeding car fled/flared as it burst into flame. (escaped/blazed brightly)

dɛd/dɛrd
h. He was dead/dared when he fell silent. (lifeless/challenged)

bɪd/bɪrd
i. His bid/beard was too small to be noticed. (offer to buy/chin whiskers)

mɪ́liy/mɪ́rliy
j. When I opened the door, it was Milly/merely Jones. (Millicent/only)

fɪz/fɪrz
k. Such fizz/fears can't be necessary. (effervescence/apprehensions)

kwɪz/kwɪrz
l. The quiz/queers can wait till tomorrow. (short exam/strange fellows)

cɔt/cɔrt
2a. They both caught/court the same girl. (captured/woo)

sɔs/sɔrs
b. The meat sauce/source dried up. (gravy/origin)

sɔd/sɔrd
c. The craftsman sawed/soared for half an hour. (cut/flew)

kɔz/kɔrz
d. The cause/cores of the wormy apples could not be found. (reason/fibrous center)

5.3 (continued)

fowks/fɔrks	3a. He left his folks/forks in the kitchen. (parents/eating tools)
sowd/sɔrd	b. He sewed/soared into the night. (stitched/flew)
rowd/rɔrd	c. He rode/roared away on his motorcycle. (departed/blasted off)
mownd/mɔrnd	d. She moaned/mourned for her lost husband. (bewailed/lamented)
gəlz/gərlz	4a. He saw lots of gulls/girls on the beach. (birds/young women)
kəb/kərb	b. He kicked the cub/curb in his frustration. (young bear/edge of the street)
klək/klərk	c. That dumb cluck/clerk doesn't know anything. (stupid person/salesperson)
həld/hərld	d. They hulled/hurled the corn. (shelled/threw)
bəd/bərd	e. There was a bud/bird on the top branch. (new plant shoot/small fowl)
bən/bərn	f. He put butter on his bun/burn. (bread roll/heat lesion)
bləd/blərd	g. The thought of blood/blurred relations upset him. (kinsmen/indistinct)

The first group, the sentences in *1,* has an /r/-sound that can quite easily be distinguished from the preceding vowel with a little practice, though the r-coloring does affect the quality of the vowel. The next two groups represent an English dialect split. Some speakers will equate /ɔ/ before /r/ with /ɔ/ alone. Others will equate /ɔ/ before /r/ with /ow/, particularly since the /r/ has the effect of raising the /ɔ/ toward /ow/. Depending on dialect preference, the sentences in *2* or the sentences in *3* can be omitted, since they cover the same phonetic area. The last group, the sentences in *4,* will probably be the most difficult, since the r-coloring all but obscures the original vowel, and it is virtually impossible to perceive /r/ as a separate sound in sequence after /ə/. The result is a "modified" schwa, pronounced with the tip of the tongue turned toward the top of the mouth.

As pointed out earlier (and in Chapter 3) diphthongs do not occur immediately before /r/, at least not in the dialect assumed for description in this text. This limitation is illustrated in words like freer and bluer, meaning "more free" and "more blue," pronounced as two syllables /fríyər/ and /blúwər/, where a schwa in a distinct syllable separates the diphthong from the /r/. Thus it is not possible to directly compare /iy/ and /ɪ/ or /uw/ and /ʊ/ before /r/, since only the simple vowels are permitted in this context. However, since the /iy-ɪ/ and /uw-ʊ/ contrasts are difficult whenever either member of either pair occurs, an exercise seems useful. Note that the vowel plus a glide (/y/ or /w/) appears in the first member of the following pairs, but a simple vowel (before /r/) in the second. Be sure to listen for and to pronounce the vowels distinctly different in the pairs.

5.3a High diphthongs (/iy, uw/) contrasted with high simple vowels (before /r/ (ɪr/ and /ʊr/)

Comparison of pattern; select the appropriate paraphrase:

fiyz/fɪrz	1a. His fees/fears are excessive. (charges/apprehensions)
biyz/bɪrz	b. He's always thinking about bees/beers. (honey insects/malt beverages)
tiyz/tɪrz	c. I don't know why her teas/tears are so important. (afternoon parties/weeping)
sniyz/snɪrz	d. His sneeze/sneers attracted the entire audience's attention. (spasmodic reaction/contemptuous grimaces)
chiyz/chɪrz	e. We got cheese/cheers from the farmers. (pressed milk curd/shouts of acclamation)

5.3a (continued)

biydz/bɪrdz	f. They got their beads/beards in the soup. (strung trinkets/chin whiskers)
tuwz/turz	2a. They came here by twos/tours. (pairs/conducted trips)
yuwz/yurz	b. Are these sheep ewes/yours? (females/belonging to you)
luwz/lurz	c. Is it important that she lose/lures the detective? (elude/entices)
buwz/burz	d. If there's one thing I can't stand, it's booze/boors. (alcoholic drink/ill-mannered louts)
kyuwd/kyurd	e. He cued/cured my stammering. (signalled/remedied)

These exercise sentences will be most useful to students whose first language fails to distinguish high diphthongs from high vowels, or whose high vowels are tense, more like English /iy/ and /uw/ than like English /ɪ/ and /u/. The second set of sentences are of relatively little value if the English dialect taught does not distinguish /u/ and /ɔ/ before /r/, that is, where *lure* and *lore* are homonyms.

Since r-coloring affects all of the vowels, a separate exercise is provided to give practice in distinguishing sequences of various vowels plus /r/.

5.3b Postvocalic /r/ after contrasting vowels
Comparison of pattern; select the appropriate paraphrase:

kər/kɑr	1a. That cur/car won't run at all. (dog/automobile)
stər/stɑr	b. He often created quite a stir/star in the movies. (general excitement/leading actress)
fərm/fɑrm	c. He worked with the firm/farm for years. (business house/agricultural tract)

5.3b (continued)

wərd/wɑrd

pərt/pɑrt

dərt/dɑrt

hərt/hɑrt

shərk/shɑrk

kər/kɔr

hər/hɔr

bərd/bɔrd

hə́rdɪŋ/hɔ́rdɪŋ

hərs/hɔrs

fərst/fɔrst

shərts/shɔrts

pərch/pɔrch

bɑr/bɔr

fɑrm/fɔrm

gɑrd/gɔrd

d. The word/ward of the king is privileged. (opinion/stepchild)

e. I think she's one pert/part Navajo. (saucy/portion)

f. The dirt/dart hit him in the face. (earth/feathered pin)

g. His hurt/heart was throbbing painfully. (injury/circulatory organ)

h. He always was a shirk/shark. (work evader/swindler)

2a. He threw the cur/core out the window. (mongrel dog/apple center)

b. Is that her/whore coming here? (female/prostitute)

c. That wooden bird/board is very decorative. (avian vertebrate/thin slab)

d. They say he's herding/hoarding beef cattle. (tending/storing away)

e. His last trip was by hearse/horse. (mortician's car/equine mammal)

f. The first/forced problems are the worst. (earliest/coerced)

g. He lost his shirts/shorts in the laundry. (male upper body garment/male underwear)

h. The canary sat there on the perch/porch. (roost/veranda)

3a. They want to bar/bore the hole. (shut off/drill)

b. He worked on the farm/form all day. (agricultural tract/application document)

c. The guard/gourd was broken up by the incident. (protector/dried calabash)

5.3b (continued)

ârdər/ôrdər   d. I didn't expect the troops' ardor/order. (zeal/discipline)

pɑrt/pɔrt   e. The outer part/port of the town was attacked. (portion/harbor)

pɑrk/pɔrk   f. He enjoys the park/pork we recommended. (recreational area/swine meat)

hɪr/hər   4a. I think it's here/her. (at this place/the lady)

spɪr/spər   b. He stuck his spear/spur in the horse. (javelin/heel goad)

fɪrz/fərz   c. His fears/furs couldn't be disposed of. (terrors/animal skins)

blîriy/blə̂riy   d. His eyes were bleary/blurry. (tear-filled/indistinct)

wɪrd/wərd   e. It's a weird/word game. (freakish/language)

stɪrd/stərd   f. He steered/stirred the ship of state. (guided/agitated)

ɪr/ɛr   5a. His ear/heir caused him lots of trouble. (hearing organ/inheritor)

shɪr/shɛr   b. He says he'll shear/share the sheep tomorrow. (remove wool/divide up)

chɪr/chɛr   c. Let's have a cheer/chair for the governor. (shout of acclaim/seat)

spɪr/spɛr   d. He promised to spear/spare the fish. (pierce/save)

stɪrd/stɛrd   e. He steered/stared down the highway. (guided/gazed)

snɪrd/snɛrd   f. He sneered/snared at everything. (grimaced/entrapped)

fɪrz/fɛrz   g. Those fears/fares are excessive. (terrors/fees for conveyance)

5.3b (continued)

tɪrz/tɛrz   h. Her tears/tears were downright embarrassing. (weeping/rips)

fɛr/fər   6a. The fare/fur was too expensive. (fee for conveyance/animal skin)

pɛr/pər   b. He loved the pair/purr of cats. (group of two/throat murmur)

fɛ́riy/fə́riy   c. The fairy/furry goblin jumped out of a tree. (imaginary being/hairy)

kɛ́riyd/kə́riyd   d. He carried/curried the horse over here this morning. (transported/groomed)

fɛr/fɑr   7a. It was fair/far outside the town. (sunny/distant)

skɛrd/skɑrd   b. The dog was scared/scarred by the accident. (frightened/permanently marked)

bɛr/bɑr   c. He can't bear/bar the consequences. (withstand/prevent)

kɛr/kɑr   d. He doesn't have a care/car. (worry/automobile)

bɪr/bɑr   8a. He headed at once for the beer/bar. (fermented malt/drinks counter)

bɪrd/bɑrd   b. The beard/bard was long and slender. (chin whiskers/poet)

jɪrd/jɑrd   c. He was jeered/jarred when he entered. (derided/upset)

tɔr/tʊr   9a. They tore/tour through the city. (raced/take trips)

pɔr/pʊr   b. The pore/poor seemed to be infected. (perspiration outlet/indigent)

These sets of sentences show that some combinations of vowel plus /r/ occur more commonly than others. It is relatively easy to find pairs among /ə-ɑ-ɔ/, a little harder to compare those with /ɪ, ɛ/ and to find pairs between /ɪ/ and /ɛ/, and very difficult to find pairs of any other vowel with /ʊ/. Perhaps this is why /ʊ/ before /r/ is missing in some dialects. The widest distribution is in syllables that end in /r/ or in /r/ followed by the common affixes /d/ or /z/. Other consonants may follow some vowel-/r/ sequences, but these are unevenly distributed.

One final exercise compares /ər/ with /ʊ/. It has been observed that /r/ affects a preceding schwa by raising the tongue (and therefore the area of articulation of the schwa) toward the roof of the mouth. Another pattern of influence tends to pull the high back round vowel (the /ʊ/) forward, favoring an unrounded pronunciation. This brings the vowels /ə/ and /ʊ/ closer together, so that the main cue for differentiation is the r-coloring of the schwa. (Remember that an /r/ after schwa is not separately perceived). Thus words like /tʊk, kʊd, fʊl/ need to be distinguished from /tərk, kərd, fərl/ *(took, could, full* from *Turk, curd, furl).*

5.3c Contrast of /ʊ/ and /ər/

Comparison of pattern; select the appropriate paraphrase:

pʊl/pərl   1. She's got to pull/purl those stitches. (remove/knit backwards)

stʊd/stərd   2. He stood/stirred up the whole audience. (intentionally disappointed/agitated)

wʊdz/wərdz   3. Please spare the woods/words. (forest/excessive explanation)

bʊ́liy/bə́rliy   4. That bully/burly cat is a tom. (quarrelsome coward/husky)

wʊ́diy/wə́rdiy   5. The agreement was a little woody/wordy. (phony/verbose)

bʊ́giy/bə́rgiy   6. Do you like boogie/Burghie? (style of jazz/brand of beer)

shʊk/shərk   7. They shook/shirk every morning. (trembled/avoid duties)

5.3c (continued)
bŭks/bərks   8. The books/Burkes were very interesting. (bound writing/Burke family)

lŭking/lə́rkĭng   9. He was looking/lurking around the corner. (glancing/quietly present)

One other contrast could be a problem if minimal pairs were common: /ər/ and /ʊr/. But there are very few pairs, like /pər/ and /pʊr/ *(purr* and *poor)*. The question of similarity is even further answered by the fact that *poor* joins *pore* (and *pour*) in many dialects; furthermore after palatal consonants /ʊr/ may in some dialects become /ər/ as in /shʊr/ ⟶ /shər/. No specific drills for /ʊr/ vs /ər/ seem to be justified.

We have pointed out that weak-stressed vowels in English are of very short duration when pronounced in context. In a word like *ago* the initial /ə̆/ is very briefly pronounced in comparison to the stretched-out final /ów/. But variations in length are important to stressed vowels in English, and the following section is devoted to explanation and practice of these variations.

By length we mean duration in the time taken to pronounce a syllable. It is important to clearly understand this because long and short vowels in the traditional description of English pronunciation as found in most popular dictionaries does not refer to actual length, but to vowel quality. The contrast long/short is traditionally used to distinguish simple vowels from diphthongs; thus short "a" refers to /æ/ (as in *cat*) and long "a" refers to /ey/ (as in *Kate*). This is unfortunate terminology, especially when we want to talk about the duration in time of vowel sounds, because it leads to confusion. As a matter of fact, there *is no* difference in the length of the so-called "short *a*" and "long *a*" in the same context: *cat* and *Kate* are the same duration, relatively short compared to *can* and *cane.* We can cite the illogicality of this terminology by pointing out that "short *a*" in *can* is longer than "long *a*" in *Kate.*

These examples *(cat, Kate, can, cane)* show that actual vowel length (speaking of duration now, not of vowel identification or quality) depends on the context the vowels occur in—specifically the kind of consonant sound that follows and if a consonant does follow. The generalizations that summarize the variation of duration in single syllables in citation form are: vowels are longer before voiced than before voiceless consonants; vowels are longer before fricatives than before stops; vowels are longer before continuants than before fricatives or stops; vowels are longer in open syllables than in closed (with some consonant following in the same syllable).

This description may sound complicated, but actually the pattern is relatively simple and consistent. The following exercise illustrates for several of the English vowels and diphthongs a progression from shortest to longest syllables (and therefore shortest to longest vowels).

5.4 Vowel length as conditioned by following consonants

Presentation and comparison of pattern; read across, then down, then across:

	/t/	/s/	/d/	/z/	/n/	
/ɪ/	mɪt	mɪs	mɪd	mɪz	mɪn	
/ɛ/	sɛt	sɛs	sɛd	sɛz	sɛn	
/æ/	bæt	bæs	bæd	bæz	bæn	
/ə/	bət	bəs	bəd	bəz	bən	
/ɔ/	sɔt	sɔs	sɔd	sɔz	sɔn	
	mitt	miss	mid	Ms.	Min	
	set	cess	said	says	sen	
	bat	bass	bad	baas	ban	
	but	bus	bud	buzz	bun	
	sought	sauce	sawed	saws	sawn	
	/t/	/s/	/d/	/z/	/n/	/ø/
/iy/	siyt	siys	siyd	siyz	siyn	siy
/ey/	leyt	leys	leyd	leyz	leyn	ley
/ay/	layt	lays	layd	layz	layn	lay
/ow/	dowt	dows	dowd	dowz	down	dow
/uw/	muwt	muws	muwd	muwz	muwn	muw
	seat	cease	seed	sees	seen	see
	late	lace	laid	lays	lain	lay
	light	lice	lied	lies	line	lie
	dote	dose	doe'd	doze	Doan	dough
	moot	moose	mood	moos	moon	moo

Note that a following voiceless stop produces the shortest vowel, then in order: voiceless fricative, voiced stop, voiced fricative, continuant, and finally, for the longest vowel, nothing (i.e., an open

English Vowel Patterns 119

syllable). As the rows of words are pronounced, the syllables get longer and longer. Notice also that the simple vowels do not normally occur in open syllables, so the diphthongs have one length gradation beyond the simple vowels. (Actually this statement could be qualified, because there are words like /bæ/ *(baa)* and /lɔ/ *(law)*. But the generalization is ordinarily accurate and is certainly useful.)

The table at the top of page 120 shows a classification of English consonants (except /h/, which does not occur at the end of a syllable and /y, w/, which join a preceding vowel to form a dipthong) which lists together different consonant types.

In the exercise below the columns and rows match the pattern of the table for the final consonants of syllables, but randomize the vowels and initial consonants. Practice in sequence and then be prepared to accurately pronounce any word from the chart without the support of similar sets by column or progressive sequences by row.

5.4a Practice on vowel length as conditioned by following consonants

Comparison of pattern; read down, then across, then by random selection:

1.	lɪp	layf	təb	muwv	thəm	boy
2.	geyt	wɪth	wayd	swɔdh	loyn	tuw
3.	səch	maws	dɑj	gowz	fɑr	haw
4.	kowk	kæsh	rowg	beyzh	peyl	kiy
5.	chiyp	læf	tuwb	ləv	howm	gow
6.	fæt	riyth	dæd	beydh	fən	sey
7.	kawch	pʊs	keyj	gɔz	sowl	hay
8.	lʊk	liysh	dɔg	ruwzh	ræng	joy
	lip	life	tub	move	thumb	boy
	gate	with	wide	swathe	loin	two
	such	mouse	dodge	goes	far	how
	coke	cash	rogue	beige	pale	key
	cheap	laugh	tube	love	home	go
	fat	wreath	dad	bathe	fun	say
	couch	puss	cage	gauze	soul	high
	look	leash	dog	rouge	rang	joy

voiceless stops	voiceless fricatives	voiced stops	voiced fricatives	voiced continuants	∅
p	f	b	v	m	
t	th	d	dh	n	
ch	s	j	z	l	
k	sh	g	zh	r	
				ng	

It is interesting to note that there are restrictions on permitted sequences of vowels and consonants. Only a diphthong can precede a /dh/ and /zh/, and only a simple vowel can precede /r/ and /ng/.

When more than one consonant follows directly after a vowel or diphthong, it appears that the consonant associated with the greatest shortening of the vowel will govern the duration of the syllable. Thus *bent* is shorter than *Ben, kissed* is shorter than *kiss,* and *kits* is shorter than *kiss*—the /t/ in all these cases (after /n/, after /s/, and before /s/) exerting a shortening influence.

This correlation of final consonant to vowel length is extremely important to oral communication in English, for listening but especially for speaking, primarily because vowel length is the clue to accurately identifying the following consonant. Pairs of voiced/voiceless consonants are distinguished by their effect on the preceding vowel. Thus *beat* and *bead* are primarily differentiated by the longer vowel in the second word. This is particularly true of stops in sentence-final position (or in citation form) before silence, since the stops are typically unreleased, and therefore the voicing quality of the consonant is minimally noticeable. Experiments have shown that in a sentence like "She sat there in his lap/lab" the interpretation can be significantly and consistently affected by mechanically changing the length of the vowel (by cutting out or splicing in extra tape). Regardless of whether the original sentence has final /-p/ or /-b/, if the vowel is shortened, /p/ is heard; if lengthened, /b/ is heard. The chance for error is likewise high with final fricatives, since the voiced fricatives are rapidly devoiced before silence. In the minimal-pair sentences "What we really need right now is some peace/peas." the length of the last vowel tells us if the context is in the halls of diplomacy or in the kitchen.

The following exercise is designed to offer practice in context for the appropriate identification of final consonants cued by the length of the preceding vowel.

5.4b Syllable structure and contrasts of vowel length
   Patterned contrasts; select the appropriate paraphrase:

lɪmp/lɪm	1a. He always walks with a limp/limb. (irregular gait/tree branch)
peynt/peyn	b. Her work reflected that dull paint/pain. (pigment/affliction)
sæŋgk/sæŋ	c. She didn't want to but she still sank/sang. (went down/made music)
fayf/fayv	2a. I think he played the fife/five. (made music/gambled)
weyf/weyv	b. They were surprised by the waif/wave. (homeless child/undulating billow)
prays/prayz	3a. Before we compete, what's the price/prize? (cost/reward)
bəs/bəz	b. How many children have we got to bus/buzz? (transport/signal)
sərch/sərj	4a. The team continued the search/surge. (seeking/rolling on)
ɛch/ɛj	b. There was still one picture to etch/edge. (engrave with acid/furnish a border)
kæp/kæb	5a. He's gone to get a cap/cab. (headgear/taxi)
mɑp/mɑb	b. He says he's finished with the mop/mob. (deck swab/gang of criminals)
kæt/kæd	6a. He's a real cat/cad. (jazz musician/scoundrel)
bliyt/bliyd	b. Prick a sheep and he'll bleat/bleed. (baa/shed blood)

5.4b (continued)

bæk/bæg

7a. He pinned the label on her back/bag. (area of spine/sack)

liyk/liyg

b. Did they ever find the leak/league? (crack/association)

Thus we see that the length or duration of pronunciation for vowels depends to a great extent on what sound (or sounds), if any, follows in the same syllable. But there are other factors that influence vowel length. The most notable is stress. We have seen that weak-stressed syllables have vowels that are extremely short. Other levels of stress have an influence for variation. In general, other factors being equal, the stronger the stress, the longer the vowel. In the exercise that follows, the syllables are similarly structured but have different stresses, and as a consequence, different syllable lengths. Note that when contrastive emphasis (in the second column) moves the strong stress, the lengthening influence moves with it. Notice also that the device of using lines of different length above the syllables to indicate the level of stress, introduced in Chapter 1 and used again in Chapter 4, is an indirect representation of vowel length, since stress and length are to some degree correlated.

5.4c Correlation of vowel length with level of stress

Presentation and comparison of pattern; read down, then across:

/t/	wêt nêt	wêt nêt	wet net
/s/	lês chês	lês chês	less chess
/d/	rêd lêd	rêd lêd	red lead
/z/	dhôwz klôws	dhôwz klôwz	those clothes
/n/	brâwn klâwn	brâwn klâwn	brown clown
/ø/	trûw blúw	trúw blûw	true blue

In the first column the second syllable is the longest; in the second column, the first syllable—in each case, since the context is similar, the heaviest stressed syllable is longest.

In the next exercise the above pattern is generalized to include all permitted final consonants, but matched for gradation.

5.4d Correlation of vowel length with level of stress—generalized

Comparison of pattern; read across, then by random selection:

	/p, t, ch, k/	
1a. thîk sûwp	thîk sûwp	thick soup
b. tâyt mǽch	tâyt mǽch	tight match
c. îych kǽt	îych kǽt	each cat
	/f, th, s, sh/	
2a. bôwth fı́sh	bôwth fîsh	both fish
b. lûws lǽth	lúws lǽth	loose lath
c. frésh lôwf	frésh lôwf	fresh loaf
	/b, d, j, g/	
3a. gûd jêj	gúd jêj	good judge
b. hyûwj pı́g	hyúwj pîg	huge pig
c. bîg mâb	bîg mâb	big mob
	/v, dh, z, zh/	
4a. fâyv pléyz	fâyv pléyz	five plays
b. bêyzh táyz	bêyzh tâyz	beige ties
c. jôwz táydh	jówz tâydh	Joe's tithe
	/m, n, l, r, ng/	
5a. nâyn dír	náyn dîr	nine deer
b. smɔ́l pér	smɔ́l pêr	small pear
c. fâyn hówm	fáyn hôwm	fine home
d. séym sɔ́ng	séym sɔ̂ng	same song
	/ø/	
6a. nûw déy	núw dêy	new day
b. hây flów	hǎy flôw	high flow
c. frîy tóy	fríy tôy	free toy
d. lów bâw	lów bâw	low bough

One additional drill will illustrate a similar contrast, this time between secondary and medial levels of stress. In the exercise that follows both columns are contrastively stressed, but the first column is an adjective plus a noun, the second a noun compound.

5.4e Length contrasts with secondary and medial stress
Comparison of pattern; read across:

1. blǽk bɔ̂rd	blǽkbɔ̀rd	*black* board	*blackboard*
		(not a white one)	(not a textbook)
2. blúw bârd	blúwbə̀rd	*blue* bird	*bluebird*
		(not a brown one)	(not a robin)
3. rɛ́d kǽp	rɛ́dkæ̀p	*red* cap	*redcap*
		(not a yellow one)	(not an agent)
4. gríyn hâws	gríynhàws	*green* house	*greenhouse*
		(not a blue one)	(not a nursery)
5. wáyt hâws	wáyt-hàws	*white* house	*White House*
		(not a red one)	(not Congress)
6. shɔ́rt stâp	shɔ́rtstàp	*short* stop	*shortstop*
		(not a long one)	(not a pitcher)
7. lɔ́ng bôwt	lɔ́ngbòwt	*long* boat	*longboat*
		(not a short one)	(not a dinghy)
8. háy jə̂mp	háyjə̀mp	*high* jump	*high jump*
		(not a low one)	(not a broad jump)

It should be observed that in addition to the stress difference, there is an effect of rhythm: /ˊˆ/ sounds like (and is) two words, while /ˊˋ/ sounds like one word. But the difference in rhythm or timing is an *effect* of the stress contrast, not an independent factor.

There are other influences on vowel length besides type of consonant following and level of stress. Perhaps position in the sentence is one; certainly features of rhythm such as the prose equivalent to metrical feet are influential. But obviously vowel length is very complex, and the interplay of influencing features can produce very complicated combinations. For instance, in a phrase like /swíyt píy/ *(sweet pea)* the factors agree with each other (final /t/ and secondary stress produce a shorter vowel in *sweet* than does an open syllable and strong stress in *pea*), and clearly the first syllable is shorter than the second. But in a phrase like /fríy síyt/ the factors contradict. In *free* the open syllable says long but the secondary stress says short; in *seat* the syllable-closing /t/ says short but the primary stress says long. Obviously it will not be feasible to practice all the possible combinations. The student is advised rather to practice sets of words and phrases in individual patterns, as a means of internalizing the principles that underlie the patterns. The details of an acceptable interpretation should accrue as a consequence of guided practice and experience.

In many languages when vowels come together within words or across word boundaries, they influence each other. For example two vowels originally in separate syllables may join in a single syllable, becoming a diphthong. Two very similar vowels may reduce to one, etc. In general this kind of vowel assimilation is quite rare in English. Simple vowels typically occur in closed syllables and hence don't have a chance to appear in sequence. And diphthongs, which do appear in open syllables, do not seem to affect each other in any extreme way. Indeed this may be a minor problem to speakers of languages where vowels assimilate readily; they must learn to keep both vowels (or, usually, diphthongs) distinct.

The following exercise demonstrates the minimum effect of adjacent identical diphthongs on each other. From high and mid diphthongs with a glide on the same side of the grid as the vowel (/iy, ey, ow, uw/) the glide drops, leaving a long vowel with two distinct stress pulses. From low diphthongs or from a back one with a front glide (/ay, aw, oy/) the glide is retained.

5.5 Adjacent identical stressed diphthongs
Presentation and comparison of pattern; read across:

	/VS+VS/	/VS/		
1a.	bîîyts	bíyts	Bea eats	beats
b.	kêêyt	kéyt	Kay ate	Kate
c.	lûûwzəs	lúwzəs	Lou oozes	loses
d.	jôôwnz	jównz	Joe owns	Jones
2a.	gâyáyd	gáyd	Guy eyed	guide
b.	kôyóyld	kóyld	Coy oiled	coiled
c.	bâwáwt	báwt	bow out	bout

For the higher diphthongs, the contrast is based on length; for all, there is a separate stress.

In the exercise below the separate representation of adjacent diphthongs is contextualized.

5.5a Adjacent identical diphthongs in context
Presentation of pattern; read across:

/VS/́ + /VS/ ⟶ /V(S)VS/

1. líy   íyts   líîyts évriythíng   Lee eats everything.
2. kéy   éyt   kêêyt dínər   Kay ate dinner.
3. jów   ówpənd jô ôwpənd thə dór   Joe opened the door.
4. súw   úwzəz   sû ûwzəz kánfədənts   Sue oozes confidence.
5. gáy   áyd   gâyâyd thə gə́rl   Guy eyed the girl.
6. róy   óyld   rôyôyld thə kár   Roy oiled the car.
7. cháw áwstəd châwâwstəd thə klə́rk Chao ousted the clerk.

It would be possible to describe in detail various sequences of nonidentical diphthongs, but this doesn't seem necessary. The principle of minimal assimilation (almost nonassimilation) applies just as for identical sequences, though there would be variations of detail.

It is possible, of course, especially in very emphatic pronunciation, to separate adjacent vowels (or diphthongs) with a glottal stop, a pattern normal in many languages. This is not normal in informal English, and when glottal stop transitions are introduced the effect is usually a strong foreign accent.

The simple vowels have somewhat different patterns. The vowels /I-ε-æ-ɑ-ʊ/ almost never occur in an open syllable and hence do not have the opportunity to appear next to another vowel. The vowel /ɔ/ can appear finally and usually does not assimilate, as seen in a phrase like /lɔ́ɔ́fəs/ *(law office).* It is of interest to note in passing that some speakers of English (and most notably those who speak the so-called r-less dialects—where /r/ after vowels is regularly substituted by /h/, or length) break up a sequence of vowels by inserting an /r/ between them; thus /lɔ́rɔ́fəs/ and /lɔ́rənɔ́rdər/ *(law office, law and order).*

But the schwa, usually under weak stress, *is* very frequent in word final position. Examples are numerous, but the most common are the definite and indefinite articles *the* and *a*. Traditionally descriptions specify special forms of these articles before words beginning with a vowel, and the tradition is usually observed in formal styles. This is likely true if the article forms are stressed. In the following presentation exercise imitate the following patterns as they are modeled.

5.5b Strong-stressed and weak-stressed forms of articles
Presentation of pattern; read across:

Formal		Informal		
/ˆ/	/˘/	/ˆ/	/˘/	
dhîy ǽpəl	dhiy ǽpəl	dhâ̂ ǽpəl	dhə ǽpəl	the apple
dhâ̂ pɛ́r	dhə pɛ́r	dhâ̂ pɛ́r	dhə pɛ́r	the pear
ǽn ǽpəl	ən ǽpəl	ǽn ǽpəl	(ə)n ǽpəl	an apple
êy pɛ́r	ə pɛ́r	â̂ pɛ́r	ə pɛ́r	a pear

Keep in mind that weak-stressed schwa is very high and very short, which especially distinguishes weak-stressed articles in informal style. Note that all the above are respectable interpretations of English articles—none are substandard.

In the following exercise a final schwa occurs before various other vowels, illustrated in three styles of speech. In the first, called emphatic formal, a glottal stop (represented by the top part of a question mark, /ʔ/) intervenes as an onset to the second vowel of the sequence. This style, on the relatively rare occasions when it is appropriate, is interpreted with overloudness, overhigh pitch, and contrastive stress. The second column represents formal style, with the vowels separated, but not by so sharp a break. The third column represents informal style, where the two vowels tend to shade into each other and even fuse together. The schwa may lose its identity as a separate syllable marked with an inverted breve under the vowel: /ə̯/. When schwa precedes another schwa, one may actually disappear as the sequence is reduced.

5.5c Schwa before another vowel

Presentation of pattern; read each sentence in emphatic formal, then formal, then informal style:

	emphatic formal	formal	informal	
1a.	sôwfə ʔı̂n	sôwfə ı̂n	sôwfə̣ı̂n	Bring the sofa in.
b.	ʔæ̂nə ʔôwvər	æ̂nə ôwvər	æ̂nə̣ôwvər	Is Anna over the flu?
c.	sâlfə ʔêniy	sâlfə êniy	sâlfə̣êniy	Is sulfa any good?
d.	nəvæ̂də ʔı̂n	nəvæ̂də ı̂n	nəvæ̂də̣ın	Is Nevada in the west?
e.	tôwgə ʔân	tôwgə ân	tôwgə̣ân	He's got his toga on.
f.	gərîlə ʔâwt	gərîlə âwt	gərîlə̣âwt	Is the gorilla out?
g.	tûwbə ʔôl	tûwbə ôl	tûwbə̣ôl	He plays the tuba all day.
h.	sôwdə ʔân	sôwdə ân	sôwdə̣ân	Have a soda on me.
i.	ʔêzrə ʔêymz	êzrə êymz	êzrə̣êymz	That's Ezra Ames.
j.	rôwzə ʔâydəl	rôwzə âydəl	rôwzə̣âydəl	Is Rosa idle?
k.	ʔêkstrə ʔîygər	êkstrə îygər	êkstrə̣îygər	Tom is extra eager.
l.	ʔêlnə ʔæ̂ftər	êlnə æ̂ftər	êlnə̣æ̂ftər	What's Elna after?
2a.	dhîy ʔə̂dhər	dhə̂ ə̂dhər	dhə̂dhər	Where's the other one?
b.	dhîy ʔə̂shər	dhə̂ ə̂shər	dhə̂shər	Wait for the usher.
c.	dhîy ʔəmbrêlə	dhə̂ əmbrêlə	dhəmbrêlə	Have you got the umbrella?
d.	pɑ̂pə ʔəbâwt	pɑ̂pə əbâwt	pɑ̂pəbâwt	Tell papa about it.
e.	kâmə ʔə̂ndər	kâmə ə̂ndər	kâmə̂ndər	Put a comma under the period.
f.	pæ̂ndə ʔæ̂t	pæ̂ndə æ̂t	pæ̂ndət	There's a new panda at the zoo.

The nonsyllabic schwa (when weak-stressed and immediately before another vowel) is so short that it might not be heard at all. Indeed it may entirely drop, though usually, when there are two different vowels in sequence, there will be a trace of the schwa. This can be tested in pairs of sentences in which the presence and absence of a nonsyllabic is minimal:

Is Anna over the flu?   Is Rosa idle?
Is Ann over the flu?   Is Rose idle?

If these are distinguished in pronunciation, the schwa remains.

Also notice the final sentence, where the word *at* is pronounced /ǽt/ when it carries a higher stress but /ət/ when weak-stressed. It is typical of a small group of structure words in English that two forms are differentiated by stress. This kind of change will be treated in a later chapter when contractions are discussed. For now, the following exercise illustrates the contracted form of the preposition *to* when a vowel follows.

5.5d Schwa before another vowel in weak-stressed *to*

Presentation of pattern; read each sentence in formal, then informal style:

	formal	*informal*	
1.	tùw îyt	tə̫îyt	He wants to eat.
2.	tùw ênter	tə̫ênter	She hopes to enter the contest.
3.	tùw ǽsk	tə̫ǽsk	He expects to ask the doctor.
4.	tùw ôwpən	tə̫ôwpən	She wants to open an office.
5.	tùw âwst	tə̫âwst	They hope to oust the governor.
6.	tùw êym	tə̫êym	It's wise to aim high.

The reduction (and occasional disappearance) of weak-stressed schwa is an example, perhaps the most extreme, of the shortening and reduction of vowels in English. The integration of the stress system, weak-stressed vowels, and consonant assimilations produces other patterns of contraction which will be presented in some detail in the next chapter.

Chapter 6

ENGLISH CONSONANT PATTERNS

In Chapter 3 an inventory of the consonants of English was presented, with exercises designed to illustrate the variations associated with single consonants (such as the aspirated initial /p/ and the unreleased final /p/ of a word like *pipe*) and the contrasts between pairs of consonants sharing almost similar sets of features (like the palatal affricates /ch/ and /j/—alike except for voicing—in words like *britches* and *bridges*). In some languages this might be an adequate presentation of consonants, since they only occur one at a time. In English, however, consonants may occur in groups or clusters of three or four, and a final cluster in one word may be followed by an initial cluster in another, so that a sequence of as many as seven consonants may appear with no intervening vowel. The correct pronunciation of consonant clusters and consonant sequences is the subject of the present chapter.

I have distinguished consonant "clusters" from consonant "sequences" because the constituencies and distributions are different—hence the problems of mastery are different. Clusters of consonants occur within a single syllable, coming either before the vowel (or diphthong) or after. Sequences occur and are divided between syllables, and therefore, of course, between words. A sequence between words may consist of any consonant (or consonant cluster) permitted finally in one word plus any following consonant (or consonant cluster) permitted initially in the next word. In a language like English, where almost all consonants may appear initially or finally in a word, and where there are numerous clusters permitted, a great variety of sequences is possible. The numbers and kinds of clusters, on the other hand, are by comparison very restricted.

Another reason for separately considering clusters and sequences is that in sequences there are often features of transition that are not present in clusters. In the pair of items *nitrate* and *night rate* the sounds /t/ and /r/ occur. In *nitrate* they form a cluster which goes with the second syllable, but in *night rate* the /t/ and /r/ are separated by a feature of transition that keeps them from functioning as a unit, so that /t/ goes with *night* and /r/ goes with *rate*. We can verify this by noting that the syllable with the diphthong /ay/ in the first item is very long, which is characteristic of an open syllable, one not followed by a consonant, while the /ay/ in the second item is very short, characteristic of a syllable closed by a voiceless stop. We can further note that the first /t/ of *nitrate* is aspirated, a sign of an initial voiceless stop, but that the first /t/ of *night rate* is *not* aspirated, therefore is not initial. (It should be mentioned in passing that transition features are not limited to sequences of consonants, but can occur between any items that are "held apart" by special boundary elements: thus "a nice drink" and "an ice drink" are distinguished by the distinctive placement of a boundary or transition feature between "a" and "nice" in the first expression, and between "an" and "ice" in the second. In analyzing groups of consonants these transition features, or "junctures" as they are often called, are useful to show where syllable and word boundaries are: before, between, or after consonants that may form clusters or sequences.)

In this chapter, clusters of consonants will be presented in some detail, since they cause considerable difficulty for learners of English. Sequences will be discussed more briefly, but the discussion will include a treatment of certain learning problems, including sequences of identical consonants, not permitted as clusters in English. In addition, there will be a treatment of assimilation patterns of certain classes of consonants and of certain patterns of contraction and simplification that are characteristic of English. All these patterns which reflect the influence of adjacent consonants on each other are

English Consonant Patterns 133

important to the mastery of English and most crucial to the informal styles often neglected in the customary formality associated with classroom instruction in English.

There are three general patterns of formation for initial consonant clusters of two consonants in English, with a limited combination of these patterns to form a smaller number of three consonant clusters. The first of these is a pattern of C^1C^2 where C^1 is a stop or a voiceless fricative and C^2 is an /r/ or an /l/. A few limitations are necessary: /t,d,th,sh/ don't cluster with /l/, /s/ doesn't cluster with /r/, and /h/ doesn't cluster with either.

In the following exercise single consonants are first presented as initial in a syllable, then are combined in a cluster. Repeat the syllables as you hear them, paying special attention to modifications of the consonants when they are combined in clusters.

6.1 Two-member initial consonant clusters: /C/ plus /r, l/
Presentation of pattern; read across:

	/C¹/	/C²/	/C¹C²/			
1a.	pey	rey	prey	pay	ray	pray
b.	toy	roy	troy	toy	Roy	troy
c.	kowm	rowm	krowm	comb	roam	chrome
d.	baw	raw	braw	bough	row	brow
e.	duw	ruw	druw	due	rue	drew
f.	gow	row	grow	go	row	grow
g.	fɪl	rɪl	frɪl	fill	rill	frill
h.	thɔng	rɔng	thrɔng	thong	wrong	throng
i.	shayn	rayn	shrayn	shine	Rhine	shrine
2a.	pay	lay	play	pie	lye	ply
b.	kæd	læd	klæd	cad	lad	clad
c.	beyd	leyd	bleyd	bayed	laid	blade
d.	gayd	layd	glayd	guide	lied	glide
e.	fown	lown	flown	phone	loan	flown
f.	sæk	læk	slæk	sack	lack	slack

Note that the voiceless stops /p, t, k/, perhaps because they are aspirated, affect the quality of /r/. This is particularly true of /tr/, in which the /r/ has an almost fricative quality. The cluster /dr/ has something of the same effect, though less noticeable. Also notice that the /r/ may have a flapped articulation after /th/.

A possibly useful way to approach an acceptable pronunciation of these clusters is shown in the following exercise. In the first column are one-syllable words with a single initial consonant, an /r/ or an /l/. The next column lists a similar sounding word with an additional syllable prefixed, a syllable that has a weak-stressed vowel that is very short and very lightly pronounced. The corresponding word in the third column is identical except that the brief schwa is omitted, which has the effect of bringing together as a cluster the two consonants that previously were separated. This exercise, then, may have a double purpose; to practice the production of a very brief schwa, and, by dropping this minimal vocalic element, to produce common English consonant clusters.

6.1a Consonant clusters from a dropped intervening schwa: /C/ plus /r, l/

Comparison of pattern; read across:

	/C²-/	/C¹ₐC²-/	/C¹C²-/			
1a.	reyd	pəréyd	preyd	raid	parade	prayed
b.	reyn	təréyn	treyn	rain	terrain	train
c.	rowd	kərówd	krowd	rowed	corrode	crowed
d.	rey	bəréy	brey	ray	beret	bray
e.	rayd	dəráyd	drayd	ride	deride	dried
f.	rænd	gərǽnd	grænd	rand	Garand	grand
g.	row	θərów	throw	row	Thoreau	throw
2a.	layt	pəláyt	playt	light	polite	plight
b.	layd	kəlayd	klayd	lied	collide	Clyde
c.	læps	kəlǽps	klæps	lapse	collapse	claps
d.	low	bəlów	blow	low	below	blow
e.	lɔr	gəlɔ́r	glɔr(iy)	lore	galore	glor(y)
f.	liys	fəlíys	fliys	lease	Felice	fleece
g.	ley	fəley	fley	lay	fillet	flay
h.	layt	səláyt	slayt	light	so light	slight

It is interesting in comparing the informal pronunciation of items in columns two and three to note just how very short and lightly pronounced the weak-stressed schwa is. It takes little—if any more—

time to pronounce the two syllables of *parade* than the one syllable of *prayed*. This illustrates an important and characteristic feature of English rhythm, to which we will return in a fuller discussion in Chapter 7.

The second general pattern of formation for initial clusters of two consonants in English specifies C^1 as one of a limited and miscellaneous number of consonants and C^2 as /y/ or /w/. Specifically /p, k, b, f, v, h, m/ occur with /y/, and /t, k, d, s/ occur with /w/. The following exercise presents these clusters in a build-up format.

6.1b Two-member initial consonant clusters: /C/ plus /y, w/
Presentation of pattern; read across:

	/C¹/	/C²/	/C¹C²/			
1a.	puw	yuw	pyuw	pooh	you	pew, Pugh
b.	kuwt	yuwt	kyuwt	coot	Ute	cute
c.	buwt	yuwt	byuwt	boot	Ute	beaut, butte
d.	fuw	yuw	fyuw	phoo	you	few
e.	vuw	yuw	vyuw	voo (doo)	you	view
f.	huw	yuw	hyuw	who	you	hue, hew, Hugh
g.	muwt	yuwt	myuwt	moot	Ute	mute
2a.	tayn	wayn	twayn	tine	wine	twine
b.	kɪk	wɪk	kwɪk	kick	wick	quick
c.	dɛl	wɛl	dwɛl	dell	well	dwell
d.	siyp	wiyp	swiyp	seep	weep	sweep

It will be noticed that the /Cy/ forms all occur before the diphthong /uw/. This is an interesting limitation that suggests that the /y/ originated from the diphthong, as a sequence /yuw/, which is confirmed by the *u* spelling of *cute, mute,* etc. The only exceptions to the distribution of /Cy/ only before /uw/ are when /Cy/ precedes an /ɔr/ (apparently derived from /uw/), as in the dialect form /pyɔr/ *pure)* etc., or when /Cy/ precedes a syllable that has been weak-stressed, /ə/ derived from /uw/, as in régyələr/ *(regular),* etc.

The list of clusters in this pattern could be expanded somewhat by including a few combinations that exist, but only infrequently or in very rare words. Thus /gw, thw, zw, gy, thy/ occur in *Gwen, thwart, Zwinglian, gewgaw, thew* and a few other items, too rare to justify formal presentation and exercise. A few additional forms have appeared as recent loanwords, mostly from Spanish or German, expanding the list of clusters with /w/ as a second member; thus /pw, bw, fw, nw, shw/ in *Pueblo, Buenos Aires, Fuegian, Nuevo Leon,* and *schweppes.*

One other set deserves special mention, the series of alveolar consonants plus /y/. These are dialect variants in American English, used by some speakers; other speakers drop the /y/. The series includes /ty, dy, ny, ly, sy/—all like other consonants before /uw/, in words like: *tune, dew, new, lute, sue.* Second-language students of English can learn and adopt these clusters if they (or their teachers) wish, but following the principle that such students should not be burdened with contrasts that most native speakers (of the dialect areas represented) do not observe, it is recommended that these clusters not be taught. It is interesting to note that the alveolar plus /y/ order can appear, not as a cluster, but as a sequence in the interior of polysyllabic words. Thus *salutary* and *annual* have sequences of /ly/ and /ny/ divided between two syllables. Other possibilities in the same series (/y/ after /t, d, s, z/) do not occur because palatal assimilation patterns apply. (These will be presented later in this chapter.)

The same principle of not teaching an "optional" pattern applies to another cluster, the initial /hw-/ of some very commonly occurring words like the question forms *where, when, why, what, which,* plus *while, wheel, wharf, wheat, whine, whip, whirl, white,* etc. Since great numbers of speakers of American English seem to get along quite well without distinguishing *where-wear, when-wen, why-wye, which-witch, whine-wine, white-Wight,* etc., it doesn't seem important for students to try to master the contrast. It might be noted in passing, however, that many speakers of English who do not ordinarily use the cluster /hw-/ in their normal pronunciation are able to revive it and use it consistently in emphatic speech forms.

The third general pattern of formation for initial clusters of two consonants in English is /s/ plus a consonant, with this consonant limited to /p, t, k, f, m, n, l/ and marginally to /th, v/. The following exercise presents the common cluster patterns in a build-up format.

English Consonant Patterns 137

6.1c Two-member initial consonant clusters: /s/ plus /C/
Presentation of pattern; read across:

	/C¹/	/C²/	/C¹C²/			
1.	sɪn	pɪn	spɪn	sin	pin	spin
2.	sɪl	tɪl	stɪl	sill	till	still
3.	sɔr	kɔr	skɔr	sore	core	score
4.	sɪr	fɪr	sfɪr	sear	fear	sphere
5.	sɔl	mɔl	smɔl	Saul	mall	small
6.	sow	now	snow	sow	know	snow
7.	sey	ley	sley	say	lay	sleigh

Marginally /sth/ and /sv/ occur *(sthenic, svelte,* etc.), but these are not numerous enough or frequent enough to warrant formal treatment.

These are particularly difficult clusters for many students whose first language does not permit an /s/-consonant cluster. Often such students add a prefixed vowel to carry the /s/. This solution won't work in English, because not only is this an unacceptable distortion of the phonological cluster patterns (converting a cluster to a sequence), but sequence patterns of /s/ closing one syllable with a consonant beginning the next also appear in English and contrast with the cluster patterns. The following exercise presents this contrast.

6.1d /sC/ as a sequence and as a cluster
Comparison of pattern; read across:

	/ĕsC/	/sC/		
1.	əspáy	spáy	espy	spy
2.	əspáyər	spáyər	aspire	spire
3.	əspéshəl	spéshəl	especial	special
4.	əspáyrənt	spáyrənt	aspirant	spirant
5.	əspáwzəl	spáwzəl	espousal	spousal
6.	əstə́r	stə́r	astir	stir
7.	əstə́rn	stə́rn	astern	stern
8.	əstéyt	steyt	estate	state
9.	əstíym	stiym	esteem	steam
10.	əstάp	stαp	estop	stop
11.	əskéyp	skeyp	escape	scape
12.	əskάr	skαr	eschar	scar
13.	əskǽnts	skænts	askance	scants
14.	əskάlləp	skάlləp	escallop	scallop

Some of these can be contextualized in minimal-pair sentences, though in general the pattern doesn't lend itself well to this type of exercise:

əslíyp/sliyp	I saw John asleep/sleep on the floor. (in a slumbering state/fall into slumber)
əstéyt/steyt	All his money went to the estate/state. (landed property/government)

The following exercise follows the format of exercise *6.1a*. A reference word appears in the first column, to which a very short, weak-stressed syllable is prefixed in column two; then in column three the weak-stressed schwa is omitted, which has the effect of bringing the preceding and following consonants together as a cluster. In pronouncing the items in the second column, be sure the schwa is very weak and very short, lightly articulated, as a means of facilitating its omission.

6.1e Consonant clusters from a dropped intervening schwa: /s/ plus /C/

Comparison of pattern; read across:

	/C²-/	/C¹əC²-/	/C¹C²-/			
1.	pɔrt	səpɔ́rt	spɔrt	port	support	sport
2.	tɑr	sətɑ́r	stɑr	tar	sitar	star
3.	tǽnɪk	sətǽnɪk	stǽnɪk	tannic	Satanic	stannic
4.	kəm	səkə́m	skəm	come	succumb	scum
5.	láynəs	səláynəs	sláynəs	Linus	salinas	slyness
6.	pɔn	səpɔ́n	spɔn	pawn	Sapon	spawn
7.	tɪr	sətɪ́rɪk	stɪr	tear	satiric	steer
8.	nɔ́rə	sənɔ́rə	snɔr	Nora	Sonora	snore
9.	lísət	səlísət	slídhər	licit	solicit	slither
10.	líyzhən	səlíyzhən	slíyziy	lesion	Silesian	sleazy

These examples are even more difficult to identify than those like *terrain, polite,* etc., because the weak-stressed schwa, coming between two voiceless consonants (in /səpówz-səkə́m/ *suppose, succumb,* etc.) can be devoiced or whispered.

Again contextualization is possible, but somewhat difficult to contrive:

səpɔrtɪng/spɔrtɪng   He's supporting/sporting a new wife.
(assuming expenses of/showing off)

In addition to the two-consonant initial clusters in English there are a few three-consonant ones. These consist of /s/ plus a voiceless stop (/p, t, k/) plus a liquid or semiconsonant (/r, l, y, w/). Not all possible combinations occur, only the following: /spr, str, skr, spl, spy, sky, skw/. Even among this number, some are very rare. The following drill in build-up format presents some of the possibilities.

6.1f Three-member initial consonant clusters
Presentation of pattern; read across:

	/C¹/	/C²/	/C³/	/C¹C²/	/C²C³/	/C¹C²C³/
1.	say	pay	ray	spay	pray	spray
2.	seyt	teyt	reyt	steyt	treyt	streyt
3.	sowl	kowl	rowl	skowl	krowl	skrowl
4.	sey	pey	ley	spey	pley	spley
5.	sɪd	kɪd	wɪd(ow)	skɪd	kwɪd	skwɪd
6.	suw	puw	yuw	spuw(l)	pyuw	spyuw
7.	suw	kuw	yuw	skuw(l)	kyuw	skyuw
	sigh	pie	rye	spy	pry	spry
	sate	Tate	rate	state	trait	straight
	soul	coal	roll	skoal	Crowell	scroll
	say	pay	lay	spay	play	splay
	Syd	kid	wid(ow)	skid	quid	squid
	sue	pooh	you	spoo(l)	pew	spew
	sue	coo	ewe	skoo(l)	cue	skew

Initial clusters with three consonants are relatively infrequent in English, and it is somewhat harder to find matching examples in contrasting patterns. The following exercise attempts to equate the patterns of the cluster /sCC/ with the sequence /əsCC/, patterned on the format of exercise *6.1d.* The practice given should be useful to a student who has trouble making this complex cluster.

6.1g /sCC/ as a sequence and as a cluster
Comparison of pattern; read across:

	/əsCC/	/sCC/		
1.	əspríy	spriy	esprit	spree
2.	əstréy	strey	astray, estray	stray
3.	əstráyd	strayd	astride	stride
4.	əstréynj	streynj	estrange	strange
5.	əstríyt	striyt	estreat	street
6.	əskráyb	skrayb	ascribe	scribe
7.	əskwáyər	skwáyər	esquire	squire

This concludes the presentation of consonant clusters at the beginnings of syllables, and the list given is reasonably complete. Consonant clusters at the ends of syllables are much more numerous, with more variety of constituents, and are consequently more difficult to describe. There are two main sources of clusters, one phonological (the inherent syllable structure) and the other morphological (produced by the addition of endings consisting of a single consonant). Both patterns can occur in the same syllable, and this accounts for some of the more complex clusters.

Looking first at the clusters designated as inherent, we note that different kinds of consonants represent a spread from more open to more close, or perhaps one could say from more "vowel-like" to more "consonant-like." the sequence, by types of consonants, is:

Semivowel - Retroflex - Lateral - Nasal - Fricative - Stop. In building an inherent final cluster of any two consonants, the above order is usually observed. Note that semivowels (the /y/ or /w/ following a vowel) are not included in consonant clusters, but are considered part of the vowel nucleus, a constituent of the diphthong. The most freely occurring C^1 of a C^1C^2 cluster, then, is /r/, which can occur before any English consonant except /dh, zh, h, ng/ which (with possible rare exceptions) do not occur with any final clusters (/h/ doesn't appear finally at all). The consonant /l/ is almost as widely distributed, but additionally not occurring before /g/ and with special restrictions (to be outlined later) before /th, s, sh/.

The nasals are more restricted, occurring only before consonants with a similar point of articulation, thus: /mp, nt, nd, nz, nch, nj, ngk/; (note that /mb/ and /ngg/ as clusters are missing). A few fricatives plus stops occur, namely /ft, sp, st, sk/ and two combinations of stops /pt/ and /kt/. It is interesting to note that all the fricative-stop and stop-stop combinations in inherent clusters are voiceless.

In the following exercise, representative clusters are presented in a build-up format.

6.2 Two-member final consonant clusters—inherent—1
Presentation of pattern; read across:

	/-C¹/	/-C²/	/-C¹C²/			
1a.	hər	həl	hərl	her	hull	hurl
b.	bɑr	bɑn	bɑrn	bar	Bonn	barn
c.	mɑr	mɑm	mɑrm	mar	mom	marm
d.	skɑr	skɑf	skɑrf	scar	scoff	scarf
e.	gɑr	gɑθ	gɑrθ	gar	Goth	Garth
f.	fɑr	fɑs	fɑrs	far	Foss	farce
g.	mɑr	mɑz	mɑrz	mar	ma's	Mars
h.	kɑr	kɑp	kɑrp	car	cop	carp
i.	bɑr	bɑb	bɑrb	bar	Bob	barb
j.	kɑr	kɑt	kɑrt	car	cot	cart
k.	bɪr	bɪd	bɪrd	beer	bid	beard
l.	sər	səch	sərch	sir	such	search
m.	lɑr	lɑj	lɑrj	Lar	lodge	large
n.	mɑr	mɑk	mɑrk	mar	mock	mark
o.	bər	bəg	bərg	burr	bug	berg
2a.	kɪl	kɪn	kɪln	kill	kin	kiln
b.	ɛl	ɛm	ɛlm	"l"	"m"	elm
c.	wʊl	wʊf	wʊlf	wool	woof	wolf
d.	shɛl	shɛv	shɛlv	shell	Chev	shelve
e.	fɪl	fɪch	fɪlch	fill	Fitch	filch
f.	hɛl	hɛp	hɛlp	hell	hep	help
g.	bɛl	bɛt	bɛlt	bell	bet	belt
h.	fiyl	fiyd	fiyld	feel	feed	field
i.	sɪl	sɪk	sɪlk	sill	sick	silk
3a.	læm	læp	læmp	lamb	lap	lamp
b.	bən	bət	bənt	bun	but	bunt
c.	bæn	bæd	bænd	ban	bad	band
d.	wɪn	wɪch	wɪnch	win	witch	winch
e.	reyn	reyj	reynj	rain	rage	range
f.	sɪng	sɪk	sɪngk	sing	sick	sink
4a.	rɪf	rɪt	rɪft	riff	writ	rift
b.	klæs	klæp	klæsp	class	clap	clasp
c.	kæs	kæt	kæst	Cass	cat	cast
d.	tæs	tæk	tæsk	Tass	tack	task
5a.	kɑp	kɑt	kɑpt	cop	cot	Copt
b.	pæk	pæt	pækt	pack	pat	pact

Note in the last two items that when a single stop is produced finally, it may be unreleased. But when a cluster of two stops appears, the second one must be released: *Copt, opt, pact, act,* etc.

In the following exercise the same cluster types are illustrated in contrasting pairs where a cluster is produced by dropping an intervening schwa. Not all possible clusters are included, since pairs for all could not be found.

6.2a Two-member final consonant clusters—inherent—2
Comparison of pattern; read across:

	/-CəC/	/-CC/		
1a.	wɑ́rən	wɑrn	warren	warn
b.	kə́rən	kərn	Curran	Kern
c.	tə́rən	tərn	Turin	turn
d.	yə́rən	yərn	urine	yearn
e.	də́rəm	dərm	Durham	derm
f.	fɔ́rəm	fɔrm	forum	form
g.	stə́rəp	stərp	stirrup	stirp
h.	tɔ́rɪk	tɔrk	toric	torque
i.	yɔ́rɪk	yɔrk	Yorick	York
j.	fɔ́rɪj	fɔrj	forage	forge
2a.	kɑ́ləm	kɑlm	column	calm*
b.	sɑ́ləm	sɑlm	solemn	psalm*
c.	wʊ́ləf	wʊlf	Woloff	wolf
d.	wɑ́lət	wɑlt	wallet	Walt
e.	pɛ́lət	pɛlt	pellet	pelt
f.	pṓwlək	powlk	pollack	Polk
3a.	grǽnət	grænt	granite	grant
b.	lɪ́nɪj	lɪnj	lineage	linge
4a.	tə́fət	təft	tuffet	tuft
b.	hǽsəp	hæsp	Hassup	hasp
c.	lɪ́sət	lɪst	licit	list
d.	kǽsək	kæsk	cassock	cask

The morphologically produced final consonant clusters are produced when affixes, or endings, consisting of a single consonant are added to a word ending in one or more consonants. These

---

*To fit this pattern *calm* and *psalm* have to be pronounced with an /l/, which they are in some dialects, though many speakers omit the /l/ and pronounce /kɑm, sɑm/.

endings follow certain rules: (1) sibilants are never added to sibilants and alveolar stops are never added to alveolar stops (the inherent clusters also observe this rule), and (2) the consonant added always matches the consonant it follows in the feature of voicing (voiceless /t/ or /s/ after a voiceless consonant and voiced /d/ or /z/ after a voiced consonant). Whenever rule (2) is applied in a situation described in rule (1), a neutral vowel (the schwa) is inserted between the consonants to prevent the cluster, with the effect of adding another syllable; /kwɪz-ə-z gréyd-ə-d/ *(quizzes graded)*. The two principle affixes added are the /z ~ s/, which has several functions (plural of nouns, possessive of nouns, 3rd person singular form of verbs, contractions of *is* and *has*), and /d ~ t/, which produces the past tense and the past participle forms of regular verbs.

The following exercise illustrates clusters of two or three consonants produced by adding a suffix to a word ending in a consonant or consonants.

6.2b Final consonant clusters—morphologically produced
    Comparison of pattern; read across:

	/Cᵛˡ/	/Cᵛˡs/	/Cᵛˡt/			
1a.	kæp	kæps	kæpt	cap	caps	capped
b.	layk	layks	laykt	like	likes	liked
2a.	kɔf	kɔfs	kɔft	cough	coughs	coughed
b.	læth	læths	lætht	lath	laths	lathed
c.	bæt	bæts	--	bat	bats	---
d.	mɪs	--	mɪst	miss	--	missed
e.	pʊsh	--	pʊsht	push	--	pushed
f.	hæch	--	hæcht	hatch	--	hatched
3a.	harp	harps	harpt	harp	harps	harped
b.	mɪlk	mɪlks	mɪlkt	milk	milks	milked
c.	sərf	sərfs	sərft	surf	surfs	surfed
d.	lɪmp	lɪmps	lɪmpt	limp	limps	limped
e.	wɪngk	wɪngks	wɪngkt	wink	winks	winked
f.	bɛlt	bɛlts	--	belt	belts	--
g.	baks	--	bakst	box	--	boxed
h.	rɛnch	--	rɛncht	wrench	--	wrenched
i.	læps	--	læpst	lapse	--	lapsed
j.	gæsp	gæsps	gæspt	gasp	gasps	gasped
k.	æsk	æsks	æskt	ask	asks	asked
l.	rɛst	rɛsts	--	rest	rests	--

6.2b (continued)

	/Cᵛl/	/Cᵛls/	/Cᵛlt/			
m.	ɑpt	ɑpts	--	opt	opts	--
n.	ækt	ækts	--	act	acts	--

	/Cᵛd/	/Cᵛdz/	/Cᵛdd/			
4a.	rəb	rəbz	rəbd	rub	rubs	rubbed
b.	həg	həgz	həgd	hug	hugs	hugged
c.	weyv	weyvz	weyvd	wave	waves	waved
d.	briydh	briydhz	briydhd	breathe	breathes	breathed
e.	ruwm	ruwmz	ruwmd	room	rooms	roomed
f.	lɔng	lɔngz	lɔngd	long	longs	longed
g.	feyd	feydz	--	fade	fades	--
h.	bəz	--	bəzd	buzz	--	buzzed
i.	ruwzh	--	ruwzhd	rouge	--	rouged
j.	wɛj	--	wɛjd	wedge	--	wedged
5a.	hərl	hərlz	hərld	hurl	hurls	hurled
b.	kərb	kərbz	kərbd	curb	curbs	curbed
c.	kɑrv	kɑrvz	kɑrvd	carve	carves	carved
d.	sɑlv	sɑlvz	sɑlvd	solve	solves	solved
e.	lænd	lændz	--	land	lands	--
f.	brɑnz	--	brɑnzd	bronze	--	bronzed
g.	cheynj	--	cheynjd	change	--	changed
h.	ərj	--	ərjd	urge	--	urged
i.	ædz	--	ædzd	adze	--	adzed

There is some duplication between inherent and morphologically produced clusters, but they are mentioned only in passing, since in terms of the clusters produced there are no significant differences. Thus /læps/ is the pronunciation of both *lapse* and *laps,* /ædz/ of both *adze* and *adds,* /læks/ of both *lax* and *lacks,* /pækt/ of both *pact* and *packed,* /kɑpt/ of both *Copt* and *copped,* /rɪft/ of both *rift* and *riffed,* /bænd/ of both *band* and *banned,* /bowld/ of both *bold* and *bowled,* /wɑltz/ of both *waltz* and *Walt's,* etc.

The following exercise mixes inherent and morphologically produced clusters, making clusters by dropping an intervening schwa.

6.2c Two-member final consonant clusters—inherent and morphologically produced
Comparison of pattern; read across:

	/-CəC/	/-CC/		
1a.	ówtəs	owts	Otis	oats
b.	brúwtəs	bruwts	Brutus	brutes
c.	hówkəs	howks	hokus	hoax
d.	krówkəs	krowks	crocus	croaks
e.	lúwkəs	luwks	Lucas	Luke's
f.	wɪ́pət	wɪpt	whippet	whipped
g.	mɑ́pət	mɑpt	moppet	mopped
h.	tǽpət	tæpt	tappet	tapped
i.	jǽkət	jækt	jacket	jacked
j.	pɛ́lət	pɛlt	pellet	pelt
k.	wɑ́lət	wɑlt	wallet	Walt
l.	rə́sət	rəst	russet	rust
m.	fǽsət	fæst	facet	fast
n.	lɪ́sət	lɪst	licit	list
o.	kǽsək	kæsk	Cassock	cask
p.	hǽsəp	hæsp	Hassup	hasp
2a.	kɔ́rpəs	kɔrps	corpus	corpse
b.	fɔ́rtəs	fɔrts	fortis	forts
c.	kǽmpəs	kæmps	campus	camps
d.	hówstəs	howsts	hostess	hosts
e.	prɪ́ystəs	prɪysts	priestess	priests
f.	kɑ́rpət	kɑrpt	carpet	carped
g.	trə́mpət	trəmpt	trumpet	trumped
3a.	hɔ́rəd	hɔrd	horrid	hoard
b.	ɛ́rəd	ɛrd	arid	aired
c.	lʊ́rəd	lʊrd	lurid	lured
d.	pǽləd	pæld	pallid	palled
e.	skwɑ́ləd	skwɑld	squalid	squalled
f.	lɪ́vəd	lɪvd	livid	lived
g.	rǽgəd	rægd	ragged	ragged (cf., dragged)
h.	rə́gəd	rəgd	rugged	rugged (cf., drugged)
i.	rɪ́jəd	rɪjd	rigid	ridged

Perhaps this is an appropriate place to call attention to a pattern that involves final consonant clusters, the comparison of certain past participles with similarly spelled adjective forms, where the adjectives are pronounced with an additional syllable. Also there are some adjective forms that end in *-ed* for which there are no corresponding verbs. These patterns are illustrated in the following exercise.

6.2d Adjectives that end in *-ed* and related past participles

Presentation and comparison of pattern; read the following sentences, observing pronunciation cues:

éyjəd
eyjd

1a. My aged father lives with me.
 b. He has aged considerably in the last few years.

biyləvəd

biyləvd

2a. My beloved friends, how I've missed you.
 b. You are beloved by the entire community.

lə́rnəd
lərnd

3a. He is a very learned scholar.
b. All he knows he learned by himself.

dɔ́gəd

dɔ́gd

4a. He worked with dogged determination.
 b. But bad luck dogged his footsteps.

lɛ́gəd
lɛgd

5a. Where's the three-legged stool?
 b. He legged it over to the barn after another one.

blɛ́səd
blɛst

6a. Not one blessed cent do you get!
 b. My life has been blessed in many ways.

kə́rsəd

kərst

7a. With my cursed luck, what can you expect?
 b. He cursed his luck and left.

6.2d (continued)

bɛ́ndəd   8a. He asked her forgiveness on bended knee.

bɛnt   b. He bent the paper clip out of shape.

néykəd   9. You can see it with the naked eye.

rɛ́chəd   10. They manage to eke out a wretched existence.

wíkəd   11. I've never seen such a wicked city.

In general the *a* sentences show an adjective use of this set of *-ed* words, the *b* a verb use. Some of these forms are optional; for example *beloved* in *2a* could be pronounced as in *2b* (but not vice versa). Sentence *8a* is probably limited to the phrase "on bended knees," *bent* being used elsewhere. Sentences *9, 10,* and *11* look like the others, but have no parallel verb forms, though there is an unrelated phonetic correlate for *wretched:* /rɛcht/ "After nine hours of nausea he still retched."

As illustrated earlier, most of the three-consonant clusters are a combination of inherent plus morphologically produced clustering. But there is another source: the intrusive consonant that is automatically inserted between two consonants to facilitate the transition from one consonant sound to another. These are largely predictable and can be described by specifying the pairs of consonants that need transition help—always from voiced continuant to voiceless fricative or stop, with the inserted sound matching the preceding continuant in point of articulation and the following fricative or stop in voicing. Thus for example if the verb *dream* is (irregularly) inflected for past tense by adding /t/, the sequence /mt/ is converted to the cluster /mpt/: /drɛmpt/ *(dreamt).* The clusters produced are: /mpt, mpf, mpth, ntth, nts, ngkth, ltth, lts, ltsh/.

The following exercise illustrates the insertion requirements for these clusters.

6.2e Clusters with intrusive stop consonants
Comparison of pattern; read across:

	/CC/	/CCstopC/		
1.	drɛm	drɛmpt	*	dreamt
2.	tɛm	tɛmpt	*	tempt
3.	ɛgzɛ́m	ɛgzɛ́mpt	*	exempt
4.	ənkɛ́m	ənkɛ́mpt	*	unkempt
5.	ətɛ́m	ətɛ́mpt	*	attempt
6.	pram	prampt	prom	prompt
7.	nɪm	nɪmpf	*	nymph
8.	lɪm	lɪmpf	limb	lymph
9.	tráyəm	tráyəmpf	try 'em	triumph
10.	warm	warmpth	warm	warmth
11.	sɛ́vən	sɛ́vəntth	seven	seventh
12.	nayn	nayntth	nine	ninth
13.	tɛn	tɛntth	ten	tenth
14.	mən	məntth	Mon	month
15.	fɛn	fɛnts	fen	fence
16.	dæn	dænts	Dan	dance
17.	tɛn	tɛnts	ten	tense, tents
18.	wən	wənts	one	once
19.	awn	awnts	*	ounce
20.	chæn	chænts	Chan	chance, chants
21.	dɛn	dɛnts	den	dense, dents
22.	lɛng	lɛngkth	*	length
23.	strɛng	strɛngkth	*	strength
24.	sfɪng	sfɪngks	*	sphinx
25.	wɛl	wɛltth	well	wealth
26.	hɛl	hɛltth	hell	health
27.	stɛl	stɛltth	*	stealth
28.	twɛl	twɛltth	*	twelfth
29.	fɪl	fɪltth	fill	filth
30.	fɔl	fɔlts	fall	false, faults
31.	ɛl	ɛlts	"l"	else
32.	riypɛ́l	riypɛ́lts	*	repulse
33.	wɛl	wɛltsh	well	welsh
34.	wɔl	wɔltsh	wall	Walsh

*structurally permissible but nonoccurring

Not all of these insertions necessarily occur in all dialects of English. The last two, for example, may not require the intrusive /t/, and if it is required, /ltsh/ will likely become /lch/, and we will then classify the cluster /tsh/ as nonoccurring.

Some of the forms cited in the drill above illustrate the relic /-th/ noun-forming suffix that is added to make ordinal numerals from cardinals and to numerous measure adjectives. Some of the forms cited below show the frequent vowel change that accompanies this formation.

6.2f Clusters with the suffix /-th/
Comparison of pattern; read across:

	/-C/	/-Cth/		
1a.	truw	truwth	true	truth
b.	grow	growth	grow	growth
c.	fɔr	fɔrth	four	fourth
d.	sɪks	sɪksth	six	sixth
e.	eyt	eytth	eight	eighth
2a.	wayd	wɪtth	wide	width
b.	brɔd	brɛtth	broad	breadth
c.	hǎndrəd	hǎndrətth	hundred	hundredth
d.	tháwzənd	tháwzəntth	thousand	thousandth
e.	fayv	fɪfth	five	fifth
3a.	wɑrm	wɑrmpth	warm	warmth
b.	muwn	məntth	moon	month
c.	sɛ́vən	sɛ́vəntth	seven	seventh
d.	nayn	nayntth	nine	ninth
e.	tɛn	tɛntth	ten	tenth
f.	lɔng	lɛngkth	long	length
g.	strɔng	strɛngkth	strong	strength
h.	hiyl	hɛltth	heal	health
i.	wiyl	wɛltth	weal	wealth
j.	stiyl	stɛltth	steal	stealth
k.	twɛlv	twɛltth	twelve	twelfth

The last item *might* be pronounced /twɛlfth/, but this would be a very careful articulation.

There are, as indicated by some of the examples above, some instances of final four-consonant clusters in English. These always have a suffix (occasionally two suffixes), and the suffix is always voiceless. The preceding three (or two) consonants may be inherent clusters (/kst, rst/), but usually the three-member cluster is the product of an intrusive stop. Thus clusters like the following appear, listed for practice. Suffixes are separated by hyphens and intrusive stops are in brackets.

6.2g Four-member consonant clusters
Presentation of pattern; read down:

Cluster	Examples
1a. ks-th-s	sixths
b. kst-s	texts
c. rst-s	bursts, thirsts, firsts
2a. rm[p]-th	warmth
b. m[p]t-s	tempts, prompts
c. m[p]f-s	nymphs, lymphs
d. m[p]f-t	triumphed
e. m[p]s-t	glimpsed
f. n[t]-th-s	thousandths, ninths, tenths, months
g. n[t]s-t	danced, pranced, fenced, chanced
h. ng[k]-th-s	lengths, strengths
i. ng[k]-st	amongst
j. l[t]s-t	waltzed, pulsed
k. l[t]-th-s	wealths, twelfths

Obviously a cluster of four consonants is very difficult to pronounce, even for native speakers. There are common patterns of reduction that apply, especially in informal styles. It is very difficult to systematize the reductions: some reduce and some resist simplification. Furthermore there are differences ascribed to context; an especially important condition is whether or not the following word begins with a consonant or a vowel. The full complexities cannot be described and presented in this text, but a few examples are listed to show representative types of reduction.

6.2h Reductions of consonant clusters
Presentation of pattern; read across:

	Components	Reduction	Examples
1.	mpts	⟶ mps	It really tempts me.
2.	mpfs	⟶ mps	They dance around the two nymphs.
3.	ntths	⟶ nts	two months ago, four tenths of a cent, The tolerance is seven thousandths of an inch.
4.	ngkths	⟶ ngks*	Two lengths of rope, please.
5.	fths	⟶ fs	I need two fifths of a gallon.
6.	tθs	⟶ ts	Three eighths of a point. Two widths of material.
7.	ksθs	⟶ ks	He lacks five sixths of an inch.
8.	ksθ	⟶ ks	He's in the sixth grade.
9.	ksts	⟶ ks	We need two texts for linguistics.
10.	kst	⟶ ks	Where's your textbook?
11..	sts	⟶ ss	He bruised both his fists. Naturally it rusts if you leave it out in the rain.
12.	rsts	⟶ rs	Every time he blows up a balloon, it bursts.
13.	pts	⟶ ps	Where are the scripts? They explored the crypts.
14.	kts	⟶ ks	He acts like a child.
15.	fts	⟶ fs	He lifts his eyes to the sky.
16.	sks	⟶ ss	He always asks first. How many desks did he bring?
17	skt	⟶ st	I asked the same question yesterday.

There are a few generalizations that can be made. Once an intrusive consonant appears, it usually stays. The following consonant is likely to drop, particularly if it's a /th/, which is especially vulnerable, or a /t/. Between /s/'s a /t/ or a /k/ may be dropped, leaving behind a long /s/. Usually (but not always) a medial consonant in the cluster drops.

---

*reduced by some speakers to /nths/: /lɛnths/

These reductions probably need not be taught. The student will likely experience enough difficulty with the more complex clusters, that reduction in some form will happen anyway. In any case there is considerable variation in the reduction patterns, and teaching any specific pattern will arouse skepticism among teachers, if not students. The discussion on reductions of consonant clusters is included at this point to illustrate the *kinds* of phonetic simplification that can occur, which will possibly be an encouragement to the student who may be struggling with clusters, to tell him that native speakers also struggle and solve their problems on a more or less consistent basis, making allowances for different levels of style. The application is to not expect more by way of precision and careful articulation from a second-language student than one normally gets from a native American.

One final generalization: clusters are simplified whenever possible by converting them to sequences. Thus in *act* /kt/ is a cluster (pronounced within a syllable), but in *actor* it is a sequence (divided between syllables). This kind of simplification takes place constantly, but needs no special practice. The student will rarely force into clusters what he can distribute in sequence.

There are a few problems associated with the pronunciation of consonant sequences (as opposed to clusters) that should be presented. One is the production of consonant geminates, or sequences of two instances of the same consonant. We have noted that not even voiced-voiceless pairs of consonants are allowed to cluster; thus when voiced /z/ follows voiceless /s/ in /klǽsəz/ *(classes)* or voiced /d/ follows voiceless /t/ in /hə́ntəd/ *(hunted)*, a syllable-carrying schwa intervenes. Likewise for two instances of /z/ or /d/: /kɔ́zəz - treydəd/ *(causes, traded)*. Sequences of identical consonants are rare within words (nonexistent within syllables—i.e., no clusters—except in the case of a few reduced clusters as cited earlier: /bərsts→bərss/ *(bursts)*, but they do occur across word boundaries. When they occur, the realization is a single long consonant, a consonant articulation with a delayed release.

Note the following phrases where a specific consonant is first final, then initial, then both. Listen for the differences in pronunciation in the first two columns, for the transition features that indicate whether the consonant is final or initial. Then in the third column listen for the long sound as the consonant is doubled.

6.3 Sequences of identical consonants

Presentation and comparison of pattern; read across:

/-C/	/C-/	/-C C-/			
sêym ǽn	sêy mǽn	sêym mǽn	same Ann	say man	same man
pêyd éy	pêy déy	pêyd déy	paid A	pay day	paid day
rûwp ǽker	rûw pǽker	rûwp pǽker	Rupe Acker	Rue Packer	Rupe Packer
kêyt áyler	kêy táyler	kêyt táyler	Kate Eiler	Kay Tyler	Kate Tyler
zîyk rǽndel	zîy krǽndel	zîyk krǽndel	Zeke Randall	Zee Crandall	Zeke Crandall
gêyb ówen	gêy bówen	gêyb bówen	Gabe Owen	Gay Bowen	Gabe Bowen
lóyd ɛ́venz	lóy dɛ́venz	lóyd dɛ́venz	Lloyd Evans	Loy Devons	Lloyd Devons
hôwg rǽnd	hôw grǽnd	hôwg grǽnd	Hoag Rand	Ho Grand	Hoag Grand
jôwzef ɛ́rel	jôwze fɛ́rel	jôwzef fɛ́rel	Joseph Errol	Josa Farrell	Joseph Farrell
kíyth éyer	kíy théyer	kíyth théyer	Keith Ayer	Kee Thayer	Keith Thayer
jôwnes ɔ́lk	jôwne sɔ́lk	jôwnes sɔ́lk	Jonas Aulk	Jonah Salk	Jonas Salk
klíyv ǽliy	klíy vǽliy	klíyv vǽliy	Cleve Alley	Clee Valley	Cleve Valley
fêyz ɔ́rn	fêy zɔ́rn	fêyz zɔ́rn	Faze Orn	Fay Zorn	Faze Zorn
mêym ǽsterz	mêy mǽsterz	mêym mǽsterz	Mame Astors	May Masters	Mame Masters
jôwn ɛ́lsen	jôw nɛ́lsen	jôwn nɛ́lsen	Joan Elson	Joe Nelson	Joan Nelson
êlener ówen	êlene rówen	êlener rówen	Eleanor Owen	Elena Rowan	Eleanor Rowan
gêyl ǽnderz	gêy lǽnderz	gêyl lǽnderz	Gail Anders	Gay Landers	Gail Landers

This pattern does not apply well to the affricates /ch/ and /j/, which are complex sounds consisting of a stop plus a strongly fricative release. Two affricates in sequence are usually heard as two distinct articulations.

Sometimes, and this is illustrated by the varying length of the vowels in words above like *Kate* and *Kay,* etc., syllable boundaries and the resulting syllable structures can have a crucial influence on the recognition of vocabulary items. This is particularly true in the case of long (drilled) /s/ and /sC/ clusters, which are presented in doubled contextual contrast in the following exercise.

6.3a Double /s/ and /sC/

Comparison of pattern; identify by paraphrase each member of the following pairs:

/C/ - /sC/

1. puwl/spuwl — This pool/spool is oversize. (tank of water/cylinder for thread)

2. tuwl/stuwl — This tool/stool is ours. (workman's implement/backless seat)

3. kuwl/skuwl — This Kool/school is not very good. (brand of cigarette/institution of learning)

4. peys/speys — This pace/space is too demanding. (rate of work/area)

5. trǎmpət/strǎmpət — This trumpet/strumpet makes too much noise. (wind instrument/harlot)

6. kɛch/skɛch — This ketch/sketch is a real inspiration. (sailing boat/drawing)

7. fɪr/sfɪr — This fear/sphere is hard to explain. (alarmed concern/globular body)

8. mɪth/smɪth — This myth/smith can't be believed. (traditional story/horse-shoer)

6.3a (continued)

/C/ - /sC/

9. neyl/sneyl — This nail/snail went through the wall. (iron fastener/slow-moving mollusk)

10. laym/slaym — This lime/slime will get you dirty. (calcium oxide/sticky muck)

11. mət/smət — This mutt/smut is intolerable. (mongrel dog/pornography)

12. nuwz/snuwz — This news/snooze is just what I needed. (information/short sleep)

13. liyp/sliyp — This leap/sleep restored my confidence. (jump/slumber)

14. wæg/swæg — This wag/swag is hard to get rid of. (humorous fellow/booty)

This exercise is designed to offer practice in identifying a doubled /s/ before a consonant. When the consonant that follows is a voiceless stop (a /p,t,k/), another feature of distinction is present, illustrated in the first six sentences. Coming at the beginning of a stressed syllable, as in *pool, tool, cool,* etc., the voiceless stop is strongly aspirated; but when /p,t,k/ come after a syllable-initial /s/, as in *spool, stool, school,* etc., this feature is greatly diminished, to a point where these consonants are usually described as unaspirated.

One very special articulation of a consonant sequence characterizes American pronunciation: the linked /nt/ after stress, in a word like /wíntər/ *(winter)*. Actually this sequence (it doesn't happen as a cluster, except finally in a word like /vɛnt/ *vent*) is produced as a nasal or nasalized flap, like /t/ in the same stress pattern and syllable environment. Comparing /wítər/ *(Witter)* and /wíntər/ *(winter)*, a listener distinguishes the two only by the presence of nasality in the second. This means that /wíntər/ *(winter)* and /wínər/ *(winner)* may not be distinguished at all, since the /n/ of *winner* may also be realized as a nasalized flap.

Listen to the comparisons made in the following exercise of /t, n, nt/.

6.3b Flapped /́nt-/
Presentation and comparison of pattern; read across:

/́t-/	/́n-/	/́nt-/			
1. wítər	wínər	wín(t)ər	Witter	winner	winter
2. bǽtər	bǽnər	bǽn(t)ər	batter	banner	banter
3. gə́tər	gə́nər	gə́n(t)ər	gutter	gunner	Gunter
4. sétər	sénər	sén(t)ər	setter	Senner	center
5. péytər	péynər	péyn(t)ər	pater	painer	painter
6. plǽtər	plǽnər	plǽn(t)ər	platter	planner	planter
7. mítiy	míniy	mín(t)iy	Mitty	mini	minty
8. métəl	ménəl	mén(t)əl	metal	Mennel	mental

The *nt* flap pattern is not limited to words of the structure shown in the above exercise. There are many commonly occurring words that have this sequence: *identify, quantity, panty, dainty, plenty, twenty, county, renter, printer, interurban, hunter, counter, entertain, elementary, oriental, dental, dentist, Atlanta, parental, lentil, pointer*. Occasionally the *nt* flap may cause a misunderstanding: "The real problem in Los Angeles is the lack of inner city/intercity transportation." These are not normally distinguished in informal speech. The student who is not familiar with this pronunciation will have predictable difficulty attempting to understand informal (and even formal) spoken American English. We will have occasion to return to this very important pattern in a discussion of contractions later in this chapter.

As shown in the linked *nt,* the consonant /n/ has the capacity to respond to its environment. Sometimes the nasal (any nasal, /m, n, ng/) assimilates to the following sound; sometimes it doesn't. Both possibilities can be observed with the prefixes /kɑn-/, which assimilates, and /ən-/, which doesn't. The following exercise permits a comparison of these two prefixes.

6.3c Patterns of assimilation—the prefixes /kɑn-/ and /ən-/
Comparison of pattern; read across:

	/kəN-/	/ən-/		
1a.	kənsɛ́nt	ənsɛ́nt	consent	unsent
b.	kənsə́rvd	ənsə́rvd	conserved	unserved
c.	kənsáynd	ənsáynd	consigned	unsigned
d.	kənsówld	ənsówld	consoled	unsold
e.	kənstrı́kt	ənstrı́kt	constrict	unstrict
f.	kənskrı́ptəd	ənskrı́ptəd	conscripted	unscripted
g.	kəntɛ́mpərɛ̀riy	əntɛ́mpərɛ̀riy	contemporary	untemporary
h.	kəntɛ́ndəd	əntɛ́ndəd	contended	untended
i.	kəndɛ́nts	əndɛ́nts	condense	undense
j.	kəndə́kt	əndə́kt	conduct	unducked
k.	kənfáynd	ənfáynd	confined	unfined
l.	kənfɔ́rmd	ənfɔ́rmd	conformed	unformed
m.	kənfáwndəd	ənfáwndəd	confounded	unfounded
2a.	kəmpáyl	ənpáyl	compile	unpile
b.	kəmpówzd	ənpówzd	composed	unposed
c.	kəmpáwndəd	ənpáwndəd	compounded	unpounded
d.	kəmpǽtəbəl	ənpǽtəbəl	compatible	unpattable
e.	kəmpláyəbəl	ənpláyəbəl	compliable	unpliable
f.	kəmpɛ́rd	ənpɛ́rd	compared	unpaired
g.	kəmbáynd	ənbáynd	combined	unbind
h.	kəmbə́stəbəl	ənbə́stəbəl	combustible	unbustable
3a.	kəmǽnd	ənmǽnd	command	unmanned
b.	kəmyúwtəd	ənmyúwtəd	commuted	unmuted
c.	kəmɛ́ndəd	ənmɛ́ndəd	commended	unmended
d.	kəmı́kst	ənmı́kst	commixed	unmixed

	/káng-/	/-n-/		
4a.	kánggrəgèyt	əngréytfəl	congregate	ungrateful
b.	kángkər	kənkə́r	conquer	concur
c.	kánggrəs	kəngrɛ́shənəl	congress	congressional
d.	kánggruwənt	kəngrǽchuwlənt	congruent	congratulant

6.3c (continued)

	/ng ~ n/	/n/		
5a.	kăngkêyv ~ kănkêyv ~ kὰngkêyv ~ kὰnkêyv	kənklûwd	concave	conclude
b.	kăngkɔ̀rd ~ kănkɔ̀rd	kənkɔ́rdənts	Concord	concordance
c.	kăngkyəbὰyn ~ kănkyəbὰyn	kənkə́rənts	concubine	concurrence
d.	kăngkwɛ̀st kănkwɛ̀st	kənklûwd	conquest	conclude
e.	kăngkɔ̀rs ~ kănkɔ̀rs	kənkɑ́kt	concourse	concoct

The prefix /kɑN-/ shows an assimilation in point of articulation to the following consonants: /n/ before /s, t, d, f/, /m/ before /p, b/. The nasal also becomes /m/ before /m/, but then the two /m/'s are reduced to one. The logical extension of the pattern to /ng/ before /k, g/ is ambivalent: sometimes /ng/, sometimes /n/, with /ng/ preferred if the prefix carries strong stress. The prefix /ən-/ on the other hand never assimilates, and /n/ always appears. This pattern, and the lack of consistent rules in the velar area, makes the mastery of the prefixes containing nasal sounds very difficult for speakers of other languages: those that do not have nasal assimilation as well as those that do. The prefix /iN-/ is similar in its distribution to /kɑN-/.

The patterns of nasal assimilation show clearly that neighboring sounds affect each other. When these effects are noticeable, we speak of patterns of assimilation. One of the clearest examples of reciprocal assimilation, where sounds and sequence affect each other, both changing, is a pattern generally referred to as palatalization. In palatal assimilations an alveolar fricative or stop sound, specifically /s, z, t, d/, is followed directly by a palatal semiconsonant, the onglide /y/. Note the following comparisons, where the items in the first two columns rhyme with each other, providing the item in the first column is pronounced in informal style.

géshər	préshər	I *guess you're* coming, right?	pressure
híyzhər	síyzhər	So *he's your* brother?	seizure
éychər	néychər	You *ate your* lunch?	nature
hə́rjər	və́rjər	I *heard your* talk.	verdure

The palatal assimilation pattern, illustrated in the above sentences, is as follows:

$$/s/ + /y/ \rightarrow /sh/$$
$$/z/ + /y/ \rightarrow /zh/$$
$$/t/ + /y/ \rightarrow /ch/$$
$$/d/ + /y/ \rightarrow /j/$$

To be more accurate, this formula would have to be expanded to something like: /s/ followed without junctural break by a /y/ that begins a weak-stressed syllable becomes an /sh/, and so on for the other combinations. The formula could be extended to include two more sequences:

$$/ts/ + /y/ \rightarrow /ch/$$
$$/dz/ + /y/ \rightarrow /j/$$

This pattern of palatalizing an alveolar stop or fricative when followed by /y/ is not something recently introduced into modern English. It extends back a long time as can be seen in the derivational noun forms that are built from a verb stem and the suffix /-yər/. Note the following, where the derivational suffix /-yər/ is compared to the informal pronunciation /yər/ of *your* or *you're:*

iyréys	iyréyshər	erase	erasure	Please *erase your* mistakes.
klowz	klówzhər	close	closure	Please *close your* books.
diypárt	diypárchər	depart	departure	If you *depart you're* safe.
prowsíyd	prowsíyjər	proceed	procedure	If you *proceed you're* lost.

Note the similar combinations with the clusters /ts/ and /dz/ followed by /y/:

heyts	héychər	hates	He *hates your* brother.
niydz	nîyjər	needs	He *needs your* help.

Other patterns of combination, such as /l/ plus /y/ in /feyl ~ féylyər/ or /n/ plus /y/ in /ətéyn ~ tényər/ *(fail - failure, attain - tenure)*, indicate that palatal changes are not automatically produced by the suffix /-yər/, but only by the combination of the /y/ of that suffix with a preceding alveolar stop or fricative.

These patterns of changes are illustrated in the following exercise. Listen to the bits and pieces of phrases, then put them together in normal sentences in informal style, making sure to provide for the assimilations.

6.3d Patterns of assimilation—alveolar consonants plus /y/ before weak-stressed vowels

Presentation of pattern; combine the fragments into full sentences:

dhîs . . . yŭr	dhîshər	1. Is this . . . your book?	Is this your book?
iyrêys . . . yŭr	iyrêyshər	2. Erase . . . your answers.	Erase your answers.
blês . . . yŭr	blêshər	3. Well bless . . . your heart.	Well bless your heart.
îz . . . yŭr	îzhər	4. Is . . . your brother coming?	Is your brother coming?
hûwz . . . yŭr	hûwzhər	5. Who's . . . your partner?	Who's your partner?
gôwz . . . yŭr	gôwzhər	6. There goes . . . your teacher.	There goes your teacher.

6.3d (continued)

êyt ... y̌ʊr	êychər	7. So you ate ... your lunch.	So you ate your lunch.
dhǽt ... y̌ʊr	dhǽchər	8. Is that ... your own car?	Is that your own car?
kât ... y̌ʊr	kâchər	9. He cut ... your lip!	He cut your lip!
dîd ... y̌ʊr	dîjər	10. Did ... your uncle come?	Did your uncle come?
hûwd ... y̌ʊr	hûwjər	11. Who'd ... your brother bring?	Who'd your brother bring?
hâyd ... y̌ʊr	hâyjər	12. Hide ... your camera.	Hide your camera.
wêts ... y̌ʊr	wêchər	13. What's ... your name?	What's your name?
dhǽts ... y̌ʊr	dhǽchər	14. That's ... your only tie?	That's your only tie?
wânts ... y̌ʊr	wânchər	15. He wants ... your answer.	He wants your answer.
gûdz ... y̌ʊr	gûjər	16. What good's ... your argument?	What good's your argument?
mêndz ... y̌ʊr	mênjər	17. Who mends ... your sox?	Who mends your sox?
fîydz ... y̌ʊr	fîyjər	18. He feeds ... your dog?	He feeds your dog?

In exercise 6.3e a palatal fricative (/sh, zh/) or affricate (/ch, j/) is constructed at word boundaries from combinations that show a higher level stress in both preceding and following syllables. For drill purposes the palatalization is assumed to occur, although in actual usage the assimilation may in fact be optional, depending on level of formality, relative emphasis, speed of pronunciation, etc.

6.3e Patterns of assimilation—alveolar consonant plus /y/ before strong-stressed vowels
Comparison of pattern; read across with two voices:

1.	dhîs wât	yîr	dhîshîr	This what?	Year. This year.
2.	dhîyz hûw	yǽngkiyz	dhîyzhǽnkiyz	These who?	Yankees. These Yankees.
3.	It dîd wât	yɛ́lpt	îchɛ́lpt	It did what?	Yelped. It yelped.
4.	frɛ̂d dîd wât	yîylded	frɛ̂jîylded	Fred did what?	Yielded. Fred yielded.
5.	Its wât kâlər	yɛ́low	îchɛ́low	It's what color?	Yellow. It's yellow.
6.	hiy nîydz hûw	yûw	hiy nîyjûw	He needs who?	You. He needs you.
7.	hiy lâyks wât	yǽmz	hiy lâykshǽmz	He likes what?	Yams. He likes yams.
8.	hîyz In Iz wât	yârd	în Izhârd	He's in his what?	Yard. In his yard.
9.	pîyt hûw	yâng	pîychâng	Pete who?	Young. Pete Young.
10.	shiy sɛ̂d wât	yɛ́s	shîy sɛ̂jɛ̂s	She said what?	Yes. She said yes.
11.	hiy wânts wât	yôwgərt	hiy wânchôwgərt	He wants what?	Yogurt. He wants yogurt.
12.	hiy râydz wât	yɛ́rlIngz	hiy râyjîrlIngz	He rides what?	Yearlings. He rides yearlings.

The palatalization patterns described and practiced above are extremely important to the second-language student of English who hopes to be able to readily comprehend informal spoken English. These assimilations are very natural, in spite of the feeling some may have that such pronunciations are careless or sloppy. As a matter of fact, native speakers of English who consistently avoid them may sound strange and affected.

The following exercise utilizes an echo-answer technique to contextualize palatal assimilations.

6.3f Patterns of assimilation—palatalizations cued by questions

Pattern practice; answer the following questions fully and affirmatively:

1.	míshuw	Jane will miss me?	Yes, she'll really *miss you*.
2.	héychər	He hates my brother?	Yes, he really *hates your* brother.
3.	wánchuw	He wants me to come?	Yes, he really *wants you* to come.
4.	níyjər	He needs my vote?	Yes, he really *needs your* vote.
5.	yúwzhuw	He expects to use me?	Yes, he really expects to *use you*.
6.	déychər	He wants to date my sister?	Yes, he really wants to *date your* sister.
7.	níyjuw	He thinks he'll need me?	Yes, he really thinks he'll *need you*.
8.	slǽshchər	He slashed my tires?	Yes, he really *slashed your* tires.
9.	fɔ́rshuw	He'll force me to come?	Yes, he'll really *force you* to come.
10.	ənjɔ́yzhər	He enjoys my playing?	Yes, he really *enjoys your* playing.

One final exercise presents the palatal assimilations, this time in a reading drill.

6.3g Patterns of assimilation—miscellaneous palatalizations
Oral interpretation; read the following sentences, observing all appropriate palatal assimilations:
1. Did you say his name's Young?
2. What's your uncle say about yodelling?
3. When's your class yearbook coming out?
4. It was your brother who ate your lunch.
5. That's yesterday's paper he left you.
6. Well, did you eat yet or didn't you?
7. What'd your mother say about your new car?
8. I thought you meant you were staying longer.
9. He needs you, and I need you.
10. Is your schedule fixed yet?

One bit of advice to students practicing this pattern: these articulations should not be exaggerated or they will be overly conspicuous. They should be pronounced lightly and rapidly. Any break in the sequence will violate the conditions under which such assimilations occur.

One special kind of assimilation is a set of contractions formed of verbs plus a weak-stressed particle, usually the preposition *to*. Note the following pairs of sentences which illustrate the contexts where contractions occur.

6.4 Verb-particle contractions
Presentation of pattern; listen to and imitate the following pairs of sentences:

1a.	I'm going to Gallup.	(destination)
b.	I'm gonna gallop.	(intention)
2a.	What do you want to play?	(how much?)
b.	What do you wanna play?	(what music?)
3a.	So you got to go.	(yesterday)
b.	So you gotta go.	(tomorrow)
4a.	What do you have to eat?	(available)
b.	What do you hafta eat?	(diet requirement)
5a.	That's what he has to do.	(has remaining)
b.	That's what he hasta do.	(is required)
6a.	He's supposed to be sick.	(is presumed to be)
b.	He's supposta be sick.	(ought to be)
7a.	This dog is used to fish.	(for the purpose of)
b.	This dog is usta fish.	(accustomed to eating)

Contractions involve specific sets of words, where assimilations occur whenever specified sounds are brought together in a sequence. Thus a sequence of *going* plus *to* may produce /gə́nə/, which may be informally spelled *gonna,* whereas similarly structured words, such as *knowing, showing, doing,* etc. never contract with a following *to.* Actually as sentences *1a* and *b* above show, *going* and *to* don't always contract, and there is a contrast of meaning when they do. This can of course be seen in all seven pairs of sentences.

These contractions, while in common use in English, particularly in informal styles, are not always admitted into formal English and especially into formal written English. The spellings used above to represent the contractions are not really acknowledged, often do not appear in standard dictionaries of current use. Some of them, especially *gonna, wanna, gotta, hafta, hasta,* are widely used when informal spoken dialogue is represented, as in comic strips, plays, and quoted dialogue in novels. Their use in personal letters is also frequent. The other two spellings, *supposta* and *usta,* have probably never been used outside of some special context, such as the present presentation which attempts to correlate their structure and distribution with the first five that *do* have informal spellings.

The use of all seven forms in informal speech is virtually universal, and in fact the contrasts of meaning illustrated in the sentences can hardly be represented without using the appropriate contractions. Nevertheless, well-meaning language teachers may feel that using these contractions is evidence of sloppy or vulgar usage. This is nonsense, an example of inexplicable folk mythology about language. The second-language student who cannot handle these contractions on an oral receptive level will be seriously crippled in the skill of listening comprehension. Furthermore, he will be able to communicate in his own speaking only on a level that will inevitably be considered very formal by his native, English-speaking communicants, who will forgive his "accent" because he is a "foreigner," but who will be to some extent distracted by the way he talks. Any student of English who expects to have any occasion to use the oral language should invest some time and effort in at least familiarization, if not mastery, of these contractions.

The following exercise is designed to offer practice in putting the constituent verbs and the particle *to* into the appropriate contracted form.

6.4a Forms of contractions—verbs plus *to*

Presentation of pattern; combine the fragments into complete sentences, employing the contractions:

gôwɪŋ ... tùw	gânə	1. John and Mary are going ... to come tomorrow.
gôwɪŋ ... tùw	gânə	2. Who's going ... to pick them up at the airport?
wânt ... tùw	wânə	3. Don't you two want ... to get them?
wânt ... tùw	wânə	4. We really want ... to go, but we can't.
gât ... tùw	gâtə	5. I'd like to get them but I've got ... to go to work.
gât ... tùw	gâtə	6. Well, somebody's got ... to go after them.
hǽv ... tùw	hǽftə	7. Why do they have ... to come at 3:00 A.M.?
hǽv ... tùw	hǽftə	8. They don't have ... to come then, but the fares are cheaper.
hǽz ... tùw	hǽstə	9. John has ... to save money whenever he can.
hǽz ... tùw	hǽstə	10. Since he lost his job he has ... to follow a strict budget.
səpôwzd ... tùw	səpôwstə	11. But isn't a wife supposed ... to help her husband?
səpôwzd ... tùw	səpôwstə	12. Marriage is supposed ... to be a fifty-fifty proposition.
yûwz ... tùw	yûwstə	13. Mary used ... to have a lot of money.
yûwz ... tùw	yûwstə	14. She used ... to be very wealthy before she married John.

To do justice to this drill it should be borne in mind that the informal level of speaking should be maintained through all of the sentence, not just the part that is contracted. In sentence three, for example, if *want to* becomes *wanna,* then surely *don't you* will become *dôwnchûw.* In sentence five the use of *gotta* implies *get them* pronounced as /gɛ́təm/, *go to* pronounced as /gôwtə/, with a flapped /t/ in /gɛ́təm/ and /gôwtə/ just as in /gâtə/. Every sentence in the exercise has similar assimilations that could be cited.

It is interesting to examine some of the changes that take place in these contractions of verbs and particles. As we have seen earlier, /gówɪŋ/ *(going)* in formal speech tends to become /gówən/ *(goin')* in less formal speech. The particle /tuw/ *(to)* with the stress reduced becomes /tə/; /gówən/ plus /tə/ brings together an /nt/ sequence, which becomes a nasal flap—described earlier in this chapter in words like *winter, twenty, entertain,* etc., which we represented as a single /n/ between vowels. *Want* plus *to* is similar; the /t/ plus /t/ sequence reduces to a single /t/, which combines with the preceding /n/ to produce an /nt/, which then becomes /n/. In *got to* the two /t/'s reduce to one, which after a stressed syllable becomes a flapped /t/. *Have to* and *has to* are made up of verbs ending in a voiced consonant (/v/ and /z/ in /hæv/ and /hæz/) which is devoiced before the /t/ of weak-stressed /tə/ to produce /hǽftə/ and /hǽstə/. *Supposed* and *used* end in /zd/ (/səpówzd/ and /yuwzd/) which devoices to /st/; then the following /t/ of weak-stressed /tə/ combines with the verbs to produce /səpówstə/ and /yúwstə/.

It should be noted that the particle /tuw/ (which becomes /tə/ in the full contraction) may maintain a medial level of stress if it is the last word of a sentence. The following exercise shows this distribution.

6.4b Full and partial contraction of verb plus *to*

Comparison of pattern; read across:

gânə	gówən tùw	1. He wants to eat, but he's not gonna eat now.	He wants to eat, but he's not going to.
hǽstə	hǽs tùw	2. He thinks he should go, and he really hasta go right now.	He thinks he should go, and he really has to.
wânə	wânt tùw	3. They say they should go, but they don't wanna go now.	They say they should go, but they don't want to.
gâtə	gât tùw	4. They say they should go, that they've really gotta go right now.	They say they should go, and they've really got to.

6.4b (continued)

yúwstə	yúws tùw	5. She says she eats lots of fish, that anyway she usta eat a lot.	She says she eats lots of fish, that anyway she used to.
hǽftə	hǽf tùw	6. She shouldn't go, and anyway she doesn't hafta go right now.	She shouldn't go, and anyway she doesn't have to.
səpówstə	səpóws tùw	7. They say they really should go to the premiere, that anyway they're supposta go.	They say they really should go to the premiere, that anyway they're supposed to.
wânə	wânt tùw	8. They'd like to go, and anyway they really wanna go right now.	They'd like to go, and anyway they really want to.
gânə	gówən tùw	9. We'd love to have another piece of chicken, but we're not gonna have any more right now.	We'd love to have another piece of chicken, but we're not going to.
gâtə	gât tùw	10. We really should leave; we've just gotta leave right now.	We really should leave we've just got to.

It is normal *not* to make the assimilations when the particle *to* comes at the end of the sentence. However this is actually optional, and a very informal style would accept a sentence like "I really wanna." Perhaps it is a bit more natural in most situations to say "I really want to."

Note, however, that the verb-particle construction at the end of a sentence represents a partial assimilation, a step toward the contracted forms. Thus in this context the middle forms appear from sets like the following: /hǽz tùw ~ hǽs tùw ~ hǽstə - hǽv tùw ~ hǽf tùw ~ hǽftə - yúwzd tùw ~ yúws tùw ~ yústə - səpówzd tùw ~ səpóws tùw ~ səpówstə - gówɪŋ tùw ~ gówən tùw ~ gânə/. There seems to be no such clear middle ground for /wânt tùw/ and /gât tùw/, though there is no doubt a less clear separate articulation for the double /t/'s. The /t/'s become a flap only when clearly assimilated to a single /t/, with *wanta* moving on to a normal /nt/ development into a nasal flap, the characteristic articulation for intervocalic /n/ when followed by weak stress.

English Consonant Patterns 169

The important feature to keep in mind when considering these contractions is that their use and meaning contrasts in many minimal constructions with the corresponding full forms. This was illustrated in exercise *6.4* and is now the subject of a separate exercise. Note that no informal spellings are used in the suggested answers, though this does not affect the use of contracted forms, which are needed to differentiate meanings. Note that the particle *to* is also pronounced /tə/ in both sentences of each pair.

6.4c Verb-particle contractions in contrast with full forms

Comparison of pattern; ask information questions beginning with *what* (based on the statements given) that inquire for more details:

hâev tə	1a. She *has* something *to* say.	What does she *have to* say?
hâeftə	b. She *has to* say something.	What does she *have to* say?
wânt tə	2a. He *wants* some amount (of money) *to* sing.	What does he *want to* sing?
wânə	b. He *wants to* sing some number.	What does he *want to* sing?
gôwɪng tə	3a. I am *going* in order *to* do something.	What are you *going to* do?
gânə	b. I am *going to* do something.	What are you *going to* do?
gât tə	4a. We've *got* something *to* do.	What have you *got to* do?
gâtə	b. We've *got to* do something.	What have you *got to* do?
hâez tə	5a. He says he *has* something *to* eat.	What does he say he *has to* eat?
hâestə	b. He says he *has to* eat something.	What does he say he *has to* eat?
yûwz tə	6a. My pet baboon is *used to* do something.	What is he *used to* do?
yûwstə	b. My pet baboon is *used to* doing something.	What is he *used to* doing?
səpôwzd tə	7a. He's *supposed to* be something.	What is he *supposed to* be?
səpôwstə	b. He's *supposed to* be something.	What is he *supposed to* be?

The next exercise changes roles, with the question preceding the answer. The answer should reflect the appropriate meaning signaled by the question.

6.4d The interpretation of verb-particle contractions

Comparison of pattern; answer the following questions with an expanded comment that utilizes the verb-particle contractions presented above:

səpôwzd tə	1a. Is he thought to be rich?	Yes, he's *supposed to* be very wealthy.
səpôwstə	b. Is he expected to be here tomorrow?	Yes, he's *supposed to* be coming in the morning.
yûwzd tə	2a. Are her talents well used?	Yes, she's *used to* produce television shows.
yûwstə	b. Is she accustomed to waiting?	Yes, she's *used to* waiting for her husband.
gât tə	3a. What has she *got to* eat?	She's *got* lots of things *to* eat.
gâtə	b. What has she *got to* eat?	She's *got to* eat lots of yogurt and liver.
gôwıng tə	4a. What is she *going* for?	She's *going to* help her sick sister.
gânə	b. What's she *going to* do?	She's *going to* leave early tomorrow.
hæz tə	5a. What does he still *have to* do?	He *has* many things *to* do.
hæstə	b. What does he *have to* do?	He *has to* finish his chores.
wânt tə	6a. What (How much) do they *want to* teach?	They *want* at least $1,000 a month *to* teach here.
wânə	b. What do they *want to* teach?	They *want to* teach biological science.
hæv tə	7a. What do they *have to* drink?	They *have* milk, juice, and orangeade *to* drink.
hæftə	b. What do they *have to* drink?	They *have to* drink milk.

The contracted forms /gânə-səpôwstə/, etc. may have variant forms for some speakers of English. For example /gânə/ may be /gɔ̂nə/ or /gôwnə/ or /gôynə/ or /gwânə/, and /səpôwstə/ may be spôwstə/, two instead of three syllables. But virtually all dialects of English have some form of contractions for these verb-particle combinations, contractions which reflect the underlying unity of the various dialects of the English language.

There is another phenomenon in English, in part similar to contraction and possibly related to assimilation: the occurrence of shortened forms of some words when these are weak-stressed. The shortening may be the dropping of some sounds, the substitution of vowel sounds, or a combination of both. There are many instances of this type of modification. We have looked, for instance, at the weak-stressed forms of the definite and indefinite articles (section *5.4b*). A similar kind of weakening can be seen in the contracted forms presented in the preceding series of drills, where /tùw/ becomes /tə/ when weak-stressed. Other examples of weak-stressed forms can be seen in the contraction patterns of certain auxiliary verbs: /wîl/ becomes /əl/ in "John'll be coming soon," and /îz/ becomes /əz/ in "Bess is coming with him," etc.

These short forms or weak forms or weak-stressed forms must be experienced in context if the student is to have the opportunity of familiarization that will help develop confidence when participating in the spoken form of the language as a speaker and even more particularly as a listener. Yet these forms are often neglected or even ignored, with the result that second-language students are completely lost when they first have to function as communicants with the spoken language in real-life situations. The following exercises are designed to provide the necessary experience in a structural format.

The particular weak-stressed forms presented and drilled below are some of the commonly occurring pronouns, which are systematically modified (1) when weak-stressed and (2) with some forms, when not initial in a phrase or sentence. The forms are listed and presented in the following exercise.

6.5 Weak-stressed forms of certain pronouns

Presentation of pattern; listen to and imitate the following pairs of sentences:

/hîy/	1a. He's coming.
/iy/	b. John said he's coming.
/hîz/	2a. His father's coming also.
/ɪz/	b. John said his father's coming too.
/hîm/	3a. Did you really see *him?*
/ɪm/	b. Yes, I saw him yesterday.
/hə̀r/	4a. Her father left Friday.
/ər/	b. Joan said her father left on Friday.

6.5 (continued)

/dhêm/	5a.	You have just seen *them?*
/əm/	b.	I saw them not five minutes ago.
/ît/	6a.	It isn't my turn.
/ət/	b.	Do it anyway.
/áwər/	7a.	Is this really *our* new car?
/ɑr/	b.	We left our car on the street.
/mây/	8a.	*My* order already came.
/mə/	b.	I lost my book.
dhêr/	9a.	Where's *their* tent?
/dhər/	b.	They left their kids home.
/yŭr/	10a.	*Your* money is no good.
/yər/	b.	Give me your hand.
/yûw/	11a.	That's what *you* say!
/yə/	b.	You just can't *do* that.

The short forms of the first six examples cited normally occur under weak stress when not initial in a sentence. (Of course *him* and *them* are rarely if ever initial in any case.) The reduced forms of the last five examples are not restricted to noninitial. Note the very minimal potential difference between:

ày sô ɪm yÉstərdèy	I saw him yesterday.
ày sô əm yÉstərdèy	I saw them yesterday.

The very small difference between /ĭ/ and /ă/ carries the number contrast between singular *him* and plural *them.* Even this difference may be obscured if the context is clear, but it can always be emphasized if clarity requires the distinction. And of course, if needed, the full forms can always be revived.

Note that there are rarely any spellings, even in informal writing, to indicate these contractions. Occasionally one sees *'em* for *them* or *ya* for *you* or *yer* for *your* in a comic strip, maybe *'im* for *him,* but rarely if ever a spelling to indicate /ĕr-ĭy-ĭz-ɑr-mə-dhər-ət/. Yet these pronunciations are normal and current in spoken English.

In the following exercise, sentence fragments are listed to provide practice in hearing and producing short forms of pronouns.

6.5a Short forms of personal pronouns

Pattern practice; combine the fragments into complete sentences, using the short forms of pronouns when appropriate:

hɪm	ɪm	1. I'll see . . . him tomorrow.
hər	ər	2. Where's . . . her mother living?
hiy	iy	3. I think . . . he won't mind.
hɪz	ɪz	4. Is . . . his brother coming?
dhɛm	əm	5. I saw . . . them just yesterday.
ɪt	ət	6. Why don't you give . . . it a try?
hɪz	ɪz	7. Have you got . . . his number?
hiy	iy	8. Where does . . . . he live?
dhɛm	əm	9. Will you take . . . them this note?
hɪm	ɪm	10. Give . . . him my very best regards.
hər	ər	11. I haven't seen . . . her all day.
ɪt	ət	12. Take . . . it with you.
yuw	yə	13. What are . . . you trying to do?
yɔr	yər	14. Is this . . . your other daughter?
dhɛr	dhər	15. They offered us the use of . . . their boat.
may	mə	16. I gave . . . my mother a new watch.
awər	ɑr	17. That's really . . . our only solution.
dhɛr	dhər	18. Tell me, what are . . . their chances?
yuw	yə	19. I'll see . . . you tomorrow then.
awər	ɑr	20. Can we give John . . . our only key?
may	mə	21. He says . . . my son's in there.
yʊr	yər	22. I hope you can bring . . . your car.

All these contractions sound natural, though some speakers might question whether /mə/ is an acceptable interpretation of *my*, even under weak stress. Perhaps it is not standard to all dialects of American English. Also there is a possible further weakening of /ɑ̂r/ to /ə̆r/ as an interpretation of *our*, as in "That's our only hope." But *our* realized as /ə̆r/ is not distinguished from weak-stressed *her*, and any need to prevent misinterpretation will quickly produce /ɑ̂r/.

These then are some of the problems presented by English consonant patterns: consonant clusters and sequences, reductions of complex clusters, assimilations, contractions, and short forms, all subjects of considerable complexity. As can be seen from several examples, it is increasingly difficult to confine patterns to the classifications "intonation, vowels, consonants." These systems interact with each other to produce more complex patterns, which belie simple categorizations. In the next chapters an attempt will be made to present additional miscellaneous patterns of behavior for the pronunciation and interpretation of the language, again grouped by the categories previously used, but recognizing the longer patterns that integrate diverse details into the overall system of the language.

Chapter 7

CONSTRUCTS OF ENGLISH INTONATION

The term intonation as used in this book is intended to cover a number of separate phenomena, including stress, pitch, juncture (the transitions between phrases or from sound to silence at the ends of phrases), and rhythm. These phenomena combine with each other in patterns that signal (along with the vowel and consonant sounds) the meanings intended by the speaker. Sometimes these phenomena are referred to as suprasegmental features, since they cannot be easily placed in the sequential stream of sounds, but rather affect whole syllables or phrases or indeed entire utterances. It will be the aim of the present chapter to examine and attempt to describe some of the features of intonation and some of the patterns into which these features combine, particularly those that are characteristic of informal spoken English.

One feature that differentiates English from many other languages is the rhythm pattern of its syllables. This can perhaps best be understood by a brief examination of English prosody, or patterns of

English versification. Prosody can be defined as "the science of poetical forms, including quantity and accent of syllables, meter, versification, and metrical composition." Poetry can be described and identified by its content, imagery, intensity, beauty, etc., but part of the effect is due to its metrical form. Poetic form tends to recognize the regularity of the inherent rhythm patterns of a language and to heighten and further regularize these. In some languages, for example, poetic form implies successive lines of a specified number of syllables; the syllable is the unit of regular recurrence, i.e., the basis of poetic form. In English the basic unit is the metrical foot, which can be regular even when the number of syllables varies. Actually, as we have seen in Chapter 4 and more specifically in Chapter 5, the lengths of syllables can vary enormously with weak-stressed syllables closed by a voiceless stop that are exceedingly brief and strong-stressed open syllables that are very long. It would be difficult, perhaps impossible, to define a "standard-length" syllable in English that could be the basis of regular recurrence implied by poetic form.

English poetry is rather based on a unit usually called a "metrical foot," which can be defined simplistically as a strong-stressed syllable and its associated weak-stressed syllables. This is not the place to attempt a detailed description of English metrics, which can be very complicated, but the basic metrical pattern can provide a rationale for what can be described as the inherent rhythm patterns of English.

Various descriptions of English rhythm characterize English as having a stress-timed rhythm pattern. That is to say the recurring unit of regularity is a strong stress, with weak-stressed syllables somehow crowded in without "counting" in the rhythmic patterns. This can be illustrated by an example, as follows:

(a) Joan can't wear Ann's ring.

This is not exactly a typical English sentence; in fact it is rather unusual to see a sentence with all words carrying a lexical stress, a total of five. Compare this sentence to the following one:

(b) Jenny isn't wearing Karen's bracelet.

In a syllable-timed language, sentence *(b)* with ten syllables could be expected to be twice as long as sentence *(a)'s* five syllables. Yet in

English both sentences are virtually equal in length of time required to pronounce them. Other sentences can have even more weak-stressed syllables scattered among the five strong stresses. Note the following:

    (c) Jennifer isn't demolishing Carolee's argument.

Sentence *(c)* adds another five syllables, again somehow articulated in approximately the same two seconds used in a normal rendition of sentence *(a)* and of sentence *(b)*.

It is a slight exaggeration to say that sentence *(c)* is produced in the same amount of time as sentence *(a)*. Sentence *(c)* takes a little longer, maybe ten per cent longer, but nothing like the additional 300 per cent implied by fifteen syllables of sentence *(c)* as compared to five syllables of sentence *(a)*. The explanation for the apparent squeezing is that time for the weak-stressed syllables is subtracted from the allocation for the preceding strong-stressed syllable. Note in the following sentence how the one-syllable words, the girls' names, are very much longer than the other strong-stressed syllables (is-, -mol-, ar-), because since no weak-stressed syllables occur to share the foot, they get the full time allocation:

    (d) Joan isn't demolishing Ann's argument.

And, conversely, note in the following sentence how the strong-stressed syllables in the girls' names (Jen-, Car-) are much shorter than the other strong-stressed syllables (can't, wear, ring):

    (e) Jennifer can't wear Carolee's ring.

So the length of individual syllables in English is influenced not only by syllable structure, stress, position in the sentence, etc., but additionally by rhythm patterns, the presence and number of following weak-stressed syllables that must share the metrical foot in the prosodic phrases.

The following exercise is designed to provide practice in the normal rhythm patterns of English sentences. As the sentences become longer, try to maintain, within reasonable limits, the length and timing of the original sentence. The strong-stressed syllables are marked for visual reference.

7.1 The rhythm pattern of English sentences

Presentation of pattern; repeat the following series of sentences, observing a pattern of pronunciation that permits only a slightly longer time to say the longer sentences:

1a. Bèars cáme.
 b. Lîons ćame.
 c. The lîoness ćame.
 d. The lîonesses ćame.
 e. The lîonesses appéared.
 f. The lîonesses've appéared.

2a. Jôhn câme hôme láte.
 b. Bîlly arrîved at tên o'clóck.
 c. Jônathan arrîved on Tûesday mórning.
 d. Cârolyn had arrîved by the ênd of the mórning.
 e. Jênnifer had arrîved by the begînning of the évening.

3a. Kârl broûght bóoks.
 b. Hênry broûght pápers.
 c. Ânthony ôffered a dĭctionary.
 d. Nîcholas provîded some réferences.
 e. Gâbriel blêw on his hórn.

It is interesting to note that people normally react to a rhythm system different from their own by overestimating the tempo or speed of normal pronunciation in the unfamiliar language. So the judgment "they speak so fast in language X" is common. Well, perhaps they do. A syllable-timed language sounds very fast, if you listen to the strong-stressed syllables. And a stress-timed language sounds comparably fast if you listen to the weak-stressed syllables.

In the following exercise, sentences with comparable lexical content but contrasting rhythm patterns are juxtaposed to facilitate the comparison of different rhythms.

7.1a Comparisons of English rhythm patterns—sentences

Comparison of pattern; read across:

1. Jîm cân't wêar Ânn's hát.   But he can wêar her ćoat.
2. Cân't Jîm wêar Ânn's hát?   Can he bôrrow her ćoat?

7.1a (continued)

3. Jôhn wôn't rêad Bîll's thême.   But he êdited the réferences.
4. Mâke Bîll reâd thrêe bóoks.   Has he fínished the óthers?
5. Âbe cân't rîde Jîll's hórse.   But he lâssoed the bróncos.

Notice that while the sentences in the left column have fewer syllables, they are all stressed syllables, and the result is a longer sentence. This is conspicuous in sentence *3*, where the five-syllable sentence on the left takes substantially longer to pronounce than the ten-syllable sentence on the right. Where the sentences on the left have five *stressed* syllables, those on the right have only two, and in spite of more syllables, are correspondingly shorter.

Another exercise illustrates the essential features of stress-timed rhythm on the word level. The comparison also shows the very brief and light pronunciation of a minimal schwa in an internal position.

7.1b Comparisons of English rhythm patterns—words
Comparison of pattern; read across:

/-ə-/	/-∅-/		
mǽdəsən	mǽdsən	Madison	Madsen
hə́ŋgəriy	hə́ŋgriy	Hungary	hungry
έlənə	έlnə	Elena	Elna
láytənɪŋ	láytnɪŋ	lightening	lightning
ɔ́rəgən	ɔ́rgən	Oregon	organ
kǽnədiy	kǽndiy	Cannady	candy
láyəbəl	láybəl	liable	libel
hǽpəliy	hǽpliy	happily	haply
kɔ́rəliy	kɔ́rliy	Coralee	Corley
ǽnəsən	ǽntsən	Anacin	Anson
sέnətər	sέntər	senator	center

We have seen earlier that there are relationships not only in the meanings, but in the stress patterns of certain forms in English, as in the verb *éducàte* and the derived noun *èducátion*. In fact we can with a usefully high degree of accuracy predict the stress pattern of English nouns ending in /-shən/ spelled *-tion* or *-sion*: the strong stress will fall on the syllable immediately preceding the suffix /-shən/. This stress placement will occur despite differences in the verb forms from which the /-shən/ form is derived. Note the following comparisons:

• —	• —	— • •
constitute		constitution
educate		education
	contribute	contribution
	sequestrate	sequestration

The pattern correlation of the first and third columns is the most general though the correlations shown in columns two and three are possible. The purpose of citing these patterns is to call attention to the regularity of the abstract noun forms in column three. It is comforting in describing languages to find a rule that works virtually one hundred per cent of the time.

The following exercise employs the stress placement rule for nouns that end in /-shən/.

7.2 Abstract nouns with the suffix /-shən/

Presentation of pattern; be prepared to complete the following sentences:

Cue	Response
1. If someone procrastinates,	we speak of procrastination.
2. If something is contributed,	we speak of a contribution.
3. If something is duplicated,	we speak of duplication.
4. If a set of rules is constituted,	we speak of a constitution.
5. If something is impregnated,	we speak of impregnation.
6. If someone is persecuted,	we speak of persecution.
7. If something is authenticated,	we speak of authentication.
8. If something is distributed,	we speak of distribution.
9. If a message is communicated,	we speak of communication.
10. If something is substituted,	we speak of a substitution.
11. If an area is inundated,	we speak of inundation.
12. If something is declared,	we speak of a declaration.
13. If something is resolved,	we speak of a resolution.
14. If power is usurped,	we speak of usurpation.
15. If something evolves,	we speak of evolution.
16. If various items are exported,	we speak of exportation.

7.2 (continued)

Cue	Response
17. If something is restored,	we speak of restitution.
18. If an award is presented,	we speak of a presentation.
19. If a parliament is dissolved,	we speak of a dissolution.
20. If something is condensed,	we speak of condensation.

This is of course a very easy exercise. It can be made somewhat more difficult by moving the other direction: "We speak of substitution when ... ", in which case the form of the cue is a stable stress pattern and the student has to select from various possible patterns on the basis of individual correlations. Note that mass-count distinctions in reference to the /-shən/ nouns vary—some nouns taking mass, some count, and some either, usually with a slightly different interpretation. Note that the /-shən/ words are interpreted consistently, even if the corresponding verb forms have alternative pronunciations, such as *inundate* is /ɪnǎndèyt/ or /ínəndèyt/.

Correlations of this type are useful to a student mainly to give him experience with the rhythmic patterns of the language, acquaintance with the normal sequences of stress that apply when new words (borrowings to be adapted or coinages to be interpreted) enter the language.

We have seen earlier in this chapter that sequences of strong-stressed syllables, though they may occur, are not typical of English rhythm patterns, in fact are a little awkward. This can be demonstrated by the fact that English avoids these sequences when it can. The avoidance mechanism is related in form to the shift between /´/ and /ˆ/ illustrated in the preceding drill. More accurately, one could talk about a shift between /´/ and /ˆ/, since it is normally the modifying word (which precedes and therefore has its strong-stressed syllable reduced to /ˆ/ for syntactic reasons) that is involved.

The shift can be illustrated by the following two answers, both employing the word *seventeen:*

(a) How old is she?   She's sèventéen.
(b) How long has she lived here?   For sêventèen yeárs.

This pattern of rhythmic shift of stresses has been a serious problem for generations of second-language students of English. The teens vs the tens in the English number system are bad enough, since when people count (i.e., vocally produce a regular series of numbers) there is a strong likelihood that contrastive patterns of stress assignment will creep in, particularly shifting the stronger stress to the first syllable of the *teens* series (which increases the similarity of these forms to the *tens* series).

But why should this "contrastive" stress be used in a sentence like the answer to sentence *(b)*? The answer is that it is not contrastive stress at all, but a more or less regular shift of the heavier stressed syllable away from a position adjacent to the sentence-stressed syllable. This shift is facilitated if the word involved (the word in next-to-last position) has the stress pattern /ˆ ˇ ´/, in which the strong and medial stresses can trade places. Thus a normal citation form, sèventéen, becomes séventèen (interpreted before yéars as sêventèen yéars). This shift avoids -téen and yéars in juxtaposition, with both carrying a strong stress.

The following exercise illustrates the optional but usually regular alternation of strong and medial stress to avoid adjacent strong stresses. Stresses in relevant syllables are marked for easy reference.

7.3 Rhythmic shift of strong stress in three-syllable modifiers

Presentation and comparison of pattern; answer the following pairs of questions as indicated:

1a. What instrument does he play?   A clarinét.
 b. What did he play on the program?   A clârinèt sólo.

2a. Do they know what I'm saying?   Yes, I'm sure they understánd.
 b. How much do they understand?   They ûnderstànd éverything.

3a. How old is Marcella?   She's seventéen.
 b. How long has she lived in Montebello?   For sêventèen yéars.

4a. What did you ask me?   What Joe underwént.
 b. Don't you know?   Not for sure; is it true he ûnderwènt súrgery?

5a. Did he buy it new?   No, it was secónd hánd.
 b. Did he get a motorcycle?   No, he got a sécondhànd cár.

6a. Did she come this morning?   No, she came this afternóon.
 b. Did she come by bus?   No, she was on the âfternòon tráin.

7a. Is there a floor lamp in this room?   No, just the light òverhéad.
 b. How do you close your garage?   It has an óverhèad dóor.

7.3 (continued)

8a. Was it a normal birth?
    No, the baby was prêmatúre.
b. Will there be any trouble?
    Well, you can't always tell with a prêmatùre báby.

9a. Was it a beautiful valley?
    Yes, it was very pîcturésque.
b. Did you enjoy your vacation in Maine?
    Yes, such a pîcturèsque átmospħere!

10a. Do you think I should go?
    Âbsolútely.
b. You agree with me, then?
    Yes, you're âbsolùtely rígħt.

This stress shift is optional, but very normal in English. As the sentences in *10* show, the shift may occur even when the two strong-stressed syllables are separated by a weak-stressed syllable: *-lútely* and *rígħt*.

As the following exercise shows, a similar shift may occur with two-syllable modifiers.

7.3a Rhythmic shift of strong stress in two-syllable modifiers
Comparison of pattern; read the following sentences, observing the stress markings given:

1. This ântîque cár is a real ântíque.
2. The bâmbòo órgan is really made of bàmbóo.
3. This sârdîne sándwich needs more sàrdínes.
4. The Bêrlîn wáll separates East and West Bèrlín.
5. This Chînèse púzzle isn't really Chìnése.
6. Naturally the úpstaîrs róoms are ùpstáirs.
7. The ûnknòwn sóldier is really ùnknówn.
8. His mâde-òver súit was really màde óver.
9. The thîrtèen girls were all thìrtéen.
10. It was an ûphîll strúggle, all the way ùp híll.

We now turn to another aspect of intonation, the patterns which apply to entire phrases or sentences. These patterns include sequences of pitches that are applied to the syllables of the utterance, usually with changes of pitch coordinated closely with the occurrence of strong-stressed syllables. Then there is the transition feature of juncture at the end of the sentence, the pitch turn that characterizes the way the sentence terminates. We can generalize by noting that when a final juncture is falling, this is a sign of completion, where another speaker may enter the conversation, or where the topic of conversation may be changed. If the final juncture is not falling, it may be hanging (left on the same pitch) or rising. A hanging juncture implies "more to come," and a rising juncture usually specifically asks for information from the listener. These are generalizations for which there are exceptions. A desire for information, for example, can be expressed by the use of a question word ("Who just came in?"), rather than by a rising juncture. But like most generalizations, they are useful and can provide the basis for a discussion of patterns in specific sets of sentences.

Intonation patterns can be described as neutral vs contrastive. The neutral intonation conveys no *special* meaning, just supports the semantic content of the sentence. The contrastive intonation adds something to the meaning, often an affective interpretation. We can illustrate the difference with examples:

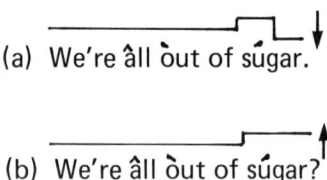

(a) We're åll òut of súgar.

(b) We're åll òut of súgar?

Sentence *(a)* is uncolored, neutral, just delivers the message that there's no more sugar. Sentence *(b)* adds to this meaning the information that the speaker is surprised, that he didn't expect the sugar to be all used up. Thus, sentence *(b)* is really a question asking the listener to confirm the unexpected information, or perhaps, if the question is not serious, merely to convey the speaker's surprise. It is not uncommon for sentences *(a)* and *(b)* to occur in sequence: speaker *(a)* makes a statement, and speaker *(b)* expresses surprise on hearing the information.

The following exercise practices these meanings. On hearing a bit of information expressed with the /231↓/ pattern, the student repeats the same utterance, using a /233↑/ pattern to express surprise or disbelief and/or disappointment.

7.4 Normal statement pattern vs surprise

Presentation and comparison of pattern; read across with two voices:

	/231↓/	/233↑/
1a.	We're all out of sugar.	Really? We're all out of sugar?
b.	We don't have any lemons.	Really? We don't have any lemons?
c.	We can't make any lemonade.	Really? We can't make any lemonade?
d.	We won't be able to have a party.	Really? We won't be able to have a party?
e.	We can't invite our friends over.	Really? We can't invite our friends over?
2a.	I got here at 7:45 this morning.	Really? You got here at 7:45 this morning?
b.	I came on my bicycle.	Really? You came on your bicycle?
c.	I rode on the sidewalk.	Really? You rode on the sidewalk?
d.	I passed hundreds of stalled cars.	Really? You passed hundreds of stalled cars?
e.	I'm going to come by bicycle every day.	Really? You're going to come by bicycle every day?
3a.	You are through for the day.	Really? I'm through for the day?
b.	You can have the rest of the day off.	Really? I can have the rest of the day off?
c.	You can leave as soon as the cash is counted.	Really? I can leave as soon as the cash is counted?
d.	You won't have to come in tomorrow.	Really? I won't have to come in tomorrow?
e.	You are being promoted to head cashier.	Really? I'm being promoted to head cashier?
4a.	He's a musician.	Oh? He's a musician?
b.	She's a football player.	Oh? She's a football player?
c.	He's a ballet dancer.	Oh? He's a ballet dancer?
d.	They're trapeze artists.	Oh? They're trapeze artists?
e.	She's a race driver.	Oh? She's a race driver?

186 Patterns of English Pronunciation

Naturally it is not intended to suggest that in real-life conversation these statements and rejoinders come in bundles. Probably only one is used at a time, but the series are offered as a means of contextualizing practice.

The next pattern is yes-no questions, or questions that can minimally be answered with a simple *yes* or *no*. The normal pattern is to use a rising final juncture, though there are exceptions (for instance, a falling intonation is common when a series of questions is asked in a formal interview). In some circumstances, and especially when the question is accompanied by appropriate vocal qualifiers (modulations of the voice) a yes-no question asked with a falling intonation will express impatience and even rudeness, associated with officious behavior. It is naturally recommended that second-language learners avoid this pattern until they can handle it in appropriate situations with confidence.

The following exercise presents yes-no questions using a normal /233↑/ pattern. These are contrasted with a /331↓/ pattern, pronounced to convey impatience or rudeness or disinterest.

7.4a Normal yes-no questions

Presentation and comparison of patterns; read across with two voices:

/233↑/   /331↓/
1. Is the plumber coming tomorrow?
2. Do you want breakfast now?
3. Would you like the red one?
4. Can you come back tomorrow?
5. Have you finished yet?

6. Will you please take a seat?
7. Do you have an appointment?
8. Can you take off your shirt?
9. Will next Tuesday be all right?
10. Can you pay your bill today?

Note that questions six and eight do not really call for a yes-no answer, but are in effect requests (in question form) for the listener to do something. The more reason to avoid a pattern that, improperly handled, may be interpreted as impatient, curt, or rude.

Information questions, those asked with a *wh*-form, normally take a falling pattern. A rising pattern may indicate worry or anxiety. The following exercise specifies that questions should be repeated, changing only the intonation pattern, for the practice of manipulating combinations of pitch-stress-juncture sequences.

7.4b Normal information questions
Presentation and comparison of patterns; read across with two voices:

/231↓/   /233↑/
1. Where did Nancy go?
2. Who went with her?
3. How long will she be gone?
4. How is she travelling?
5. When will she return?

6. What was the news today?
7. How did the stock market do?
8. Why did the World Trade Board convene?
9. When will the Security Council vote?
10. Where is the Tripartite Committee meeting?

Where the preceding two exercises are mostly cautionary, to help the student avoid being misunderstood or having his intentions misinterpreted, the next pattern is more useful—one that can be employed functionally. It is the echo question pattern, essentially asking the listener to confirm (or correct) what the speaker thinks he has heard. The echo question can query a statement, a yes-no question, or an information question. It is characterized by a pronunciation on pitch level 4, with a rising final juncture. Essentially it means: "Did you say . . . ?" In fact an echo can be requested by "What?" alone. Note the following:

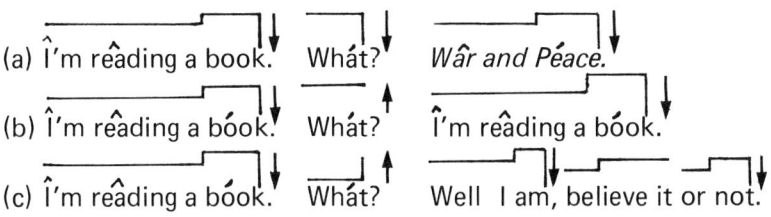

188   Patterns of English Pronunciation

The first *what* is an information question, asking the title of the book. The second *what* is an echo question, asking for a repetition of the assertion. The third, included to complete the comparison, is an expression of disbelief—"What? *You* reading something?"

Exercise 7.4c compares statements and questions with the echo-question pattern, which is typically a repetition of the basic yes-no question pattern, but shifted to a higher pitch register.

7.4c Echo questions
Presentation and comparison of pattern; read across with two voices:

/231↑/	/344↑/
1a. I'm going home now.	You're going home now? OK.
b. Lisa just came in.	Lisa just came in? Good.
c. She says they're through with the mailing.	She says they're through with the mailing? Fine.
d. We've finished the auditing.	You've finished the auditing? Excellent.
e. You're supposed to stay and lock up.	I'm supposed to stay and lock up? All right.
2a. Who's coming tomorrow?	Who's coming tomorrow? Joan is.
b. When will she be here?	When will she be here? At ten o'clock.
c. What does she want of us?	What does she want of us? Who knows.
d. Where will we see her?	Where will we see her? She'll come here.
e. Why is she coming?	Why is she coming? Search me.

/233↑/	/344↑/
3a. Is the salad ready?	Is the salad ready? Yes, it is.
b. Have you finished the carrot sticks?	Have I finished the carrot sticks? Not yet.
c. Are there enough sandwiches?	Are there enough sandwiches? I don't know; I think so.
d. Shall I pack the soda pop?	Should you pack the soda pop? Yes, would you please.
e. Is there a dessert planned?	Is there a dessert planned? Yes, chocolate cake.

The patterns presented, discussed, and practiced in the above series of exercises could be called universals, or near universals. They will be found in most languages in much the same form, with perhaps differences in details. These patterns will need little practice, perhaps none, though possibly they can be useful to illustrate pattern construction and manipulation. And there may be some languages which structure these basic patterns in significantly different ways.

But the next sets of exercises present intonation patterns that come closer to being idiosyncratic to English, patterns that are less generally utilized in a large number of the world's languages. These patterns may justify more time for practice (though, again, specific other languages may structure like English and therefore present only minor problems, or no problems). The first of these is the question which asks the listener to select between alternative answers. The pattern consists of two phrases, the first rising (or sustained on a high pitch), the second falling, which presumes that a choice is being offered, either that suggested in the first phase or the one in the second. This pattern can be contrasted with a yes-no pattern that includes an option, either of which may be chosen without forcing the choice. Note the following:

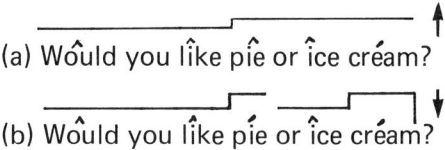

Sentence *(a)* really asks if you would like dessert and very incidentally mentions what the dessert may be. It is a yes-no question and can readily be answered "Yes, please" or "No, thank you." Sentence *(b)* asks the listener to express a choice, selecting one or the other: "I'll take ice cream please."

Drill 7.5 compares choice questions with yes-no questions of similar form.

In sentences *6-10* the phrase "more or less" is used with the meaning "reasonably well" or "approximately" with no choice implied (sentences *a*) contrasting with the meaning "in a higher/lower degree" with an alternative to be selected (sentences *b*). Not all sentences that use "more or less" can be interpreted either as a yes-no question or as a choice question, as sentences *6* and *7* can. In all cases where a choice of alternatives is being offered the listener,

7.5 Choice questions vs. yes-no questions
Presentation and comparison of pattern; answer each question with an appropriate response:

(a) /233↘/   (b) /233↘ 231↘/

1a.	Would you like pie or ice cream?	Yes, please.
b.	Would you like pie, or ice cream?	I'd like pie.
2a.	Will you have some milk or orange juice?	No, thank you.
b.	Will you have some milk, or orange juice?	Neither thanks, but I could go for a glass of cold water.
3a.	Would you care for tea or coffee?	No, thank you, nothing to drink right now.
b.	Would you care for tea, or coffee?	I'll take tea, please.
4a.	Will you be here Sunday or Monday?	Yes, early next week.
b.	Will you be here Sunday, or Monday?	Monday, early in the morning.
5a.	Can I get this book at the library or the bookstore?	Yes, there are lots of copies around.
b.	Can I get this book at the library, or the bookstore?	I'd try the bookstore; it's too new for the library to have ordered it.
6a.	Is she more or less happy?	Yes, I think she's reasonably well satisfied.
b.	Is she more, or less happy?	She's happier than she's ever been.
7a.	Is he more or less resigned to staying here?	Yes, I think he won't mind staying.
b.	Is he more, or less resigned to staying here?	He's less resigned than ever.
8a.	Doesn't he more or less handle German?	Well, yes, if the conversation's kept simple.
9a.	Is that more or less the way you saw it?	Yes, that's a pretty fair description.
10b.	Does he have more, or less money than he used to?	Oh, he has much more since investing in bonds.

the intonation will signal the choice: a rising phrase, then a falling phrase.

Another area of potential confusion for the second-language learner of English is the tag question. These are tremendously complicated grammatically, but we will assume the grammar has been mastered and will concentrate only on intonation features. Tag questions always begin with a statement, which is followed by a short phrase that queries the truth of the statement. The tag generally consists of a minimum part of the verb auxiliary, the negative particle (if the statement was affirmative), and an appropriate subject pronoun. The two main possible patterns are:

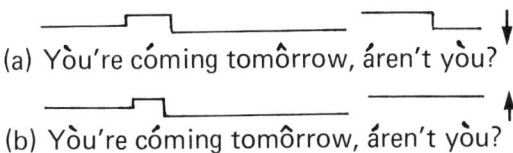

(a) You're coming tomôrrow, áren't yòu?

(b) You're coming tomôrrow, áren't yòu?

Both of these expressions lean toward the presumption of an answer that agrees with the initial statement or at least expresses a hope that it is an accurate statement. But in sentence *(a)* the presumption is very strong; it is not really a question, but an invitation for the listener to confirm what the speaker has said. A disagreeing answer would surprise the speaker of sentence *(a)*, and such an answer would probably employ contrastive pitch and stress. Sentence *(a)* is what has been called a conversation question: it doesn't ask a real question for information, but keeps the conversation moving. Sentence *(b)* is closer to a real question form, though the speaker believes, or wants to believe that the answer will be affirmative—or for purposes of courtesy wants the listener to assume that an agreeing answer will be appreciated.

An appropriate answer pattern would be as follows:

		Agreeing	*Disagreeing*
(a)	You're coming tomorrow, áren't you?	Yes, of course, I'll be here.	Oh no. I told the chief I had to be in Yuma.
(b)	You're coming tomorrow, áren't you?	Yes, I expect to be here.	No, I'm sorry but I can't.

192   Patterns of English Pronunciation

In the following exercise the stimulus will be a tag question. The response will be an agreeing or a disagreeing answer (possibly as signalled by a head shake or nod by the questioner) that is appropriate to the form of the tag used.

7.5a Tag questions and answers

Presentation and comparison of pattern; answer appropriately as indicated:

1a.	He's gonna be elected, isn't he? ↘↓	Yes, of course.	On the contrary, I think he'll lose.
b.	He's gonna be elected, isn't he? ↑	Yes, I think so.	No, I think he won't be.
2a.	John can come, can't he? ↘↓	Oh yes, he'll be here.	No, he won't be able to come this time.
b.	John can come, can't he? ↑	Yes, I believe so.	No, I don't think he can.
3a.	You've been there, haven't you? ↘↓	Oh yes, many times.	No, I've never even seen the place.
b.	You've been there, haven't you? ↑	Yes, I have.	No, not yet.
4a.	She'll make it to the party, won't she? ↘↓	Yes, she'll be there.	No, she told me she couldn't come.
b.	She'll make it to the party, won't she? ↑	Yes, I think so.	No, she has other plans.
5a.	You go there every year, don't you? ↘↓	Yes, I never miss.	Oh no. I've never been there.
b.	You go there every year, don't you? ↑	Yes, almost every year.	No, I've only been there once.

7.5a (continued)

6a.	He had already eaten, hadn't he? ↘	Oh yes.	No, he hadn't had a bite.
b.	He had already eaten, hadn't he? ↗	Yes, I think so.	No, he was on his way to dinner.
7a.	He wasn't going, was he? ↘	No, he wasn't.	Oh yes, he was going all right.
b.	He wasn't going, was he? ↗	No, I think not.	Well, I think he was.
8a.	We shouldn't wait, should we? ↘	No, by no means.	Oh, I think we better wait until she comes.
b.	We shouldn't wait, should we? ↗	No, I don't think so.	Well, maybe a little longer.
9a.	He doesn't want the job, does he? ↘	No, he certainly doesn't.	Yes. He'll take *any* job.
b.	He doesn't want the job, does he? ↗	I think he doesn't.	He *might* be willing to take it.
10a.	You're not hungry, are you? ↘	No, I just ate.	Indeed I am. I'm starved.
b.	You're not hungry, are you? ↗	No, I'm not.	Well, I could take a bite.

In the correct and effective use of tag questions a great deal depends on the communication context (what the real circumstances and facts are) and on the oral interpretation given the suggested answers. The exercise above will be successful only if the speakers ask and answer these questions with a feel for what has been called the "context of situation."

There are many contrasts that are expressed by intonation patterns. We can't hope to illustrate all of them. One for illustrative purposes is presented in exercise 7.5b.

7.5b Contrastive tags

Presentation and comparison of pattern; repeat and complete the following sentences with the two words "did too":

1a. He said he'd come early, and they .... He said he'd come early, and thêy díd tóo.
 b. He said he'd come early, and he .... He said he'd come early, and he díd, tóo.

2a. She wanted to go to the party, and he .... She wanted to go to the party, and he did too.
 b. She wanted to go to the party, and she .... She wanted to go to the party, and she did, too.

3a. They planned to visit Laguna, and you .... They planned to visit Laguna, and you did too.
 b. They planned to visit Laguna, and they .... They planned to visit Laguna, and they did, too.

4a. He felt he had to mow the lawn, and I .... He felt he had to mow the lawn, and I did too.
 b. He felt he had to mow the lawn, and he .... He felt he had to mow the lawn, and he did, too.

5a. I hoped I'd get to help her, and he .... I hoped I'd get to help her, and he did too.
 b. I hoped I'd get to help her, and I .... I hoped I'd get to help her, and I did, too.

The selection of the pattern on which to pronounce "did too" is cued by the second pronoun. If the second pronoun is different from the first, it is in contrast and is therefore stressed. If the second pronoun repeats the first, the contrast (and the main stress) falls on the pro-verb *did. Too* is stressed in both patterns.

Another pattern characteristic of English that differs in many other languages is the intonation of vocatives, particularly those that occur at the end of a sentence. The typical polite vocative may be pronounced on low or mid pitch or, after a yes-no question, on high pitch (less frequently on overhigh), but whatever the level of pitch, the polite vocative has a rising final juncture. In fact the use of a falling juncture on a vocative signals social distance or even curtness or annoyance. Note the following "polite" vocatives:

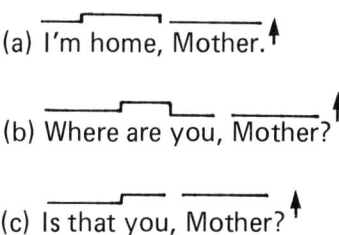

If one enquires about the content of the main meal of the day, the courteous, considerate way to do so is shown in sentence *(d)*. Sentence *(e)* will likely be interpreted as lack of respect to Mother as a person or as a cook.

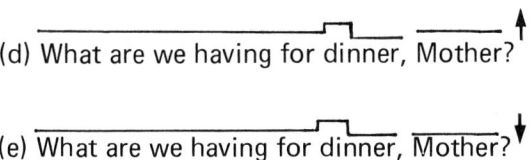

The following exercise offers practice with vocatives. The stimulus sentence uses a falling pattern (connoting annoyance, superior status, haughtiness) which should be changed in the response sentence by a rising pattern (indicating friendliness, respect, courtesy).

7.5c Intonation for vocatives

Presentation and comparison of pattern; read across with two voices:

/111↓/	/111↑/ or /222↑/ or /333↑/
1. Come in, Miss Johnson.	
2. Have a cookie, Mrs. Brown.	
3. Are you coming, Mary?	
4. Have you finished, Marilyn?	
5. What are you doing, Kenneth?	
6. Where are your shoes, Christina?	
7. I have your pencil, Annabelle.	
8. Here's your lemonade, Freddie.	

Sometimes the /111↓/ vocative is appropriate. It is one normal way to show disapproval to a misbehaving child (Don't do that, Johnny); it is the correct way to address a military superior (Yes, sir); it is a quite normal way to respond in very formal situations, such as the meeting of the board of directors (May we have your report now, Mr. Perkins). But all of these circumstances are unlikely in the lives of typical second-language students, who will have more use for forms connoting warmth and courtesy. In any case, students should be aware of the meanings of the forms they use.

One final pattern characteristic of English is associated with informal greetings and leavetakings. These are important in that they set or summarize the tone of a conversational exchange, and an inappropriate intonation can undo the good intentions of a well-meaning participant. Exercise 7.5d is intended to display a few

---

7.6 Two-word verbs

Presentation of pattern; repeat the following pairs of sentences:

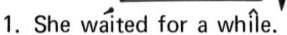

1. She waited for a while.	She waited for the light.
2. He sat for a while.	He sat for a picture.
3. He listened for a minute.	He listened for an airplane.
4. He looked for a few minutes.	He looked for an exit.
5. He read for an hour.	He read for a living.
6. He ran for a spell.	He ran for an office.
7. He rang for a second.	He rang for a bellboy.
8. He hoped for a while.	He hoped for an answer.
9. He worked for a time.	He worked for a promotion.
10. He wrote for an hour.	He wrote for an application.

greetings, phatic phrases, and leavetakings for student repetition and practice.

7.5d Greetings and leavetakings

Presentation of pattern; repeat the following forms as you interpret or hear them:

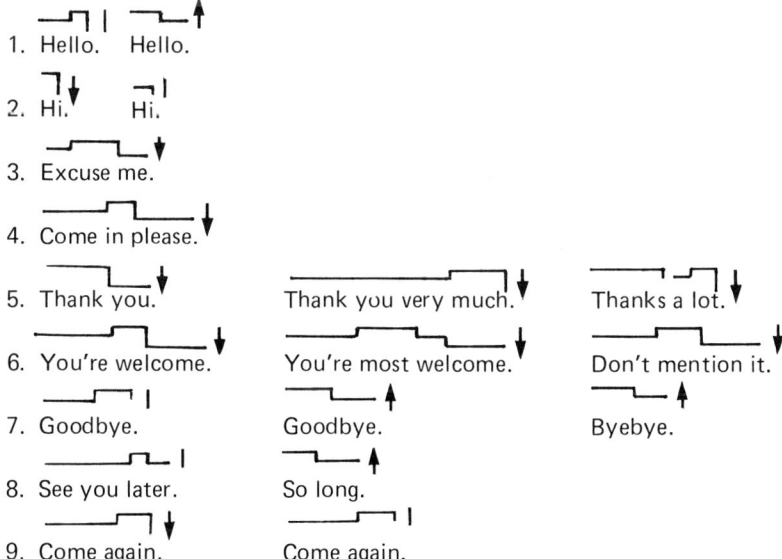

Finally, exercise 7.6 involves an intonation pattern associated with two-word verbs. The expressions (verb plus particle) can be interpreted as a two-word verb (followed by a direct object) or as a verb plus a preposition (followed by an object of the preposition).

7.6 (continued)

11. He looked up the street.   He looked up the word.
12. He glanced over the wall.   He glanced over the project.
13. He sent down the street.   He sent down the orders.
14. He wrote in the office.   He wrote in the answers.
15. He turned off the highway.   He turned off the lights.
16. He passed by the window.   He passed by the opportunity.
17. He checked over the weekend.   He checked over the inventory.
18. He turned on a dime.   He turned on the radio.
19. He pitched in the evening.   He pitched in his contribution.
20. He passed on Saturday.   He passed on the news.

The two-word verb pattern is very extensive in English. It is probably the most active derivational process in English, one that daily creates new forms. Not all can be conveniently matched with verbs taking prepositional phrases to produce potentially ambiguous pairs like those cited above, but the alert student will be aware of the possibility of more than one interpretation and will listen for the phrase breaks that help identify constituents in a construction.

These then are some of the details of intonational features and patterns that are to be found in English. The list is by no means exhaustive, but the patterns presented can serve as examples for the student, to sensitize him to the kinds of phenomena that pattern together to produce (or perhaps more often to support or contribute to) the total range of linguistic data used for human communication.

Chapter 8
CONSTRUCTS OF ENGLISH VOWELS AND CONSONANTS

In this text suprasegmental (or intonational) features have been treated apart from segmental (or sequential) features, with a separate chapter on intonational phenomena in each of the three cycles (Chapters 1, 4, 7). Additionally, in the first two cycles, the segmental features have been separately treated as vowels (Chapters 2, 5) and consonants (Chapters 3, 6). In dealing with segmental features it has occasionally been difficult to consistently and meaningfully differentiate between vowels and consonants, to assign a phenomenon to one category or the other, for example to treat contraction as affecting vowels or consonants, since typically it involves both. In this third cycle it seems justified to treat vowels and consonants together, which is done in the present chapter.

The first topic for discussion is vowel reduction, which was introduced earlier when treating vowel reductions associated with weak stress (Chapter 5), where a separate *system* of vowels was shown to operate under weak stress. Since English morphological patterns often shift the location of strong stress, sometimes with assignments to one syllable (or set of syllables), sometimes to another (or others), the realized values of English vowels may change. This is best illustrated by examples. The following examples will be cited in conventional spelling for reasons that should become clear. The English word *graph* can be combined with the prefix *tele-* to form *telegraph.* Three suffixes are possible, *-y, -er,* or *-ic,* giving *telegraphy, telegrapher, telegraphic.* (Other suffixes can be added on to *-ic,* to produce *telegraphical, telegraphically,* etc., and still further forms are possible.) Since these forms are related in meaning, they obviously belong to a semantic set, a fact that is conveniently shown and usefully recognized by common spellings, especially of the elements *graph* and *tele-.* But the pronunciation of vowels in these syllables varies, depending on which syllables are assigned weak and strong stress. Note the following:

tĕləgræ̀f təlĕgrəfiy tĕləgræ̀fɪk   telegraph telegraphy telegraphic

We observe *tele-* is pronounced /tɛ́lə-/ or /təlɛ́-/ and *-graph* is pronounced /-græf-/ or /-grəf-/, which suggests (1) that the conventional spellings represent meaning relationship more consistently than do pronunciations and (2) that strong-stressed syllables are pronounced with full vowels (from the stressed vowel system) while weak-stressed syllables are pronounced with reduced vowels (from the weak-stressed vowel system).

Native speakers of English of course have these vowel alternations built into their reflexes, so the conventional spelling representations seem normal. In fact the pronunciation variations are felt to be so normal that it would come as a surprise to many English speakers to learn that the pronunciation alternations even exist. But of course the pronunciations do not come naturally and normally to second-language speakers of English, since their first language doesn't have these built-in systems of alternation; they have to learn each word separately until with increased exposure and familiarity they gradually assimilate the patterns (that is, until they gain fluency in the underlying systems of English). This suggests that conventional spelling—with all its supposed shortcomings, inconsistencies, and limitations—is most appropriate as a representation of English for native speakers (and for second-language speakers who have achieved a "systematic" control of the language), while the more accurate phonetic transcription is more helpful to students who have not formed English habits and still need guidance on the pronunciation of individual words and syllables.

The present chapter will serve to illustrate how English spelling closely represents the underlying forms of English, which are then interpreted by speakers who have achieved competence in the system of "phonological representation" by having mastered the rules of interpretation. The rule presently illustrated specifies that vowels under weak stress are reduced, and that the weak-stressed vowel that typically appears is schwa.

The exercise that follows is designed to show alternations that correlate with stress. It can be used as a repetition drill, to familiarize students with forms that illustrate vowel alternations, or as a transformation drill, where a form in one pattern is used to cue a related form in the other pattern, or as a reading interpretation exercise, to provide practice in interpreting sounds from writing symbols (which implies mastery of the rules of underlying representations).

8.1 Vowel reductions correlated with stress—1
Presentation and comparison of pattern; read across:

1a.	télǝgrǽf	tǝlégrǝfiy	telegraph	telegraphy
b.	fówtǝgrǽf	fǝtágrǝfiy	photograph	photography
c.	líthǝgrǽf	lǝthágrǝfiy	lithograph	lithography
d.	sténǝgrǽf	stǝnágrǝfiy	stenograph	stenography
e.	épǝgrǽf	ǝpígrǝfiy	epigraph	epigraphy
f.	sérǝgrǽf	sǝrígrǝfiy	serigraph	serigraphy
g.	tǽkǝgrǽf	tǝkígrǝfiy	tachygraph	tachygraphy
2a.	kóriyǝgrǽf	kòriy.ágrǝfiy	choreograph	choreography
b.	ídiyǝgrǽf	ìdiyágrǝfiy	ideograph	ideography
c.	kárdiyǝgrǽf	kàrdiyágrǝfiy	cardiograph	cardiography
d.	híyliyǝgrǽf	hìyliyágrǝfiy	heliograph	heliography
3a.	sáyzmǝgrǽf	sàyzmágrǝfiy	seismograph	seismography
b.	lówgǝgrǽf	lòwgágrǝfiy	logograph	logography
c.	ótǝgrǽf	òtógrǝfiy	autograph	autography
d.	pǽntǝgrǽf	pæ̀ntógrǝfiy	pantograph	pantography

Three patterns are illustrated above, with different patterns of syllable sequence and syllable structure. In each the pronunciation can be predicted (even if one is not sure of the meanings). They have in common a stress on the stem -*graph* which is shifted to the next syllable earlier when -*y* is added to -*graph-* to form -*graphy.* The examples in the first set alternate stress on the prefix, while in the second and third sets the stress on the first syllable is retained. The second set shows an extra syllable enabling the -*graphy-* form to maintain a pattern of alternating strong and weak stressed syllables not present in the third set.

Exercise *8.1* (and others in this chapter) illustrate the "morphophonemic" type of spelling system characteristic of English, where a set of related forms will be similarly spelled, even when there are changes in the pronunciation of these forms. In other words English does *not* have a strict one-sound-one-symbol (or "phonemic") spelling system; a morphophonemic system is more relevantly related to meaning than to pronunciation. The phonemic transcription, included in this book and other specialized books, (including many dictionaries) as a help or guide to pronunciation, is useful mainly to second-language students, and to native speakers when they encounter a totally unfamiliar word or a completely anomalous form.

There are numerous words similar to those in the exercise above that do not occur in pairs. Knowing the pattern illustrated, it is possible to predict with comfortable confidence how these words will be stressed and pronounced. Try the following: *paragraph, phonograph, dictograph, monograph, multigraph, mimeograph* and *biography, bibliography, orthography, geography, ethnography, lexicography,* and many others. Knowing how the rule for alternation works allows a consistent production of a new form, as illustrated in the following humorously intended exchange: "Have you got any pornography in this store? — Goodness no. I haven't even got a pornograph." An understanding of how the patterns work also helps us to understand and orally interpret more complex forms, such as *telephotography, biobibliography,* or *electrocardiographic.*

The following exercise illustrates another "morphophonemic" alternation, related to the preceding patterns, that is very common to English. Again it can be used in various ways, for repetition, transformation, or interpretation.

8.1a Vowel reductions correlated with stress—2
Presentation and comparison of pattern; read across:

1a.	təlégrəfiy	tèləgrǽfək(əl)	telegraphy	telegraphic(al)
b.	stənágrəfiy	stènəgrǽfək(əl)	stenography	stenographic(al)
c.	fətágrəfiy	fòwtəgrǽfək(əl)	photography	photographic(al)
d.	krənágrəfiy	krànəgrǽfək(əl)	chronography	chronographic(al)
e.	kəlígrəfiy	kæ̀ləgrǽfək(əl)	calligraphy	calligraphic(al)
2a.	bàyágrəfiy	bàyəgrǽfək(əl)	biography	biographic(al)
b.	ɔ̀rthágrəfiy	ɔ̀rthəgrǽfək(əl)	orthography	orthographic(al)
c.	jìyágrəfiy	jìyəgrǽfək(əl)	geography	geographic(al)
d.	tàypágrəfiy	tàypəgrǽfək(əl)	typography	typographic(al)
e.	kàrtágrəfiy	kàrtəgrǽfək(əl)	cartography	cartographic(al)
f.	krìptágrəfiy	krìptəgrǽfək(əl)	cryptography	cryptographic(al)
g.	rèydiyágrəfiy	rèydiyəgrǽfək(əl)	radiography	radiographic(al)
h.	bìbliyágrəfiy	bìbliyəgrǽfək(əl)	bibliography	bibliographic(al)
i.	kàzmágrəfiy	kàzməgrǽfək(əl)	cosmography	cosmographic(al)

Constructs of English Vowels and Consonants 203

There are other patterns of related words in English which illustrate patterns of vowel reduction (morphophonemic alternations) correlated with the location of the stressed syllable. A pattern with very extensive membership is shown below.

8.1b Vowel reductions correlated with stress—3
Presentation and comparison of pattern; read across:

1a.	éybəl	əbílətiy	able	ability
b.	stéybəl	stəbílətiy	stable	stability
c.	fǽsəl	fəsílətiy	facile	facility
d.	ǽjəl	əjílətiy	agile	agility
e.	frǽjəl	frəjílətiy	fragile	fragility
f.	stérəl	stərílətiy	sterile	sterility
g.	vírəl	vərílətiy	virile	virility
h.	sívəl	səvílətiy	civil	civility
i.	pyúrəl	pyərílətiy	puerile	puerility
j.	fə́rtəl	fərtílətiy	fertile	fertility
k.	də́ktəl	dəktílətiy	ductile	ductility
2a.	mówbəl	mowbílətiy	mobile	mobility
b.	nówbəl	nowbílətiy	noble	nobility
c.	dɑ́səl	dɑwsílətiy	docile	docility
d.	hɑ́stəl	hɑstílətiy	hostile	hostility
e.	fyúwtəl	fyùwtílətiy	futile	futility
f.	tǽktəl	tæktílətiy	tactile	tactility
g.	núwbəl	nùwbílətiy	nubile	nubility
3a.	sìynáyl	sənílətiy	senile	senility
b.	sə̀rváyl	sərvílətiy	servile	servility
c.	jɛ̀ntíyl	jɛntílətiy	genteel	gentility

A similar pattern occurs with words that end in the suffix -al, which is /-əl/ under weak stress, but becomes /-æl-/ when strong-stressed.

8.1c Vowel reductions correlated with stress—4
Presentation and comparison of pattern; read across:

1a. plŭrəl	plərǽlətiy	plural	plurality
b. fáynəl	fənǽlətiy	final	finality
c. mɔ́rəl	mərǽlətiy	moral	morality
d. lŏwkəl	lowkǽlətiy	local	locality
e. lĭygəl	liygǽlətiy	legal	legality
f. rĭyəl	riyǽlətiy	real	reality
g. frŭwgəl	fruwgǽlətiy	frugal	frugality
h. mŏwdəl	mowdǽlətiy	modal	modality
i. tŏwtəl	towtǽlətiy	total	totality
2a. vàytəl	vàytǽlətiy	vital	vitality
b. fèytəl	fèytǽlətiy	fatal	fatality
c. nèyzəl	nèyzǽlətiy	nasal	nasality
d. pàrshəl	pàrshǽlətiy	partial	partiality
e. kɔ̀rjəl	kɔ̀rjǽlətiy	cordial	cordiality
3a. nǽshənəl	nǽshənǽlətiy	national	nationality
b. ǽkchəwəl	ǽkchəwǽlətiy	actual	actuality
c. tɑ́pəkəl	tɑ́pəkǽlətiy	topical	topicality
d. lɑ́jəkəl	lɑ́jəkǽlətiy	logical	logicality
e. mĭthəkəl	mĭthəkǽlətiy	mythical	mythicality
f. jŏwviyəl	jŏwviyǽlətiy	jovial	joviality

There's not much reason to separate items *1* from items *2* above, only that the first group changes the strong-stressed vowel that may also occur under weak stress. The second group clearly maintains a strong-stressed vowel, which presumes at least medial stress in the first syllable of the second column. The third group conspicuously maintains the strong-stressed vowel in the first column, which is converted to a medial stress in the second column. It is easier to preserve the original stress pattern when a weak-stressed syllable occurs between the two stressed syllables as in the third group of items, producing the typical alternating rhythm of English.

The preceding exercises illustrate stress alternations in English, where vowels are reduced, usually to schwa, when the location of the strong stress changes. The next section presents another type of vowel alternation in English, where stress is not the conditioning factor associated with the change.

Anyone who has studied English following traditional patterns of instruction, where vowel sounds are presumed to be the consequences of pronouncing vowel letters, is aware of a set of correlations usually referred to as short vowels and long vowels. Virtually all English dictionaries accept this convention in marking pronunciations for their entries. (They do indeed "show" the pronunciation of traditional spellings, with diacritical marks and rules to guide the student from written forms to oral interpretation.)

We spent considerable time in Chapters 6 and 7 demonstrating that vowel length is a complex function of syllable structure, stress, and rhythm—which conclusively contradicts the dictionary tradition that vowel length is a function of the vowels themselves, that somehow some vowels are "long" and others are "short." We are now ready to show that while the terminology of short and long may be badly chosen and misleading, the correlations which the dictionary classification makes (which indeed reflect the conventions of the English writing system) are a valid and very useful explanation of vowel alternation in English.

These correlations are listed below, using the breve and macron diacritics of the dictionary with the letters of English. The sounds are illustrated by key words:

ā	ă	hate	hat	heyt	hæt	ey	æ
ē	ĕ	Pete	pet	piyt	pɛt	iy	ɛ
ī	ĭ	kite	kit	kayt	kɪt	ay	ɪ
ō	ŏ	note	not	nowt	nɑt	ow	ɑ
ū	ŭ	jute	jut	juwt	jət	uw	ə

This at first glance seems to be a strange set of correlations, matching a selection of diphthongs against a selection of simple vowels. Furthermore, four are left out, /aw, oy, ɔ, U/, which have to be represented by the same five vowels of the writing system, or by combinations of these vowels. But the correlations are very important to English, as we shall presently see. But first, let's take a look at the correlations as they occur on the standard vowel grid.

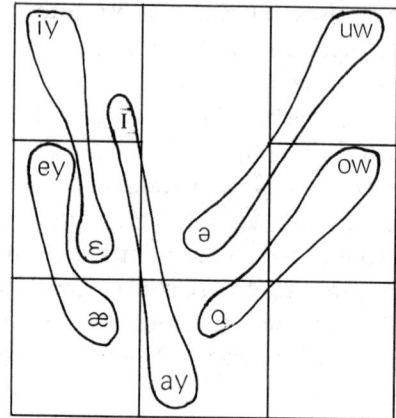

This is a very interesting pattern, which can be explained by the history of the development of the English language, representing relationships that have been present in the language for many hundreds of years. We note that in all cases a simple vowel is in correspondence with a diphthong; in most cases the relationship is between adjacent boxes. The missing vowels and diphthongs are in a sense peripheral to English—low frequency of occurrence, absence in some dialects of English, unusual in combining a back vowel with a front glide, etc. What is displayed by the correlations is clearly the heart of the English vowel system.

It is well to remember that the vowel alternations in the exercises that follow differ from those that precede by not being directly correlated with a shift in stress. Rather the alternations correspond to different sets of suffixes, with no change of stress. Note the following:

ā	ă	grade	gradual	greyd	grǽjəwəl	ey	æ
ē	ĕ	meter	metrical	mīytər	mɛ́trəkəl	iy	ɛ
ī	ĭ	mine	mineral	mayn	mínərəl	ay	I
ō	ŏ	cone	conical	kown	kɑ́nəkəl	ow	ɑ
ū	ŭ	duke	duchess	duwk	də́chəs	uw	ə

The exercises which follow will present lexical items in pairs or groups which illustrate the vowel alternations listed above. These exercises, like the set presented earlier in this chapter, can be used for repetition, transformation, pattern elicitation, or oral interpretation. They offer experience for familiarization that will facilitate for the advanced student the handling of this morphophonemic pattern of vowel alternation, applied to stressed vowels.

8.2 Vowel alternation in stressed syllables—/ey ~ æ/

Presentation and comparison of pattern; read down within an item, then across and down within the same item:

	/ey/	/æ/		
1.	gréyd	grǽjəwəl	grade	gradual
	gréydiyənt	grǽjəwèyt	gradient	graduate
		grǽjəwéyshən		graduation
2.	seyn	sǽnətiy	sane	sanity
	séynnəs	sǽnətὲriy	saneness	sanitary
		sænətɔ́riyəm		sanitorium
		sænətéyshən		sanitation
3.	prowféyn	prowfǽnətiy	profane	profanity
	prowféynər	prowfǽnətɔ̀riy	profaner	profanatory
4.	gréytfəl	grǽtətùwd	grateful	gratitude
	gréytfəliy	grǽtəfày	gratefully	gratify
	gréytfəlnəs	grǽtəfəkéyshən	gratefulness	gratification
5.	seyt	sǽtəsfày	sate	satisfy
	séyshiyèyt	sǽtəsfǽktəriy	satiate	satisfactory
	séyshəbəl	sǽtəsfǽkshən	satiable	satisfaction
6.	ərbéyn	ərbǽnətiy	urbane	urbanity
7.	méyjər	mǽjəstiy	major	majesty
	mèyjərὲt		majorette	
8.	peyl	pǽləd	pale	pallid
	péylnəs	pǽlər	paleness	pallor
	péylfèys		paleface	
9.	veyl	vǽliy	vale	valley
10.	kɑ́leyt	kəlǽtərəl	collate	collateral
	kəléyshən	lǽtərəl	collation	lateral

8.2a Vowel alternation in stressed syllables—/iy ~ ɛ/

Presentation and comparison of pattern; read down and within an item, then across and down:

/iy/	/ɛ/		
1. míytər míytərɪj	mɛ́trəkəl mɛ́trɪks	meter meterage	metrical metrics
2. səríyn	sərɛ́nətiy	serene	serenity
3. səpríym səpríymliy	səprɛ́məsiy	supreme supremely	supremacy
4. əpíyl əpíyləbəl riypíyl	əpɛ́lət əpɛ́lənt əpɛ́lətəv	appeal appealable repeal	appellate appellant appellative
5. riypíyt riypíytər	rəpɛ́tətəv rəpɛ́tətəvliy	repeat repeater	repetitive repetitively
6. səksíyd səksíydər səksíydɪŋ	səksɛ́s səksɛ́shən səksɛ́sfəl səksɛ́sər	succeed succeeder succeeding	success succession successful successor
7. riysíyd riysíydɪŋ	riysɛ́shən riysɛ́səv riysɛ́shənəl	recede receding	recession recessive recessional
8. hàyjíyn	hàyjɛ́nək hàyjɛ́nəks	hygiene	hygienic hygienics
9. àbsíyn àbsíynliy	àbsɛ́nətiy	obscene obscenely	obscenity
10. dəskríyt dəskríytliy	dəskrɛ́shən dəskrɛ́shənəl dəskrɛ́shənɛ̀riy	discreet discreetly	discretion discretional discretionar

8.2b Vowel alternation in stressed syllables—/ay ~ ɪ/
Presentation and comparison of pattern; read down within an item, then across and down again:

/ay/	/ɪ/		
1. mayn	mínərəl	mine	mineral
máynər	mínərəlàyz	miner	mineralize
	mìnərálǝgiy		mineralogy
2. dəváyn	dəvínətiy	divine	divinity
dəváynliy	dəvínətòriy	divinely	divinatory
dəváynər		diviner	
3. sǽtàyr	sətírək	satire	satiric
	sətírəkəl		satirical
4. dəráyv	dərívətəv	derive	derivative
dəráyvəbəl	dərívətəvliy	derivable	derivatively
5. layn	líniyər	line	linear
láynɪŋ	línɪj	lining	lineage
láynər	líniyəl	liner	lineal
láynmən	dəlíniyèyt	lineman	delineate
6. rɛ̀kənsàyl	kənsìliyéyshən	reconcile	conciliation
rɛ̀kənsáylmənt	kənsíliyətòriy	reconcilement	conciliatory
rɛ̀kənsáyləbəl	rɛ̀kənsìliyéyshən	reconcilable	reconciliation
7. wayld	wíldərnəs	wild	wilderness
wáyldkæ̀t	biywíldər	wildcat	bewilder
8. sáykəl	síkləkəl	cycle	cyclical
sáyklək	báysíkəl	cyclic	bicycle
sáykləst	tráysɪkəl	cyclist	tricycle
sáykləstàyl		cyclostyle	
9. dəsáyd	dəsízhən	decide	decision
dəsáydɪŋ		deciding	
dəsáysəv		decisive	
10. táytəl	tíchələr	title	titular
táytəld	tíchəlèriy	titled	titulary
	tíchələrliy		titularly

8.2c Vowel alternation in stressed syllables—/ow ~ a/

Presentation and comparison of pattern; read down within an item, then across and down again:

	/ow/	/a/		
1.	kówn	kánək	cone	conic
	kównɪng	kánəkəl	coning	conical
	nówzkòwn	kánəfər	nose cone	conifer
2.	vərbóws	vərbásətiy	verbose	verbosity
	vərbówsliy		verbosely	
3.	hàrmówniyəs	hàrmánək	harmonious	harmonic
	hàrmówniyəsliy	hàrmánəks	harmoniously	harmonics
	hàrmówniyəm	hàrmánəkə	harmonium	harmonica
		hàrmánəkən		harmonican
4.	sówl	sáləs	sole	solace
	sówlliy	sálətùwd	solely	solitude
		sálətɛ̀r		solitaire
		sálətɛ̀riy		solitary
5.	vówkəl	vákətəv	vocal	vocative
	iyvówk	iyvákətəv	evoke	evocative
	riyvówk	prəvákətəv	revoke	provocative
	pròwvówk		provoke	
	vòwsífərəs		vociferous	
	vòwkéyshən		vocation	
6.	prówtɛ̀st	prátəstənt	protest	protestant
		pràtəstéyshən		protestation
7.	jowk	jákyələr	joke	jocular
	jówkər	jàkyəlérətiy	joker	jocularity
	jówkɪngliy		jokingly	
	jòwkóws		jocose	
8.	kowd	kádəfày	code	codify
	kówdɛ̀ks	kádəfàyər	codex	codifier
	kówdəsìyz	kàdəfəkéyshən	codices	codification
	diykówd	kádəsəl	decode	codicil

Constructs of English Vowels and Consonants 211

8.2c (continued)

	/ow/	/ɑ/		
9.	town	tɑ́nək	tone	tonic
	tównəl	dàyətɑ́nək	tonal	diatonic
	tównləs		toneless	
10.	fown	fɑ́nək	phone	phonic
	tɛ̀ləfówn	tɛ̀ləfɑ́nək	telephone	telephonic
	fównìym	fɑ́nəks	phoneme	phonics
	fównəgræ̀m		phonogram	
	fównəlɑ̀jəkəl		phonological	

8.2d Vowel alternation in stressed syllables—/uw ~ ə/

Presentation and comparison of pattern; read down within an item, then across and down again:

	/uw/	/ə/		
1.	duwk	də́chəs	duke	duchess
	dúwkdəm	də́chiy	dukedom	duchy
2.	kənsúwm	kənsə́mpshən	consume	consumption
	kənsúwmər	kənsə́mptəv	consumer	consumptive
		kənsə́mptəvnəs		consumptiveness
3.	riyzúwm	riyzə́mpshən	resume	resumption
	riyzúwməbəl		resumable	
4.	əjúwdəkèyt	jəj	adjudicate	judge
	júwdəkəbəl	jə́jmənt	judicable	judgment
	júwdəkətəv	jə́jmǽtɪk	judicative	judgmatic
	júwdəkèytər	jə́jshɪ̀p	judicator	judgeship
	júwdəkətɔ̀riy		judicatory	
	júwdəkəchər		judicature	
5.	pyúwnətəv	pə́nɪsh	punitive	punish
	pyúwnətəvliy	pə́nɪshmənt	punitively	punishment
	pyúwnətɔ̀riy	pə́nɪshəbəl	punitory	punishable

8.2d (continued)

/uw/	/ə/		
6. kúwkùw	kə́kəld	cuckoo	cuckold
	kə́kəldriy		cuckoldry
7. núwmərəl	nə́mbər	numeral	number
núwmərəs	nə́mbərləs	numerous	numberless
núwmərèyt		numerate	
núwmərèytər		numerator	
nùwmərèyshən		numeration	
8. əsúwm	əsə́mpshən	assume	assumption
əsúwməbəl	əsə́mptəv	assumable	assumptive
	əsə́mpsət		assumpsit
9. priyzúwm	priyzə́mpshən	presume	presumption
priyzúwmər	priyzə́mptəv	presumer	presumptive
priyzúwməbəl	priyzə́mpchəwəs	presumable	presumptuous
priyzúwmədliy		presumedly	
10. prowdúws	prowdə́kshən	produce	production
riydúws	riydə́kshən	reduce	reduction
siydúws	siydə́kshən	seduce	seduction
ɪndúws	ɪndə́kshən	induce	induction
diydúws	diydə́kshən	deduce	deduction
kəndúwsəv	kəndə́kshən	conducive	conduction

A few generalizations about the distribution of this pattern are possible. Assuming a diphthong in the base form, certain suffixes usually do not cause a shift: *-ing, -er, -less, -ness, -able, -ment, -ive.* Others usually accompany a shift: *-ity, -ify, -itude, -tion, -eral, -ative, -ical, -id, -ish.* Many of this latter group are two syllables, of which the first (and sometimes the second also) is weak-stressed. It is interesting to note that this typical multisyllabic unstressed ending lends support to the dictionary terminology that specifies a "long vowel" in *sane, profane,* but a "short vowel" in *sanity, profanity,* though as we have seen (Chapter 7) this is a question of metrics, supported by examples like *aim, am* (both long in duration) and *claimable, crammable* (both shorter in duration).

The vowel alternations shown in the above exercises are very common in English. Many irregular verbs follow the /iy - ɛ/ alternation *(feed-fed, keep-kept,* etc.) and the /ay - ɪ/ *(bite-bit, ride-ridden,* etc.). Other pairs that illustrate these alternations are *do-does* for /uw - ə/, and *bathe-bath* for /ey - æ/. There are other examples. Sometimes the same word may have variant pronunciations reflecting the pairs, such as *economics* /iykənámɪks ~ ɛkənámɪks/, *rations* /réyshənz ~ ræshənz/, *deluxe* /dəlúwks ~ dəláks/, etc. There are other alternations in English, of course, many of them. One that seems worth calling attention to is /aw - ə/, limited to a selection of forms ending in *-ounce* and *-ound.*

8.2e Vowel alternation in stressed syllables—/aw ~ ə/
Presentation and comparison of pattern; read down within an item, then across and down again:

	/aw/	/ə/		
1.	prənáwnts	prənə́nsiyéyshən	pronounce	pronunciation
	iynáwnts	iynə́nsiyéyshən	enounce	enunciation
	ənáwnts	ənə́nsiyéyshən	announce	annunciation
	riynáwnts	riynə́nsiyéyshən	renounce	renunciation
	diynáwnts	diynə́nsiyéyshən	denounce	denunciation
2.	əbáwnd	əbə́ndənt	abound	abundant
	riydáwnd	riydə́ndənt	redound	redundant
	prowfáwnd	prowfə́ndətiy	profound	profundity

Exercises of this kind, illustrating the typical, common alternations of the language, provide an opportunity of familiarization and help students to learn the distributions of vowel variations, thus raising confidence in their ability to use and interpret English. These alternations, like most derivational patterns, can be only partially predicted—thus familiarity rather than total mastery is a legitimate pedagogical aim.

One other comment seems worth offering, that patterns of vowel reduction (obscuring vowels in weak-stressed syllables) and patterns of vowel alternation (variation of vowels in strong-stressed syllables) often occur in sets of related forms. An extremely large number of examples could be cited, but for our present purposes an illustration will suffice to call attention to the very common interaction of these patterns: *major - majesty - majestic* (/éy ~ ǽ ~ ə̆/, *satire - satirical - satirist* (/áy ~ í ~ ə̆/).

There are alternation patterns in English for consonants as well as for vowels. Some of the regular patterns have been presented (Chapter 6) in the discussion of palatal assimilations (/s ~ sh - z ~ zh - t ~ ch - d ~ j/). There are a number of others, of which only a small sample is offered here, with no attempt at exhaustive explanation.

The first pattern is the alternation of the final /k/ on the suffix /-ɪk/ with an /s/ before the suffix /-ətiy/. Both /-ɪk/ and /-ɪtiy/ are very active suffixes, so this alternation can be seen in hundreds of words, with new ones frequently added as technical terms are developed. The following exercise starts with very simple terms and proceeds to more complex examples.

8.3 Consonant alternations—/k ~ s/
Presentation and comparison of pattern; read across:

	/-k/	/-s-/		
1a;	pə́blɪk	pəblɪ́sətiy	public	publicity
b.	éthnɪk	èthnɪ́sətiy	ethnic	ethnicity
c.	tɑ́ksɪk	tɑ̀ksɪ́sətiy	toxic	toxicity
d.	rə́stɪk	rə̀stɪ́sətiy	rustic	rusticity
e.	séntrɪk	sèntrɪ́sətiy	centric	centricity
f.	plǽstɪk	plæ̀stɪ́sətiy	plastic	plasticity
2a.	əléktrɪk	əlèktrɪ́sətiy	electric	electricity
b.	əlǽstɪk	əlæ̀stɪ́sətiy	elastic	elasticity
c.	dəméstɪk	dɔ̀wmestɪ́sətiy	domestic	domesticity
d.	həstɔ́rɪk	hìstərɪ́sətiy	historic	historicity
e.	ɔthéntɪk	ɔ̀thəntɪ́sətiy	authentic	authenticity
f.	səlǽbɪk	sìləbɪ́sətiy	syllablic	syllabicity
g.	spəsɪ́fɪk	spèsəfɪ́sətiy	specific	specificity
h.	əkséntrɪk	èksəntrɪ́sətiy	eccentric	eccentricity
3a.	pìriyɑ́dɪk	pìriyədɪ́sətiy	periodic	periodicity
b.	ɔtəmǽtɪk	ɔ̀təmətɪ́sətiy	automatic	automaticity
c.	èpədémɪk	èpədəmɪ́sətiy	epidemic	epidemicity
d.	hàydrəskɑ́pɪk	hàydrəskəpɪ́sətiy	hydroscopic	hydroscopicity

This list could be greatly expanded, and other similar lists could be added, illustrated by such pairs as /médɪk ~ médəsən - krítɪk ~

krítəsìzəm - ɪndə́kshən ~ ɪndúws/ *(medic - medicine, critic - criticism, induction - induce)*, etc. It is instructive to note that the spelling rules of English are often described using the terms "hard *c*" and "soft *c*," another way of saying /k/ and /s/, both sounds frequently represented by the letter *c*.

Another frequent alternation is between /s/ and /z/. The following drill illustrates several patterns of related words, one with /s/ and the other with /z/.

8.3a Consonant alternations—/s ~ z/
    Presentation and comparison of pattern; read down within an item, then across and down:

	/s/	/z/		
1a.	əsíst	riyzíst	assist	resist
	kənsíst		consist	
	pərsíst		persist	(persist)
b.	əsémbəl	riyzémbəl	assemble	resemble
	dɪsémbəl		dissemble	
	sémbləntS		semblance	
c.	əsúwm	riyzúwm	assume	resume
	kənsúwm	priyzúwm	consume	presume
d.	əsáyn	riyzáyn	assign	resign
	kənsáyn	diyzáyn	consign	design
	sayn		sign	
e.	sɑlv	riyzɑ́lv	solve	resolve
		dɪzɑ́lv		dissolve
f.	kənsə́rv	riyzə́rv	conserve	reserve
	sərv	priyzə́rv	serve	preserve
		diyzə́rv		deserve
g.	əsə́rt	diyzə́rt	assert	dessert

8.3a (continued)

	/s/	/z/		
2a.	ənǽləsəs	ǽnəlàyz	analysis	analyze
	pərǽləsəs	pɛ́rəlàyz	paralysis	paralyze
b.	ri͐yələst	ri͐yəlàyz	realist	realize
	àydi͐yələst	àydi͐yəlàyz	idealist	idealize
	mɔ́rələst	mɔ́rəlàyz	moralist	moralize
	nŭwtrələst	nŭwtrəlàyz	neutralist	neutralize
	ə́rbənəst	ə́rbənàyz	urbanist	urbanize

In the first set, under *1*, a stem beginning with /s/ is assumed. This /s/ is voiced to /z/ when vowels occur on both sides: /sáyn ~ diyzáyn/ *(sign - design)*, but an /n/ before the /s/ prevents the voicing, as in /kənsayn/ *consign).* The form /əsayn/ *(assign)* seems to be an exception, but the double *ss* of the spelling is the evidence of a one-time consonant sequence *ds* (*ad signare* etymologically), which presumably became *ss,* later pronounced as a single /s/. Apparently the /r/ of *per-* is ambivalent, may or may not cause voicing. Note in *1a* the form is in both the /s/ and the /z/ columns. The /s - z/ contrasts of the second set seem to be differences of suffixes, though these two are related.

The following exercise contrasts voiceless-voiced pairs of English sounds correlated with the categories noun and verb.

8.3b Consonant alternations correlated with noun and verb classes—/Cvl ~ Cvd/

Presentation and comparison of pattern; read across:

	Noun	Verb		
1a.	yuws	yuwz	use	use
	əbyŭws	əbyŭwz	abuse	abuse
	ɛkskyŭws	ɛkskyŭwz	excuse	excuse
	haws	hawz	house	house
	maws	mawz	mouse	mouse
b.	rɛ̂fyŭws	riyfŭwz	refuse	refuse
	spaws	əspáwz	spouse	espouse
	lɑs	luwz	loss	lose

8.3b (continued)

	Noun	Verb		
2a.	shɛlf	shɛlv	shelf	shelve
	hæf	hæv	half	halve
	kæf	kæv	calf	calve
	wayf	wayv	wife	wive
	seyf	seyv	safe	save
	griyf	griyv	grief	grieve
	thiyf	thiyv	theif	thieve
	biylĭyf	biylĭyv	belief	believe
	riylĭyf	riylĭyv	relief	relieve
	pruwf	pruwv	proof	prove
b.	layf	lıv	life	live
3a.	tiyth	tiydh	teeth	teethe
	mawth	mawdh	mouth	mouthe
	shiyth	shiydh	sheath	sheathe
	riyth	riydh	wreath	wreathe
b.	klɑth	klowdh	cloth	clothe
	swɑth	sweydh	swath	swathe
	bæth	beydh	bath	bathe

This contrast in voicing (voiceless fricative for nouns, voiced fricative for verbs) is a quite general pattern that could be extended to other forms, but those cited are illustrative. Other patterns of consonant variation could be cited, such as the /g - j/ of /ǽnəlɑ̀g ~ ǽnəlɑ́jəkəl - pɛ́dəgɑ̀g ~ pɛ̀dəgɑ́jəkəl - dáyəlɑ̀g ~ dáyələjəst - mǽnəlɑ̀g ~ mǽnəlɑ́jɪk/ /analogue - analogical, pedagogue - pedagogical, dialogue - dialogist, monolog - monologic), etc.

Another kind of consonant alternation is patterns in which a consonant is suppressed, apparently because it occurs as an unpronounceable cluster. The word *sign,* for example is pronounced

/sayn/, since /gn/ is not a permitted cluster in English. But /gn/ is permitted as a consonant sequence, and when suffixes are added, the /g/ is restored, with a syllable boundary between the /g/ and the /n/, as in /sígnəl - sígnət - sígnəfay - sígnətɔriy - sígnəchər - sıgnífəkənt/ *(signal, signet, signify, signatory, signature, significant)*, etc. Functionally the *gn* in word final position serves as an indication of a preceding diphthong, of an /ay/ pronunciation for the preceding *i*, which becomes /ɪ/ when the /g/ is restored, in the forms with suffixes, illustrating the /ay - ɪ/ alternation presented earlier in this chapter.

The following exercise presents a set of words with cluster/sequence /gn/.

8.4 Consonant suppression—/n - gn/
Presentation and comparison of pattern; read across:

/n/	/gn/		
sayn	sígnəchər	sign	signature
əsáyn	æ̀səgnéyshən	assign	assignation
kənsáyn	kɑ̀nsəgnéyshən	consign	consignation
diyzáyn	dɛ̀zəgnéyshən	design	designation
riyzáyn	rɛ̀səgnéyshən	resign	resignation
biynáyn	biynígnənt	benign	benignant
məláyn	məlígnənt	malign	malignant
ɛ́nzən ~ ɛ́nzàyn	ɪnsígniyə	ensign	insignia
ɪmpyúwn	ɪ̀mpəgnéyshən	impugn	impugnation
riypyúwn	riypágnənt	repugn	repugnant
ɛ̀kspyúwn	ɛ̀kspágnətɔ̀riy	expugn	expugnatory
deyn	dígnəfày	deign	dignify
reyn	rɛ́gnəl	reign	regnal
nɑ́stɪk	æ̀gnɑ́stɪk	gnostic	agnostic
nów səs	dàyəgnówsəs	gnosis	diagnosis
nówmɪk	fìsiyágnəmiy	gnomic	physiognomy
nówmən	kɑ́gnətəv	gnomon	cognitive
nɑ́thɪk	pràgnéythəs	gnathic	prognathous

Not every possible pair occurs. Such forms as *align, arraign, campaign, feign, sovereign, foreign* appear as /n/ forms with no corresponding /gn/ forms. Nor do all /gn/ forms have corresponding /n/ forms: *cognate, agnate,* etc. In spite of these nonmatched instances, the spelling *g* (in *gn*) of a word can be thought of as an indication of the underlying form of the word, and the /g/ is then available when needed. In those instances where the consonant sequence /gn/ is necessarily interpreted as a consonant cluster, finally (groups *1, 2, 3*) or initially (group *4*), an interpretation rule (called a morphophonemic rule) specifies /gn→n/. That is to say, /gn/ (as a cluster) is "unpronounceable" in English, and is consequently reduced to /n/.

Other forms of the words in the /n - gn/ set could be cited. Both sides of the comparison yield frequent derived forms, but those cited are illustrative. Also cf. /gm-m/ in *phlegm* and *phlegmatic.*

Another example of simplification is the sequence /mn/ as a cluster, reducing to /m/ when the cluster is final, /n/ when the cluster is initial.

8.4a Consonant suppression—/m/n - mn/

Presentation and comparison of pattern; read across:

	/m/	/mn/		
1a.	dæm	dæmnéyshən	damn	damnation
b.	kəndém	kàndəmnéyshən	condemn	condemnation
c.	sáləm	səlémnətiy	solemn	solemnity
d.	kálәm	kəlámnər	column	columnar
e.	ɔ́təm	ətə́mnəl	autumn	autumnal
f.	hɪm	hɪ́mnəl	hymn	hymnal
g.	lɪm	lɪmnétɪk	limn	limnetic
	/n/			
2.	nəmánɪk	æmnı́yzhə	mnemonic	amnesia

One word ending with *mn* doesn't seem to have a corresponding /mn/ form: *contemn.* The interesting variation on the *mn* pattern is that a different consonant is retained in initial and final position—the consonant nearest the center of the word.

A few other patterns occur where one consonant of a would-be cluster is suppressed.

8.4b Consonant suppression—miscellaneous
Presentation and comparison of pattern; read across:

	/t/	/bVt/		
1a.	dɛt	débət	debt	debit
b.	dawt	dùwbətéyshən	doubt	dubitation
c.	sə́təl	sə́btəl	subtle	subtile

	/n/	/kn/		
2.	now	æ̀knálɪj	know	acknowledge

	/m/	/mb/		
3a.	pləm	plə́mbɪk	plumb	plumbic
b.	thəm	thímbəl	thumb	thimble
c.	gæm	gǽmbət	gamb	gambit
d.	jæm	jǽmbōw	jamb	jambeau
e.	klaym	klǽmbər	climb	clambor
f.	bɑm	bɑ́mbɑ́rd	bomb	bombard
g.	krəm	krə́mbəl	crumb	crumble

	/ng/	/ngg/		
4a.	yəng	yə́nggər	young	younger
b.	lɔng	lɔ́nggər	long	longer
c.	strɔng	strɔ́nggər	strong	stronger

A few notes on these patterns: The /b/ sequence in group *1* can be assured by inserting a vowel between the /b/ and the /t/. Lots of *kn*-words occur, but few have a form where the *k* is realized. Many *mb* words (pronounced /m/) occur that are not paired: *lamb, dumb, numb, tomb,* etc. Only a few /ng - ngg/ forms occur (though this combination is common as a cluster in some nonstandard dialects of English).

We have talked earlier of certain items that have variant forms when they occur under strong and weak stress, often referred to as "reduced" forms. These include the definite and indefinite articles (Chapter 5), which are *usually* weak-stressed, and certain forms of personal pronouns (Chapter 6). Normally these are words of one syllable and include (besides articles and pronouns, including possessives) prepositions, conjunctions, relatives, and various auxiliary verb forms (though many of these are fully destressed in contractions: *John has come→ John's come*).

Since in the weak-stressed forms the vowel schwa is substituted for the vowel of the full form, it occasionally happens that two words fall together, i.e., are pronounced alike, which means that the correct interpretation depends on recognizing the function of the word in a sentence. Note the following sentences:

at ⟶ /ət/   (a) The book's at home.
it ⟶ /ət/   (b) He took it home.

The third word in each sentence is pronounced /ət/ in a normal, noncontrastive pronunciation, but is interpreted *at* in sentence *(a)*, *it* in sentence *(b)*. As speakers in control of the underlying structure of English, we expect a locative phrase after the verb *be* (contracted to *-'s*) in sentence *(a)* and a noun phrase (pronominalized to *it*) after the verb *took* in sentence *(b)*. *It* could appear after *be* (*This is it*), but would then have to be stressed and could not reduce to /ət/.

Note the following:

at ⟶ /ǽt/   (c) Where's he at?
at ⟶ /ət/   (d) He's at home.
at ⟶ /ət/   (e) At home.
it ⟶ /ət/   (f) Where's the book? Who took it?
it ⟶ /ət/   (g) I saw it right here.
it ⟶ /ít/   (h) It's home.

At will not likely reduce in sentence-final position *(c)* or if otherwise stressed, but will reduce if medial or initial. On the other hand *it* will probably not be reduced in initial position, but will be medially or finally. Prepositions and pronouns obey different sets of rules specifying which positions may take weak-stressed forms, though the general rule that weak-stressed forms will take reduced vowels (the vowel will change to schwa) usually applies.

There are other examples of particles pronounced alike under weak stress:

in ⟶ /ən̆/	(i)	Put the doll in the box.
and ⟶ /ən̆/	(j)	Take the doll an' the box.
in/and ⟶ /ən̆/	(k)	Put the doll $\begin{bmatrix} \text{in} \\ \text{an'} \end{bmatrix}$ the box on the cupboard.

In sentence *(i)* /ən̆/ has to be interpreted *in,* because the verb *put* in English requires an adverb of place. In sentence *(j)* /ən̆/ is probably *and,* though *in* would be possible. Sentence *(k)* is ambiguous, with either *in* or *and* as a possible interpretation.

One additional example:

a ⟶ /ə/	(l)	Drink a cup a day.
of ⟶ /ə/	(m)	Drink a cup o' coffee.

In sentence *(l)* /ə/ is *a,* while in sentence *(m)* /ə/ is *of,* the interpretation being governed by the fact "of day" and "a coffee" do not make sense in the context "Drink a cup _____."

The particles *and* and *of* show another feature associated with reduction, the possibility of different grades or amounts of reduction. Note the following:

and: ǽnd ~ ənd ~ ən ~ n
of: ɑ́v ~ əv ~ ə

Which form appears depends on several factors, including level of stress, surrounding sounds (if consonants or vowels), and register or level of formality of the conversation. In the exercise below a few examples are given as models for practice.

8.5 Miscellaneous particle reductions

Presentation of pattern; imitate the following sentences as you hear them:

and ⟶ /ǽnd/	1a.	No, John ǽnd Bill are coming.
/ənd ~ ən̆/	b.	No, but Russ has answered, ənd he says he'll come.
/ən̆/	c.	Yes, Bob ən̆d Jerry are both coming.
/n̩/	d.	Yes, Ed n̩' Jack said they'd come.

8.5 (continued)

of	→ /ăv ~ əv/	2a. What's this box made ôf?
	/əv/	b. She's the maid ŏf honor.
	/ə/	c. I'd like a glass ŏ' milk.
in	→ /în/	3a. Did you put the car în?
	/ən/	b. Yes, it's ĭn the garage.
	/n̩/	c. Then he went ĭn the house.
to	→ /tûw/	4a. Who'd he speak tô?
	/tə/	b. He spoke tŏ John.
or	→ /ôr/	5a. It doesn't matter—take two ôr three.
	/ər/	b. He said to take two ŏr three.
are	→ /âr/	6a. He's going and he says you âre.
	/ər/	b. Who ăre you going with?
has	→ /hǽz/	7a. Andy hasn't gone, hás he?
	/həz/	b. Hăs Andy left yet?
	/əz/	c. Jess hăs just come.
	/z/	d. Bill's already come.
one	→ /wən̂/	8a. I only need ône.
	/ən/	b. This ŏne 'll do.
that	→ /dhǽt/	9a. Is thât the man?
	/dhət/	b. He's the man thăt I was telling you about.
as	→ /ǽz/	10a. Who's he as tall âs?
	/əz/	b. He's as tall ăs Brad.
was	→ /wâz ~ wâz/	11a. Is John going? He said he wâs.
	/wəz/	b. He wăs just here.
can	→ /kǽn/	12a. I hope we cân.
	/kən/	b. I'm sure they căn go.
for	→ /fôr/	13a. Who are you voting fôr?
	/fər/	b. I'm voting fŏr Jackson.
from	→ /frâm ~ frəm/	14a. Where are you frôm?
	/frəm/	b. I'm frŏm Spain.

Many additional examples could be cited for this very general pattern, but those given above provide an idea of the extent and types of reduction. The pattern applies to a large number of words, a consideration that becomes even more important when one realizes that these words are very high frequency items in a running text, perhaps as high as thirty-five per cent. Add to this the fact that very similar vowel reductions occur widely in the weak-stressed syllables of multisyllabic words, and it is easy to see how indispensably necessary it is for second-language students of English to be familiar with the alternation of vowels correlated with stress. Students who have been shielded from these normal weak-stressed reductions in the belief that such pronunciations are sloppy, careless, etc., are practically crippled when first exposed to normal English in real contexts. It is crucially important for any second-language student of English who will ever deal with the oral language to have at least the experience of hearing and practicing reduced forms as a means of developing an acceptance of these morphophonemic alternations.

As shown in some of the examples of exercise *8.5,* the pattern of reduction shades off into the patterns of contraction. This is particularly true of verb forms and the negative particle *not*. Note the following series:

is →	/íz/	(n) What *is* it?	(Verb *is* strong-stressed— full form)
	/əz/	(o) The judge is here.	(Verb *is* weak-stressed— reduced form)
	/z/	(p) So's the bailiff.	(Verb *is* contracted to /-z/)
	/s/	(q) The clerk's here too.	(Verb *is* contracted to /-s/)
not →	/nât/	(r) Really? I think not.	(particle *not* strong-stressed— full form)
	/nât/	(s) He's not coming.	(particle *not* strong-stressed— full form)
	/ənt/	(t) I wouldn't think so.	(particle *not* reduced and contracted /-ənt/)
	/-n̩t/	(u) You mightn't think so.	(particle *not* contracted to /-n̩t/)
	/-nt/	(v) He can't come.	(particle *not* contracted to /-nt/)

The following exercise presents full and reduced forms of prepositions in a question-response format. Note that position in the sentence is the determining factor—full forms are final, reduced forms nonfinal.

8.5a Particle reductions-prepositions

Comparison of pattern; reply with a confirming affirmative response:

fɔ́r ~ fǝr	1. What's he asking for? Money?	Yes, he's asking for money.
túw ~ tǝ̆	2. Where's he going to? The bank?	Yes, he's going to the bank.
ǽt ~ ǝ̆t	3. Where's he staying at? The dorm?	Yes, he's staying at the dorm.
frɑ́m ~ frǝ̆m	4. Where's he coming from? The library?	Yes, he's coming from the library.
ɑ́v ~ ǝ̆v	5. What's he thinking of? The lab?	Yes, he's thinking of the lab.
ín ~ ǝ̆n	6. What's he going in? The car?	Yes, he's going in the car.

It's perhaps worth pointing out that some particle forms resist reduction more than others. The preposition *on* is an example; *on* usually retains the vowel /ɑ/, and to do so usually attracts at least a medial level of stress. Thus "He's on the bus" would have the preposition /ɑ̀n/.

The following exercise presents fragments which are to be combined to form full sentences. The pieces, in citation form, take strong stress and full vowels. In context the stress is weakened and the vowel reduced.

8.5b Particle reductions—contextual constraints

Presentation of pattern; combine the fragments into full sentences:

fŏr ~ fər dhă ~ dhă	1. One . . . for . . . the . . . money,	One for the money,
fŏr ~ fər dhă ~ dhă	Two . . . for . . . the . . . show,	Two for the show,
tŭw ~ tă	Three . . . to . . . get ready,	Three to get ready,
ăend ~ ănd tŭw ~ tă	And . . . four . . . to . . . go.	And four to go.
dŭw ~ dă yŭw ~ yă tŭw ~ tă	2. Who do . . . you . . . want to . . . go?	Who do you want to go?
tŭw ~ tă tŭw ~ tă dhă ~ dhă	3. He wants to . . . go to . . . the . . . movie.	He wants to go to the movie.
dăz ~ dăz hĭy ~ ĭy ă ~ ă ŏr ~ ăr ă ~ ă	4. Does . . . he have . . . a . . . bike . . . or . . . a . . . car?	Does he have a bike or a car?
ăr ~ ăr dhă ~ dhă ăv ~ ăv	5. Where . . . are . . . the . . . snows of . . . yesteryear?	Where are the snows of yesteryear?
ăen ~ ăn ăend ~ ăn ăen ~ ăn	6. Get an . . . apple and . . . an . . . orange.	Get an apple and an orange.

It would be very difficult to provide exercises for all possible combinations of weak-stressed particles in sentences. Reduction and vowel alternation is literally an ever-present phenomenon in oral

English. The sentences in the preceding drills are typical of the kinds of modification common to informal oral expression in standard usage.

Reduction can occur along with other types of modification, such as palatal assimilation, to further complicate the patterns of variation common in English. The following exercise offers a few examples which illustrate a fairly extensive modification in highly informal English. This type of pronunciation is common among native speakers of English in normal conversation on a very casual level. It would not normally be judged inappropriate unless transported to much more formal contexts (or used by second-language speakers whose control of English clearly indicated unfamiliarity with this style and register).

8.5c Particle reductions combined with palatal assimilations
Presentation of pattern; combine the fragments into full sentences:

1. What . . . did . . . you . . . do?   wâdjədûw ↓
2. What . . . is . . . your . . . name?   wâchərnéym ↓
3. Did . . . you . . . eat . . . yet?   jəĭychêt ↑
4. Would . . . you . . . like . . . an . . . apricot?   djəlâykənéyprəkɑ̀t ↑
5. What . . . did . . . you . . . think . . . of . . . the . . . judge?   wâjəthîngkədhəjə̂j ↓
6. Do . . . you . . . want . . . to . . . go . . . to . . . Phoenix?   jəwɑ̂nəgôwtəffynɪks ↑

These then are some of the characteristics of informal oral English. Not every student will want to attempt the mastery of this level of speech, though anyone who expects to live and work among native English speakers would find it very useful. But an *acquaintance* with informal styles would be beneficial to most students, and would certainly help minimize the transition from the classroom to the real world for those who eventually take this step.

Chapter 9
FUNCTIONAL SYNTHESIS

The preceding eight chapters have discussed individual features or patterns, or occasionally the intersection of two patterns in a construct. The inventory of sounds, pedagogically significant variants, combinations of sounds, features of order, and related suprasegmental features, while certainly far from exhaustive, has been reasonably complete. Several hundred exercises of various kinds have been offered to present, compare, and contrast features and patterns, and the process of contextualization in the practice of pronunciation skills has been illustrated when appropriate exercises could be devised.

But in actual use, pronunciation problems seldom come in neat packages, where a single feature acts as the pivot of two otherwise rational interpretations. More typical is the case of the young man who thought, for reasons that might be difficult to specify, that he heard "rice pudding" when in fact the information "aspirin" was intended. There's a hint of similarity, but it would be difficult indeed to specify just which features are most in need of remedial attention.

The exercises in the preceding chapters are designed to improve skills in discrimination and production. Those in the present chapter are perhaps aimed more specifically at listening comprehension, concentrating on "obscure" details of pronunciation that seem to be most difficult for foreign students of English, small but crucial details. There may, of course, be some associated benefit to production skills as a result of increased familiarity with the overall rhythm patterns of the language and their effect on the sequences of sounds that make up sentences.

The student is asked to distinguish between sentences that are suggestively similar, though in fact they differ by one or two or three or several features. This sort of drill is especially appropriate to English, where weak-stressed syllables are not only pronounced very briefly, but have their phonological content obscured. As with many other exercises in this text, paraphrase is used as a device for identifying members of contrasting pairs.

Sentences are presented in pairs, and the members of the pairs are listed in a consistent order. In doing the drills, however, the order should be randomized, so that the student cannot rely on sequence as a cue to accurate identification. Thus sometimes sentence *(a)* should come first, sometimes sentence *(b)*. This randomization of sentence sequence is crucially important to the proper utilization of the exercises. Also it should be understood in pronouncing these pairs that the sentences must not be contrastively stressed or the point of difference emphasized in any special way. The purpose of the exercise is to force the student to rely on minimal cues, similar to those that will normally be present in informal speech when there is no contrast or emphasis. To highlight the differences would frustrate the purpose of the exercise.

Often it is difficult for students to distinguish between *a* and *the* in a sentence, since when weak-stressed, as they usually are, they differ so little in pronunciation. Yet the difference is normally very important, telling the listener whether any example of the noun will do or a specific referent is intended.

9.1 Utterance discrimination—*a* vs *the*
Comparison of pattern; identify the sentence heard:

1a. Someone's got to bring a car. (I'll bring mine.)
   (any car)
 b. Someone's got to bring the car. (I'll bring it.)
   (a specific car)

2a. Where can I find a minister? (There's one here now.)
   (any minister)
 b. Where can I find the minister? (He's with the president.)
   (a specific minister)

3a. Would you like a piece of pie? (OK, I'll take one.)
   (we can all have pie for dessert)
 b. Would you like the piece of pie? (OK, I'll take it.)
   (only one of us can have pie)

4a. Have you seen a can opener? (There's one on the table.)
   (there are probably several)
 b. Have you seen the can opener? (It's on the table.)
   (there's only one in the house)

5a. I saw a librarian this morning. (And I sure needed one.)
   (there are several)
 b. I saw the librarian this morning. (And I sure needed her.)
   (there's only one)

6a. Have you got a typewriter? (Yes, I have one.)
   (no special machine)
 b. Have you got the typewriter? (Yes, I have it.)
   (we both know there is a certain machine)

The next exercise concentrates on the minimal presence of a schwa, which substantially changes the structure (and therefore meaning) of the sentence.

9.1a Utterance discrimination—/ə/ vs ∅

Comparison of pattern; identify the sentence heard by selecting the appropriate paraphrase:

1a.	I saw him cross the street.	(go over)
b.	I saw him across the street.	(over there)
2a.	I saw him round the corner.	(go there)
b.	I saw him around the corner.	(already there)
3a.	I saw him peer in the cellar.	(look into)
b.	I saw him appear in the cellar.	(come into view)
4a.	I saw him sign his inheritance.	(write his name on)
b.	I saw him assign his inheritance.	(transfer)
5a.	I saw him sleep on the floor.	(go to sleep)
b.	I saw him asleep on the floor.	(already sleeping)
6a.	They proved the theory.	(demonstrated its truth)
b.	They approved the theory.	(accepted)
7a.	They praised the house.	(commented favorably on it)
b.	They appraised the house.	(set a value on it)
8a.	The lawyer tacked the announcement on the bulletin board	(affixed to)
b.	The lawyer attacked the announcement on the bulletin board	(criticized strongly)
9a.	I think they'll mend the document.	(repair it with scotch tape)
b.	I think they'll amend the document.	(officially modify)
10a.	He wants to quit the defendant.	(abandon)
b.	He wants to acquit the defendant	(declare innocent)

Many of the signals that differentiate constructions in English involve the sound schwa, which is typically weak-stressed and consequently very briefly pronounced. This makes it hard to hear, and therefore the identification of a construction is correspondingly difficult. In the following exercise the contrast involves the insertion at two places in a string of words of the indefinite article *a,* which has the effect of changing a transitive sentence to an equational sentence.

9.1b Utterance discrimination—variant insertion of *a*

Comparison of pattern; identify the sentence heard by selecting the appropriate paraphrase cue:

1a. He's chosen a candidate.	(supports a candidate)
b. He's a chosen candidate.	(is a candidate)
2a. He's toughened a fighter.	(exercised one)
b. He's a toughened fighter.	(is one)
3a. He's trained a technician.	(prepared one)
b. He's a trained technician.	(is one)
4a. He's educated a professor.	(instructed one)
b. He's an educated professor.	(is one)
5a. He's forgotten a widower.	(neglected one)
b. He's a forgotten widower.	(is one)
6a. He's appointed a spokesman.	(designated one)
b. He's an appointed spokesman.	(is one)
7a. He's invited a speaker.	(asked one)
b. He's an invited speaker.	(is one)

Sometimes weak-stressed pronoun forms are difficult to hear. In the following exercise the pronoun *it* appears in one but is absent from the other of a pair of sentences.

9.1c Utterance discrimination—*it* vs ∅

Comparison of pattern; identify the sentence heard by selecting the correct paraphrase:

1a. He went over it himself.	(examined it)
b. He went over himself.	(traveled there)
2a. He was speaking of it himself.	(referring to it)
b. He was speaking of himself.	(self reference)
3a. He looked at it himself.	(perused it)
b. He looked at himself.	(self scrutiny)
4a. He thought about it himself.	(considered it)
b. He thought about himself.	(self recollection)
5a. He listened to it himself.	(heard it)
b. He listened to himself.	(took his own counsel)
6a. He depended on it himself.	(trusted it)
b. He depended on himself.	(self reliance)

The exercise that follows below treats the contrast of the *-ed* ending on verbs (verbs that have stems ending in *t* or *d*, so that the *-ed* forms a separate syllable) and the pronoun *it*. Some of the sentence pairs also show other differences, such as an /s/ vs /z/ at some point in the verb. But these are easy to confuse.

9.1d Utterance discrimination— -ed vs *it*

Comparison of pattern; identify the sentence heard by giving the appropriate paraphrase:

1a.	He's disgusted with her.	(offended by her)
b.	He's discussed it with her.	(consulted her)
2a.	He's already busted.	(flat broke)
b.	He's already bussed it.	(sent it by bus)
3a.	He's posted at the office.	(assigned to work)
b.	He's posed it at the office.	(propounded the question)
4a.	The glass is misted.	(dim and blurry)
b.	The class has missed it.	(failed to notice it)
5a.	They banded all together.	(all joined a group)
b.	They banned it all together.	(completely prohibited it)
6a.	They spaded a month ago.	(turned the soil)
b.	They spayed it a month ago.	(removed the ovaries)
7a.	There was a proposal that we translated.	(We translated the proposal.)
b.	There was a proposal that we translate it.	(We were to translate it.)
8a.	There was a suggestion that we disregarded.	(We disregarded the suggestion.)
b.	There was a suggestion that we disregard it.	(We were to disregard it.)
9a.	There was an order that we reported.	(We reported the order.)
b.	There was an order that we report it.	(We were to report it.)
10a.	There was a request that we repeated.	(We repeated the request.)
b.	There was a request that we repeat it.	(We were to repeat it.)

Contractions with reduced forms of the verb auxiliary provide some fairly difficult problems for interpreting oral English. In the exercise that follows the modal *would* is contracted as /d/ and the

Functional Synthesis 235

modal *will* as /l/. *Would* indicates an intention that could have been carried out in the past, which can be verified by the tag rejoinder "did you?" *Will* implies that only intention is reported, which can be verified by the tag rejoinder "will you?" As you hear a statement of intention reported, address a short question asking if the intention was or still will be carried out.

9.1e Utterance discrimination—*would* vs *will*

Comparison of pattern; identify the sentence heard by giving the appropriate tag rejoinder:

1a.	He said you'd go with him.	(Did you?) or (Have you?)
b.	He said you'll go with him.	(Will you?)
2a.	He said you'd read a paper.	(Did you?)
b.	He said you'll read a paper.	(Will you?)
3a.	He said you'd take the minutes.	(Did you?)
b.	He said you'll take the minutes.	(Will you?)
4a.	He said you'd make an oral report.	(Did you?)
b.	He said you'll make an oral report.	(Will you?)
5a.	He said you'd write a summary.	(Did you?)
b.	He said you'll write a summary.	(Will you?)
6a.	He said you'd do the evaluation.	(Did you?)
b.	He said you'll do the evaluation.	(Will you?)
7a.	He said you'd clear the conference table.	(Did you?)
b.	He said you'll clear the conference table.	(Will you?)
8a.	He said you'd mail his letter.	(Did you?)
b.	He said you'll mail his letter.	(Will you?)
9a.	He said you'd empty the trash.	(Did you?)
b.	He said you'll empty the trash.	(Will you?)
10a.	He said you'd lock the building.	(Did you?)
b.	He said you'll lock the building.	(Will you?)

Past and present perfect verb forms are often used to refer to recent past time, especially when the modifier "just" appears in the sentence. Yet there is a difference in meaning, with the past separated from the present moment of time, but the present perfect emphasizing the continuing relevance of the event to the present moment. In the exercise below, past and present perfect are differentiated only by the appearance of a contracted form of *has* or *have.* Respond to the statments given by an appropriate echo question tag.

9.1f Utterance discrimination—past vs present perfect

Comparison of pattern; identify the sentence heard by asking the appropriate echo question tag:

1a. He just heard the bad news.	(Did he?)
b. He's just heard the bad news.	(Has he?)
2a. She just called the police.	(Did she?)
b. She's just called the police.	(Has she?)
3a. He just had a picture taken.	(Did he?)
b. He's just had a picture taken.	(Has he?)
4a. She just read the telegram.	(Did she?)
b. She's just read the telegram.	(Has she?)
5a. Grant just arrived.	(Did he?)
b. Grant's just arrived.	(Has he?)
6a. They just brought up the chest.	(Did they?)
b. They've just brought up the chest.	(Have they?)
7a. They just measured the skid marks.	(Did they?)
b. They've just measured the skid marks.	(Have they?)
8a. I just called Betty.	(Did you?)
b. I've just called Betty.	(Have you?)
9a. We just finished the investigation.	(Did you?)
b. We've just finished the investigation.	(Have you?)
10a. I just opened the letter.	(Did you?)
b. I've just opened the letter.	(Have you?)

Hearing the *-ed* of past participle forms of verbs is sometimes very difficult, especially when the form occurs in the middle of a sentence and is immediately followed by the word *the* (or another word beginning with a consonant). Yet of course it is important to know whether something has happened or was only planned but is still to happen, and correctly hearing the /d/ or /t/ is tremendously important to the listener. In the following exercise, use the rejoinder that corresponds with the facts of time reference. Note that the contracted form *he'd* derives from "he would" when it precedes a nonpast verb, but from "he had" when it precedes a past participle.

9.1g Utterance discrimination—past subsequent vs past perfect
Comparison of pattern; identify the sentence heard by giving the appropriate rejoinder:

1a.	He said he'd study the proposal.	(And he will.) or (And he did.)
b.	He said he'd studied the proposal.	(And he had.)
2a.	He said he'd prepare the lecture.	(And he will.)
b.	He said he'd prepared the lecture.	(And he had.)
3a.	He said he'd offer the seminar.	(And he will.)
b.	He said he'd offered the seminar.	(And he had.)
4a.	He said he'd analyze the play.	(And he will.)
b.	He said he'd analyzed the play.	(And he had.)
5a.	He said he'd open the door.	(And he will.)
b.	He said he'd opened the door.	(And he had.)
6a.	He said he'd unlock the building.	(And he will.)
b.	He said he'd unlocked the building.	(And he had.)
7a.	He said he'd ask the questions.	(And he will.)
b.	He said he'd asked the questions.	(And he had.)
8a.	He said he'd type the manuscript.	(And he will.)
b.	He said he'd typed the manuscript.	(And he had.)
9a.	He said he'd finish the lesson.	(And he will.)
b.	He said he'd finished the lesson.	(And he had.)
10a.	He said he'd pack the books.	(And he will.)
b.	He said he'd packed the books.	(And he had.)

Whose and *who's* are pronounced alike, but *who's* usually takes the article *a* after it. Hearing and identifying the /ə/ then, is the means of identifying the correct interpretation of /huwz/.

9.1h Utterance discrimination—*whose* vs *who's*

Comparison of pattern; identify the sentence heard:

1a. That's the teacher whose student's here.
   (The teacher has a student.)
 b. That's the teacher who's a student here.
   (The teacher is a student.)

2a. That's the lawyer whose client's here.
   (The lawyer has a client.)
 b. That's the lawyer who's a client here.
   (The lawyer is a client.)

3a. That's the doctor whose patient's here.
   (The doctor has a patient.)
 b. That's the doctor who's a patient here.
   (The doctor is a patient.)

4a. That's the novelist whose publisher's here.
   (The novelist has a publisher.)
 b. That's the novelist who's a publisher here.
   (The novelist is a publisher.)

5a. That's the industrialist whose consultant's here.
   (The industrialist has a consultant.)
 b. That's the industrialist who's a consultant here.
   (The industrialist is a consultant.)

9.1h (continued)

6a. That's the neighbor whose gardener's here.
   (The neighbor has a gardener.)
 b. That's the neighbor who's a gardener here.
   (The neighbor is a gardener.)

7a. That's the plumber whose helper is here.
   (The plumber has a helper.)
 b. That's the plumber who's a helper here.
   (The plumber is a helper.)

8a. That's the author whose editor's here.
   (The author has an editor.)
 b. That's the author who's an editor here.
   (The author is an editor.)

9a. That's the plasterer whose apprentice is here.
   (The plasterer has an apprentice.)
 b. That's the plasterer who's an apprentice here.
   (The plasterer is an apprentice.)

10a. That's the student whose counselor is here.
   (The student has a counselor.)
  b. That's the student who's a counselor here.
   (The student is a counselor.)

The English spelling *that* can be either a demonstrative or a relative pronoun. As a demonstrative it is pronounced with at least secondary stress as /dhæt/. As a relative it is almost always weak-stressed, pronounced as /dhət/. In the following exercise the contrast is further distinguished by a contracted form of the verb *is* after the relative.

9.1i Utterance discrimination—/ðæt/ vs /ðət/
Comparison of pattern; identify the sentence heard:

1a.	I don't like a play that sad.	(as sad as that one)
b.	I don't like a play that's sad.	(one that is sad)
2a.	I don't care for a movie that scary.	(as scary as that one)
b.	I don't care for a movie that's scary.	(one that is scary)
3a.	I don't want a house that dreary.	(as dreary as that one)
b.	I don't want a house that's dreary.	(one that is dreary)
4a.	I don't enjoy a trip that long.	(as long as that one)
b.	I don't enjoy a trip that's long.	(one that is long)
5a.	I don't want a car that worn out.	(as worn out as that one)
b.	I don't want a car that's worn out.	(one that is worn out)
6a.	I don't want an apple that wormy.	(as wormy as that one)
b.	I don't want an apple that's wormy.	(one that is wormy)

7a. I don't care for a staircase that rickety.
　　(as rickety as that one)
 b. I don't care for a staircase that's rickety.
　　(one that is rickety)

8a. I'm afraid of a windshield that cracked.
　　(as cracked as that one)
 b. I'm afraid of a windshield that's cracked.
　　(one that is cracked)

9a. I don't enjoy a flight that dangerous.
　　(as dangerous as that one)
 b. I don't enjoy a flight that's dangerous.
　　(one that is dangerous)

10a. I don't like a job that dull.
　　(as dull as that one)
  b. I don't like a job that's dull.
　　(one that is dull)

The exercise that follows contrasts the relative pronoun *that* with the conjunction *than.* Both are normally weak-stressed, and they differ only in their final consonant sound.

9.1j Utterance discrimination—*than* vs *that*

Comparison of pattern; identify the sentence heard by selecting the appropriate paraphrase cue:

1a. There's more than we can do.
(too much for us)
 b. There's more that we can do.
(some additional)

2a. There's more than he promised.
(in excess of)
 b. There's more that he promised.
(some additional)

3a. There's more than meets the eye.
(some we don't see)
 b. There's more that meets the eye.
(additional can be seen)

4a. There's more than tongue can tell.
(not time for the whole story)
 b. There's more that tongue can tell.
(the story's not finished)

5a. There's more than came yesterday.
(more is on the way)
 b. There's more that came yesterday.
(this is not all of yesterday's shipment)

6a. There's more than Eldon brought.
(didn't bring it all)
 b. There's more that Eldon brought.
(this is not all he delivered)

Short words, especially when pronounced under weak stress, are often difficult to perceive for students learning English. In the following sentences, the occurrence of "from" is minimally present in one of each pair.

9.1k Utterance discrimination—*from* vs ∅

Comparison of pattern; identify the sentence heard by paraphrasing the contrasting information:

1a. Studying has kept me going to the library. (I went.)
 b. Studying has kept me from going to the library. (I didn't go.)

2a. My assignments have kept me going to the museum. (I visited.)
 b. My assignments have kept me from going to the museum. (I didn't visit.)

3a. Playing basketball has kept me attending strategy meetings. (I attended.)
 b. Playing basketball has kept me from attending strategy meetings. (I didn't attend.)

4a. My schedule kept me running all day. (I ran.)
 b. My schedule has kept me from running all day. (I didn't run.)

5a. This play will keep me reading until midnight. (I'll read.)
 b. This play will keep me from reading until midnight. (I won't read.)

6a. My car repairs will keep me working until at least six o'clock. (I'll work.)
 b. My car repairs will keep me from working until at least six o'clock. (I won't work.)

7a. My office hours will keep me talking to students until 2:00 P.M. (I'll talk.)
 b. My office hours will keep me from talking to students until 2:00 P.M. (I won't talk.)

8a. Painting the house will keep me puttering for at least a week. (I'll putter.)
 b. Painting the house will keep me from puttering for at least a week. (I won't putter.)

Note that in addition to the negative implication of *from* in "keep from" there is another contrast implied. In *(8a)* painting is considered puttering, but in *(8b)* puttering is a separate activity that won't begin until painting ends. All the other pairs of sentences in this exercise have comparable inclusion/exclusion implications.

In the drill that follows a very short syllable (/ər/) is introduced into a sentence, requiring a reinterpretation of the preceding /z/, which was a verb but becomes a plural suffix.

9.11 Utterance discrimination—*is* vs *are*

Comparison of pattern; identify the sentence heard by specifying "one" or "more than one":

1a.	His brother's Chinese.	(one brother)
b.	His brothers 're Chinese.	(more than one)
2a.	His uncle's Spanish.	(one uncle)
b.	His uncles 're Spanish.	(more than one)
3a.	His cousin's Turkish.	(one cousin)
b.	His cousins 're Turkish.	(more than one)
4a.	His teacher's German.	(one teacher)
b.	His teachers 're German.	(More than one)
5a.	His partner's rich.	(one partner)
b.	His partners 're rich.	(more than one)
6a.	His daughter's good looking.	(one daughter)
b.	His daughters 're good looking.	(more than one)
7a.	His secretary's efficient.	(one secretary)
b.	His secretaries 're efficient.	(more than one)
8a.	His driver's well trained.	(one driver)
b.	His drivers 're well trained.	(more than one)
9a.	His employee's happy.	(one employee)
b.	His employees 're happy.	(more than one)
10a.	His supervisor's really coming tomorrow.	(one supervisor)
b.	His supervisors 're really coming tomorrow.	(more than one)

Note that the verb *are* is written *'re* to suggest the kind of contracting common in informal spoken English, an obscured pronunciation that is difficult for students to hear.

The following exercise contrasts *they* and *there,* each followed by *are.* Both of these combinations are subject to the rules of contraction, but *they* and *are* can be contracted in two ways, /dhɛr/ and /dhêyər/, depending on level of formality and speed of pronunciation. *There are* would perhaps be expected to contract to /dhɛ́rər/, but this sequence in informal speech usually comes out /dhɛ̂ər/ (cf., exercise *3.9d*) or if destressed, even /dhər/. The comparison intended in the present drill is between /dhêyər/ and /dhɛ̂ər/. The latter intention is shown in the exercise sentences by writing the contraction "there're."

9.1m Utterance discrimination—*they are* vs *there are*
Comparison of pattern; identify the sentences heard:

1a. They are excellent hotels to stay at.
   (Those hotels are excellent.)
 b. There're excellent hotels to stay at.
   (Excellent hotels are available.)
2a. They are good people to deal with.
   (Those people are good.)
 b. There're good people to deal with.
   (Good people are available.)
3a. They are some old friends of ours.
   (Those people are our friends.)
 b. There're some old friends of ours.
   (Some friends are available.)
4a. They are very interesting historical accounts.
   (Those histories are interesting.)
 b. There're very interesting historical accounts.
   (Interesting histories are available.)
5a. They are important decisions to make.
   (Those decisions are important.)
 b. There're important decisions to make.
   (Important decisions must be made.)
6a. They are dangerous streets at night.
   (Those streets are dangerous.)
 b. There're dangerous streets at night.
   (Some streets are dangerous.)

Both *is* and *as* can be pronounced /əz/, so they are hard to distinguish. In the following drill the conjunction *as* occurs twice in a correlative pair. When the verb *is* occurs, it is in its contracted form, unless a sibilant consonant (particularly /s/ or /z/) precedes it.

9.1n Utterance discrimination—*is* vs *as*

Comparison of pattern; identify the utterance heard by classifying it as a title or a sentence:

1a. A girl as sweet as candy	(title)
b. A girl's as sweet as candy.	(sentence)
2a. A sea captain as hard as nails	(title)
b. A sea captain's as hard as nails.	(sentence)
3a. A souffle as light as feathers	(title)
b. A souffle's as light as feathers.	(sentence)
4a. A salesman as smooth as syrup	(title)
b. A salesman's as smooth as syrup.	(sentence)
5a. A bank as solid as Gibraltar	(title)
b. A bank's as solid as Gibraltar.	(sentence)
6a. A poker player as cool as a cucumber	(title)
b. A poker player's as cool as a cucumber.	(sentence)
7a. A promise as good as gold	(title)
b. A promise is as good as gold.	(sentence)
8a. An excuse as thin as paper	(title)
b. An excuse is as thin as paper.	(sentence)

Note that utterances *(a)* as they are informally pronounced *could* be interpreted as sentences, with /əz/ understood as *is:* A girl is sweet as candy, etc.

Sometimes a minimal difference can signal a completely opposite meaning. This is often true for a negative prefix, which is sometimes no more than an additional schwa. This is illustrated in the following exercise.

9.1o Utterance discrimination—negative prefixes

Comparison of pattern; identify the sentence heard by selecting the appropriate paraphrase:

1a.	That argument could be very irrelevant.	(not pertinent)
b.	That argument could be very relevant.	(pertinent)
2a.	That solution could be completely illegal.	(not permitted by law)
b.	That solution could be completely legal.	(permitted by law)
3a.	That procedure is certainly immoral.	(not virtuous)
b.	That procedure is certainly moral.	(virtuous)
4a.	That action is highly irregular.	(not proper)
b.	That action is highly regular.	(proper)
5a.	His handwriting is totally illegible.	(cannot be read)
b.	His handwriting is totally legible.	(can be read)
6a.	His habits are absolutely immoderate.	(not reasonable)
b.	His habits are absolutely moderate.	(reasonable)
7a.	His attitude is reasonably irreverent.	(not respectful)
b.	His attitude is reasonably reverent.	(respectful)
8a.	His excuse is really illegitimate.	(not sanctioned by law)
b.	His excuse is really legitimate.	(sanctioned by law)

These sentences are somewhat more difficult than they might otherwise be, due to the placement of an adverb that ends in the vowel /iy/ just before the adjective. The /iy/ and the schwa tend to run together and obscure the extra syllable.

The following drill contrasts /ɪ/ and /ə/, first with a supporting difference and then without one. It will be remembered that /ɪ/ and /ə/ under weak stress are very similar and occasionally interchangeable.

9.1p Utterance discrimination—negative prefix *in-* and the article *an*

Comparison of pattern; identify the sentence heard by selecting the appropriate paraphrase:

1a.	We had inexperienced guides.	(novice leaders)
b.	We had an experienced guide.	(a practiced leader)
2a.	Use inanimate nouns.	(words for non-living things)
b.	Use an animate noun.	(word for a living thing)
3a.	He's studying inarticulate speakers.	(indistinct lecturers)
b.	He's studying an articulate speaker.	(an able lecturer)
4a.	The decision is based on inadequate theses.	(nonsuitable propositions)
b.	The decision is based on an adequate thesis.	(a suitable proposition)
5a.	That's inexpensive salmon.	(cheap seafood)
b.	That's an expensive salmon.	(a costly sea animal)
6a.	What inactive sheep!	(passive wool animals)
b.	What an active sheep!	(a lively wool animal)
7a.	It only works with inexact series.	(non-precise sequences)
b.	It only works with an exact series.	(a precise sequence)

Note that sentences *1* to *4* contain nouns with a marked plural, which supports the contrast. Sentences *5* to *8* have nouns with zero plurals which leave the interpretation of the contrast to the perception of /ɪn/ and /ən/, possibly aided by an occasional higher stress on the prefix *-in*.

The series of exercises that follow are similar to those above, but include some type of intonational clue in addition to different sequences or forms of words. In the first exercise the sentences have different sequences of stresses and also differ by contrasting *his* and *him*.

9.2 Utterance contour—stress and pronoun interpretation, masculine forms.

Comparison of pattern; identify the sentence heard by selecting the correct paraphrase:

1a. They fed his dôg bı́scuits. (The dog ate the biscuits.)
 b. They fed him dőg bı̀scuits. (He ate the biscuits.)

2a. They gave his hôrse feáthers. (The horse got the feathers.)
 b. They gave him hőrse feàthers. (He got the feathers.)

3a. They sent his beâr greáse. (The bear got the grease.)
 b. They sent him beár greáse. (He got the grease.)

4a. They offered his côw bèlls. (The cow got the bells.)
 b. They offered him côw bèlls. (He got the bells.)

5a. They brought his cât nı́p. (The cat got the nip.)
 b. They brought him cátnı̀p. (He got the nip.)

6a. They gave his goôse pı́mples. (The goose got the pimples.)
 b. They gave him goóse pı̀mples. (He got the pimples.)

7a. They sent his lôve létters. (She got the letters.)
 b. They sent him lóve lètters. (He got the letters.)

8a. They fed his dûck éggs. (The duck ate the eggs.)
 b. They fed him dúck èggs. (He ate the eggs.)

9a. They fed his gôose bérries. (The goose ate the berries.)
 b. They fed him goósebèrries. (He ate the berries.)

10a. They gave his tîger bálm. (The tiger got the balm)
 b. They gave him Tı́ger Bàlm. (He got the balm.)

When the above sentences can be distinguished readily, the exercise should be repeated using *her* instead of *his* or *him*. Since it is both a possessive and an object form, *her* can occur in both *(a)* and *(b)* sentences, leaving the listener with only the stress cue.

9.2a Utterance contour—stress interpretation, feminine forms

Comparison of pattern; identify the sentence heard by selecting the correct paraphrase:

1a.	They fed her dôg bĭscuits.	(The dog ate the biscuits.)
b.	They fed her dóg bèscuits.	(She ate the biscuits.)
2a.	They gave her hôrse féathers.	(The horse got the feathers.)
b.	They gave her hórse fèathers.	(She got the feathers.)
3a.	They sent her bêar gréase.	(The bear got the grease.)
b.	They sent her béar grèase.	(She got the grease.)
4a.	They offered her côw bèlls.	(The cow got the bells.)
b.	They offered herców bèlls.	(She got the bells.)
5a.	They brought her cât nĭp.	(The cat got the nip.)
b.	They brought her cátnĭp.	(She got the nip.)
6a.	They gave her gôose pĭmples.	(The goose got the pimples.)
b.	They gave her góose pìmples.	(She got the pimples.)
7a.	They sent her lôve létters.	(He got the letters.)
b.	They sent her lóve lètters.	(She got the letters.)
8a.	They fed her dûck éggs.	(The duck ate the eggs.)
b.	They fed her dúck èggs.	(She ate the eggs.)
9a.	They fed her gôose bérries.	(The goose ate the berries.)
b.	They fed her góosebèrries.	(She ate the berries.)
10a.	They gave her tîger bálm.	(The tiger got the balm.)
b.	They gave her Tíger Bàlm.	(She got the balm.)

The exercise which follows illustrates a different kind of problem. There is an extra syllable, a schwa, to serve as a differentiator, but there is also an intonation contrast that marks the information that is crucial for the correct interpretation of these contrasting sentences.

250   *Patterns of English Pronunciation*

9.2b Utterance contour—identification of referent vs place
    Comparison of pattern; identify the sentence heard by selecting the appropriate echo question:

1a. Is that a bank across the street? ↑
    (A what?)

 b. Is that bank across the street? ↑
    (Where?)

2a. Is that a drugstore on the corner?
    (A what?)
 b. Is that drugstore on the corner?
    (Where?)

3a. Is that a service station in the next block?
    (A what?)
 b. Is that service station in the next block?
    (Where?)

4a. Is that a soda fountain by the teacher?
    (A what?)
 b. Is that soda fountain by the teacher?
    (Where?)

5a. Is that a dry cleaners around the corner?
    (A what?)
 b. Is that dry cleaners around the corner?
    (Where?)

6a. Is that a post office across from the courthouse?
    (A what?)
 b. Is that post office across from the courthouse?
    (Where?)

7a. Is that a policeman waiting in the lobby?
    (A what?)
 b. Is that policeman waiting in the lobby?
    (Where?)

8a. Is that a salesman on the telephone?
    (A what?)
 b. Is that salesman on the telephone?
    (Where?)

"Is that a..." signals a request to identify an object. But when "that" immediately precedes the noun, we know that noun is already familiar in the context, that it therefore does not carry new information. Of course the skip up to level 3 on the intonation line also signals the new, and therefore important, information in the sentence.

In the exercise that follows there is a contrast between prominence (shown by stress and pitch) on the verb and on the following noun, depending on which carries the most information. If the noun after the verb indicates time duration, the verb will be more prominent. If the noun is a genuine direct object, the noun will carry the sentence stress.

9.2c Utterance contour—adverbial noun vs direct object
  Comparison of pattern; pronounce the following sentences, correctly locating the sentence stress:

1a. Why don't you wait for a minute? ↓

b. Why don't you wait for a message? ↓

2a. Why don't you listen for a while?
 b. Why don't you listen for a whistle?

3a. Why don't you work for a bit?
 b. Why don't you work for a promotion?

4a. Why don't you write for a while?
 b. Why don't you write for a book?

5a. Why don't you pray for a little while?
 b. Why don't you pray for a little brother?

6a. Why don't you sit for a spell?
 b. Why don't you sit for a portrait?

7a. Why don't you just look for a bit?
 b. Why don't you just look for a bat?

8a. Why don't you hope for a while yet?
 b. Why don't you hope for a white jet?

The next exercise illustrates a very common and productive pattern of English syntax: compounding. In these sentences a compound noun is further compounded.

9.2d Utterance contour—multiple compounding

Response drill; reply to the following questions, combining nouns in compounds:

1a. What do you call a hât for cówbòys?　　　A cówbòy hât.
 b. What do you call a warden for air raids?　　An air raid warden.
 c. What do you call a station for a railroad?　A railroad station.
 d. What do you call the conductor of a streetcar?　A streetcar conductor.
 e. What do you call the operator of a drill press?　A drill press operator.
 f. What do you call a bulb for a flashlight?　A flashlight bulb.
 g. What do you call a holder for flash bulbs?　A flash bulb holder.
 h. What do you call a bun for a hot dog?　A hot dog bun.
 i. What do you call an eraser for blackboards?　A blackboard eraser.
 j. What do you call a liner for trash cans?　A trash can liner.

2a. What do you call a gréenhòuse that's brôwn?　A brôwn gréenhòuse.
 b. What do you call a watchchain that's gold?　A gold watchchain.
 c. What do you call a staple remover that's new?　A new staple remover.
 d. What do you call cobblestones that are rough?　Rough cobblestones.
 e. What do you call a letter opener that's made of copper?　A copper letter opener.
 f. What do you call an alarm clock that's unreliable?　An unreliable alarm clock.
 g. What do you call a music hall that's old?　An old music hall.
 h. What do you call a rosebud that's pink?　A pink rosebud.
 i. What do you call a steering wheel that's broken?　A broken steering wheel.
 j. What do you call a rocking chair that's an antique?　An antique rocking chair.

Sentences *(1)* are multiple compounds, where a compound is compounded. Thus *raíl ròad* combines with *station* to produce *raílròad státion,* comparable to *bús stàtion.* Sentences *(2),* listed for comparison, contain simple compounds preceded by a modifier (adjective or noun). The stress patterns that identify these two constructions are shown with the models above. Multiple compounds can be built into very complex constructions, as the set below illustrates:

> áir ràid
> áir ràid wârden
> áir ràid wârden pôst
> aîr ràid wârden pòst stáirs
> aîr ràid wârden pòst stáirwày
> aîr ràid wârden pòst stáirwày êntrance
> etc.

Though the stress pattern shown for these compounds is not absolutely fixed as the length and complexity is increased, there are correlations with constituent relations, and the whole construction functions as part of a single noun phrase (can take an article, attributive adjectives, etc.), as in "the old but still functioning air raid warden post stairway entrance."

Exercise 9.2e shows how intonation features (specifically stress and pitch) can be used to signal contrastive meanings. In the following pairs of sentences, strong stress falls on an adjective, highlighting unusual quality, or on a noun, implying a better but different product.

Note that when strong stress falls on the adjective, it is normal for contrastive pitch to also mark the adjective, lifted to level 4 and dropped to level 1 for the remainder of the sentence. In its noncontrastive position (in the *b* sentences) the strong-stressed syllable occurs on level 3.

Phrasing helps the speaker to express and the listener to interpret information presented orally, since phrase contours indicate how words group together to represent meanings. Note the following pairs of sentences:

> He looked   up the hill.
> He looked up   the word.

Looked in the first sentence means "used one's sense of sight" and *up the hill* tells the orientation toward which the looking was

9.2e Utterance contour—contrastive stress

Comparison of pattern; identify the assumptions implicit in the following pairs of sentences:

1a. Use Span like órdinary sôap. (Span is an especially good soap.)

b. Use Span like órdinary sóap. (Span is another product, better than soap.)

2a. Use Spredz like órdinary mârgarine. (Spredz is an especially good margarine.)
b. Use Spredz like órdinary márgarine. (Spredz is another product, superior to margarine.)

3a. Use Cornco like régular shôrtening. (Cornco is an especially good shortening.)
b. Use Cornco like régular shórtening. (Cornco is another product, superior to shortening.)

4a. Use Powpaks like órdinary bâtteries. (Powpaks are especially good batteries.)
b. Use Powpaks like órdinary bátteries. (Powpaks are another product, better than batteries.)

5a. Use Plasticote like régular flôor wàx. (Plasticote is an especially good floor wax.)
b. Use Plasticote like régular flóor wàx. (Plasticote is another product, better than floor wax.)

6a. Use Gromor like órdinary fêrtilizer. (Gromor is an especially good fertilizer.)
b. Use Gromor like órdinary fértilizer. (Gromor is another product, better than fertilizer.)

employed. In the second sentence *looked up* means "searched for and found" (presumably in a dictionary) and *the word* identifies what was sought. If pronounced slowly, a phrase break is very natural before *up* in the first sentence and after *up* in the second. But in such short sentences there may not *be* a break. In this case the phrasing pattern will be marked by stress patterns. *Lóok úp* (or *lóok ûp* when nonfinal in a phrase) has the stress pattern / ˋ ´ /, which identifies one kind of phrasal (or two-word) verb. When *up* is a preposition, as in the first sentence, it normally carries a medial stress: "up the hill." This feature of patterning is effectively illustrated by comparison of single-word verbs (followed by a preposition) and phrasal verbs, as in Exercise 9.2f.

9.2f Utterance contour—phrasal verbs

Comparison of pattern; read the pairs of sentences in this exercise, being careful to observe appropriate stress patterns:

1a. He lôoked ùp the hill.   (gazed)

b. He lòoked ûp the word.   (found)

2a. He tûrned ìn his grave.   (rotated)
b. He tùrned în his homework.   (submitted)

3a. We rêad òver the lunch hour.   (apprehended writing)
b. We rèad ôver the proposal.   (examined)

4a. She rân dòwn the hill.   (hurried)
b. She ràn dôwn her compétitors.   (belittled)

5a. He tûrned òff the road.   (veered)
b. He tùrned ôff the radio.   (stopped)

6a. She trîed òn the stage.   (attempted)
b. She trìed ôn the dress.   (donned)

9.2f (continued)

7a. He pítched ĭn the last ball game. (threw the ball)
b. He pítched ĭn his last penny. (contributed)

8a. He lŏoked ŏver the wall. (glanced)
b. He lŏoked ŏver the project. (scrutinized)

9a. They bácked ŭp the hill. (reversed)
b. They bácked ŭp the authorities. (supported)

10a. He pŭlled ŏff the highway. (tugged)
b. He pŭlled ŏff the robbery. (perpetrated)

11a. She cálled ŭp the stairwell. (shouted)
b. She cálled ŭp the plumber. (telephoned)

12a. They mŏved ŭp the block. (transferred)
b. They mŏved ŭp the date. (advanced)

13a. She pásssed oŭt the door. (exited)
b. She pássed oŭt the exam. (distributed)

14a. He tŭrned dŏwn the road. (angled)
b. He tŭrned dŏwn the suggestion. (rejected)

The use of phrasal verbs is perhaps the most productive pattern of lexical creativeness in modern English. New combinations are constantly being added to the lexicon. In the sentences above the contrast is marked by different stress patterns (specifically the / ˋ ´/ for phrasal verbs), but is reinforced in an important way by lexical choice, the kind of noun that follows the verb. Sometimes the same sequence of noun plus preposition/particle plus object is subject to two interpretations, and the contrast must be perceived by stress differences only.

9.2g Utterance contour–phrasal verbs distinguished by stress only

Comparison of pattern; identify the sentence heard by giving the appropriate expansion of the context:

1a. He lôoked ûp the street. (and saw a car coming)
1b. He lôoked ûp the street. (and found it on a map)
2a. They ôpened ûp the road. (and did better at their new location)
2b. They ôpened ûp the road. (and immediately it was heavily traveled)
3a. They pâssed bŷ the house. (greeting each other as they met)
3b. They pâssed bŷ the house. (deciding there was no point in stopping)
4a. She lôoked ôver the wall. (and saw the garden on the other side)
4b. She lôoked ôver the wall. (and approved its design)
5a. He tûrned dôwn the new road. (traveling in that area for the first time)
5b. He tûrned dôwn the new road. (basing his disapproval on expensive cost estimates)
6a. He rôlled ûp the rug. (showing what a well-trained dog he was)
6b. He rôlled ûp the rug. (so it could more easily be stored)
7a. They plâyed dôwn the hill. (where the valley started)
7b. They plâyed dôwn the hill. (saying it really wasn't important)
8a. The painter drôpped ôff the scaffold. (and got badly hurt)
8b. The painter drôpped ôff the scaffold. (so it will be here when he comes tomorrow)

258   Patterns of English Pronunciation

Sometimes differences, typically lexical differences, are clearly made but are subject to faulty interpretation because of similar-sounding alternative sentences. The stressed vowels of a pair of polysyllable words may be the same, but the consonants (usually somewhat harder to hear) are different. The resulting pair of words may allow two possible interpretations in a single sentence frame. Usually these pairs are not hard to discriminate if one is attentive; trouble in accurate interpretation occurs when a listener is distracted, or is concentrating on another part of the sentence. A wrong interpretation is much more likely to happen early in a discourse or right after a signal for a change of common focus.

The following sentence pairs illustrate some of the tangles that may occur.

9.3 Lexical identification—similar sounding sentences
Comparison of pattern; identify the sentence heard by producing an equivalent statement as a paraphrase:

1. Dr. Jones gives a very {classical / practical} course.

2. He does complicated math problems without any apparent {concentration. / hesitation.}

3. As a leader he's very {important. / impotent.}

4. The solution you suggest is {incongruous. / in Congress.}

5. You say a {kiss fixed / fish kissed} her?

6. He had never seen {Calvary / cavalry} before.

9.3 (continued)

7. This water's not $\begin{cases} \text{potable.} \\ \text{palatable.} \end{cases}$

8. It was not the right hour for $\begin{cases} \text{reveille.} \\ \text{revelry.} \end{cases}$

This type of exercise is illustrative only, serving to alert students to the possibility of strange and often humorous misinterpretations that can happen. There is no point trying to anticipate and do exercises for specific lapses, because they can occur in almost limitless number and variety. Notice that this is different from another type of misinterpretation, where the same spoken sentence can be understood more than one way, as in:

Something should be done about $\begin{cases} \text{a tax} \\ \text{attacks} \end{cases}$ on city busses.

These, then, are samples of some globally oriented pronunciation exercises: utterance discrimination from minimal segmental clues, utterance contours where suprasegmental features combine with sound segments to signal meanings, and gross lexical similarities. Hopefully, working through these exercises as a culmination to the more specific points treated in earlier chapters will at least sensitize students to the kinds of clues that native speakers rely on to interpret oral communication.

It might be some small comfort for the student to know that some of the problems presented in this last chapter can afflict native speakers as well as foreign-speaking students. The remedy is familiarity with the kinds of problems that can occur and strategies for backing up to reprocess the data that didn't make sense, to try again for the meaning, using all available contextual clues in addition to the phonological information. It is my sincere hope that adequate useful practice has been offered through this book, and that the serious student can continue on his own to whatever perfection of the skills of speaking and comprehension he feels he would like to achieve.

INDEX

The locations of presentations, descriptions, and exercises on individual sounds, comparison of sounds, and sound features can be found in the reference matrices that follow the present index. Chart A lists consonants, chart B vowels, and chart C levels of stress.

a   232, 127
a/an, forms of   127
a ~ the   230
adverbial noun vs direct object   251
affricates   29, 31
alveolus   31
an vs negative prefix *in-*   247
are vs *is*   243
articles, stress and vowel patterns for   127
articulation
   place of   29
   type of   29
   voicing of   30
as vs *is*   245
aspiration   37-38
   contrasts for /p, k/   39, 41
   contrasts for /t/   40-41, 100
   as a recognition feature in /C ~ sC/
      contrasts   155

assimilation
    of nasal consonants to following
        sound   156-158
    palatal   158-164
    reciprocal   158
  at   128-129

centering glide before /r/   56
centering tendency of /r/   53
citation forms   75
closed syllables, simple vowels in
    15, 21
clusters, consonant (see consonant
    clusters)
compound compounds   252
compounds (see noun compounds)
compound noun (or construct)   78
    vs noun phrase (modifier plus
        noun)   79-82
consonant
    alternations   214-217
    articulation
        places of   29-31
        types of   29-31
        voicing of   30
    chart   31
    classification for effect on length
        of preceding vowel   120
    suppression   218-220
consonant clusters   32, 131
    final
        three member   147
        four member   150
        inherent   140-142
            order of openness   140
        morphologically produced
            142-145
            phonotactic rules affecting
                143
        formed by intrusive consonants
            147

reductions   150-152
  simplification to sequences
      152
  initial
    two member
      stop or voiceless fricative plus
          liquid   133-134
      consonant plus semiconson-
          ant   134-136
      /s/ plus consonant   136-137
    three member
      /s/ plus voiceless stop plus
          liquid or semiconsonant
          139-141
consonant sequences   32, 131
  geminates   152-153
  geminate /s/ with /sC/ clusters
      154-155
consonants
  alveolar liquids /l, r/   52-54
  alveolar nasal /n/   33
  alveolar sibilant /s/   33
  alveolar sibilant /z/   48
  bilabial nasal /m/   33
  bright /l/   54-56
  dark /l/   55-56
  dental fricatives /th, dh/   46-47
  flap /t/   39-40, 100, 105
  glottal /t/ before /ṇ/   43, 105
  labiodental fricatives /f, v/   45-46
  laterally released /t/   44-45
  palatal affricates /ch, j/   49-50
  palatal sibilants /sh, zh/   48-49
  pharyngeal fricative /h/   50-51
  retroflex /r/   52
  semiconsonants /y, w/   58
  syllabic /ḷ/   55
  syllabic /ṇ/   43, 105
  velar nasal /ng/   50-51
  voiced stops /b, d, g/   35-36
  voiceless stops /p, t, k/   37-45

contextual presentation   58
contraction as an "advanced" form of reduction   224
contractions with *to*   165
contrastive stress
   for identification of assumptions   253-254
   to correct, emphasize, contradict   85-86
   to frame an echo question   91-93
   to indicate information new to the context   89
   to recognize antonyms with negative prefixes   88
   used with pitch /4/   84-93
   with noun phrases and noun compounds   124

/dhæt/ vs /dhət/   240
dialect mismatches   74
diphthongs   19-28
   adjacent identical not reduced   125-126
   preceding /-ər/   111
direct object vs adverbial noun   251
downshift to pitch /1/ after contrastively stressed syllable   87

-ed, past participles vs adjectives   146
-ed vs *it*   234
/ə/ vs ∅   231
flap, nasalized   155-156
flapped /t/   39-40, 167-168
fricatives   29, 31
from vs ∅   242

glide   20-22
   (*see* semivowels)
   centering   107
glottal stop   126-128
   to separate adjacent vowels   128
   variant of /t/   43

glottis 31
gonna 164-170
gotta 164-170
"growled" /r/ 52

hafta 164-170
hasta 164-170

-ing /-ĭng -ăn/ 105
intonation (stress, pitch, juncture, rhythm) 175
    pattern for adjective plus noun 76
intonation patterns 75
    neutral vs contrastive 184
    /231↓/ neutral statements 185
           normal information questions 187
    /233↑/ normal yes-no questions (requests) 186, 190
           to express surprise, disbelief, disappointment 185
    /331↓/ to express impatience, rudeness, disinterest 186
    /344↑/ echo questions 187-188
    /233↑ 231↓/ choice questions 189-190
    /31↓/ tag questions - conversation 191-193
    /23↑/ tag questions - confirmation 191-193
    /2321↓/ and /241 | 31↓/ contrastive tags 193-195
    /111↑, 222↑, 333↑/ vocatives 195-196
    /231↓, 32↑, 21 |, 2321↓, 232 |/ greetings and leavetakings 197
intonation phrase 75
intrusive consonants 147
intrusive /r/ 126
is vs *are* 243

is vs *as*   245
it vs Ø   233
it vs *-ed*   234

juncture, final   183-184
junctures   132

lexical identification   258-259
linked *nt*   155-156
lips   31
liquids   29, 31
listening comprehension, general   229

-man   94
metrical feet   176
minimal pairs   15
morphophonemic alternation   202
morphophonemic spelling   201
mouth as a resonance chamber   13

nasal flap   167-168
nasals   29, 31
nasalized flap   155-156
nasalized vowels (adjacent to or between nasal consonants)   34
negative prefixes   246
    in- vs article *an*   247
neutralization of voicing contrast
    /t - d/   42
Nilsen, Don L. F. and Alleen Pace   74
noun compounds   248
    multiple compounding   252
nt linked   155-156

one-sound-one-symbol   32
open syllables, diphthongs in
    20, 25

palatal assimilation   158-164
palate   31

paraphrase cues   74
   for identification   16
past subsequent vs past perfect (contractions of *would* and *did*)   237
past vs present perfect (contractions of *have*)   236
pharynx   31
phonemic spelling   201-202
phonological representation, rules of   200
phrasal verbs   254-257
pitch   75
   high, mid, low /3, 2, 1/   2, 77 83
   extra high /4/   84
   patterns for adjective plus noun   77
place vs referent   250
present perfect vs past (contractions of *have*)   236
prominence (*see* stress)   1, 2
pronouns, reduced (short, weak-stressed) forms   171-173
prosody   175-176
postvocalic /r/   107-117
   dropping in informal forms   107

/r/-colored schwa   52
/r/-less dialects with a centering glide   107
/r/ plus /-ə̰r/   57
   plus /-Vsə̌r/   56
randomized order of drill sentences   229
reduced forms   171
   articles   127
   other particles (conjunctions, relatives, auxiliary verb forms, etc.)   221-227
   with palatal assimilations   227
   prepositions   221, 225

pronouns 171-173
referent vs place 250
retroflex /r/ 52
rhythm, stress-timed vs syllable-timed 176
rhythm patterns
   contrasts in 178-179
   experience with 181
rules of phonological representation 200

schwa 96, 127-128
   brevity when weak stressed 97, 100, 134, 179
   often drops before another vowel 127-128
   often drops when internal, weak-stressed 100, 129
   plus /r/ 98-99
   spellings for 97
   strong- vs weak-stressed 98-99
   with exercises that drop schwa to form consonant clusters 134, 137, 138, 140, 142, 145
segmental features 199
selective application 74
semiconsonants 29, 31
semivowels 19
sequences, consonant (see consonant sequences)
spelling, morphophonemic vs phonemic 201-202
stops 29, 31
stress
   contrast of medial and weak 4-6, 8-9
   contrast of secondary and medial 124
   and function relations 5-6, 8-9
   secondary 75
   sequences of strong and weak 2-6

sequences of strong and medial 4-6
  sequences of strong, medial, and weak 4-11
  strong, medial, weak 1, 75
stress alternations 181
  shift to negative prefix to highlight contrast 88
  shift of strong stress to avoid adjacent placement 181-183
stress patterns, predicting 179-180
supposta 164-170
suprasegmental features 175, 199
syllable length conditioned by
  features of rhythm and prosody 175-179
  position in sentence 124
  stress 122-125
  syllable structure 117-122

teens vs tens 90-91, 181-182
teeth 31
tempo of normal pronunciation, estimates of 178
-*th*, consonant clusters with the suffix 149
than vs *that* 241
the 127
the vs *a/an* 230
they are vs *there are* 244
to, weak stressed 129
  contractions with 165
transition features 75
  in consonant clusters 132

underlying representations 201, 219
unreleased stops 60
usta 164-170

velum 31

verbs, two-word or phrasal   254-257
   verb plus particle vs verb plus
      preposition   196-197
   (phrase break after particle, before
      preposition)   197
vocal cords (bands)   30
vocal qualifiers   186
vowel
   alternations in stressed syllables
      205-213
   quality vs duration   117
   reduction correlated with stress
      201-204
   (strong stress full vowels vs weak
      stress reduced vowels)   200
vowel chart or grid   13-14, 19-20
   before /r/   108
   showing morphophonemic alterna-
      tions   206
   weak stressed   96
vowel length
   classification of consonants that
      condition   120
   conditioned by features of rhythm
      and prosody   124
   conditioned by position in sen-
      tence   124
   correlated with stress   122-125
   correlated with syllable structure
      (following consonant)   117-122
   cue to identifying following con-
      sonant   120
   and syllable structure   117-122
vowels
   adjacent   125
   before /r/   96-107
   diphthongs (complex)   20-28
   "long" vs "short"   117, 205
   nucleus   32
   simple   5-19
   weak stressed   108-117

wanna 164-170
weak-stressed forms of pronouns 171
weak-stressed vowel system 95
whose vs *who's* 238
will vs *would* 235

CHART A
Presentation and Comparison of Consonants

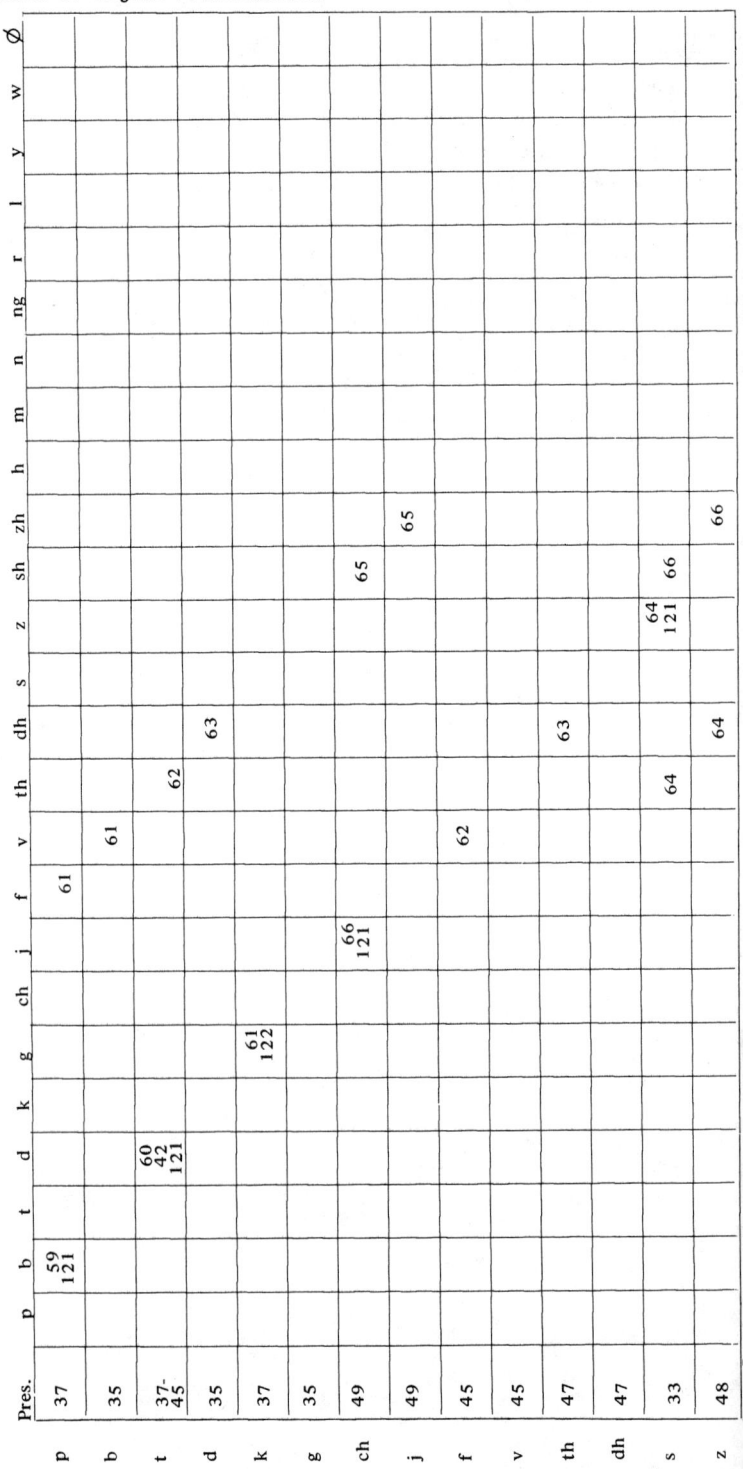

Pres. = Presentation

Page numbers at intersections refer to location of treatment or comparison exercises.

CHART B

Presentation and Comparison of Vowels Strong Stressed and Weak Stressed

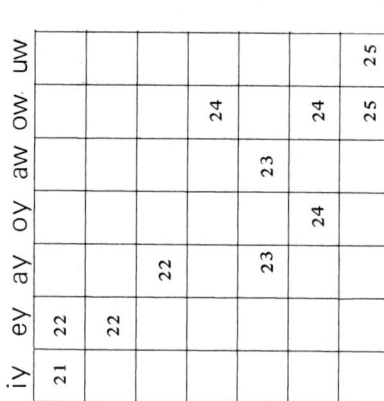

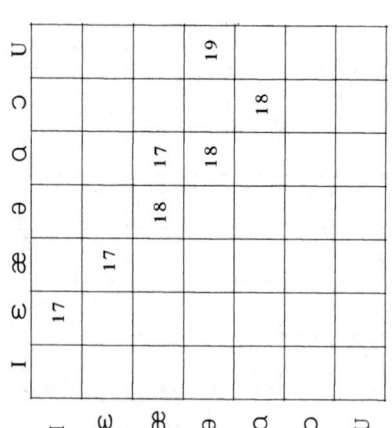

Index 275

	iy	ey	ay	oy	aw	ow	uw
iy	26						
ey		26					
ay			26				
oy				27			
aw			27				
ow				27			
uw							28

iy	106
	106
	106
	102

ow	106	102
uw	106	103

Page numbers at intersections refer to location of treatment or comparison of exercises.

Presentation and Comparison of Vowels Before /r/

Pres.	I	ɛ	e	æ	ɑ	ɔ	U
108 109 111		114	114	115			
108 109			115				

	I	ɛ	e	æ	ɑ	ɔ	U
e	108 110 116				112	113	
æ	108 109					113	
ɔ	108 109 110						
U	108 112						115

Page numbers at intersections refer to location of treatment or comparison exercises.

CHART C

Presentation and Comparison of Stress Levels

	strong ´	secondary ˆ	medial ˋ	weak ˇ
strong ´			4-10	2-10
secondary ˆ	76-77		79-82 124	
medial ˋ				4-5 8-9 94
weak ˇ				

Page numbers at intersections refer to location of treatment or comparison exercises